Dundas; Or, A Sketch Of Canadian History, And More Particularly Of The County Of Dundas, One Of The Earliest Settled Counties In Upper Canada

Croil, James, 1821-1916

Nabu Public Domain Reprints:

You are holding a reproduction of an original work published before 1923 that is in the public domain in the United States of America, and possibly other countries. You may freely copy and distribute this work as no entity (individual or corporate) has a copyright on the body of the work. This book may contain prior copyright references, and library stamps (as most of these works were scanned from library copies). These have been scanned and retained as part of the historical artifact.

This book may have occasional imperfections such as missing or blurred pages, poor pictures, errant marks, etc. that were either part of the original artifact, or were introduced by the scanning process. We believe this work is culturally important, and despite the imperfections, have elected to bring it back into print as part of our continuing commitment to the preservation of printed works worldwide. We appreciate your understanding of the imperfections in the preservation process, and hope you enjoy this valuable book.

DUNDAS;

OR,

A SKETCH OF CANADIAN HISTORY,

AND MORE PARTICULARLY OF

THE COUNTY OF DUNDAS,

One of the earliest settled Counties in Upper Canada.

BY

JAMES CROIL.

"*Quod potui, perfeci.*"

Montreal:
B. DAWSON & SON, 23 GREAT ST. JAMES STREET.
1861.

Entered according to the Act of the Provincial Parliament, in the year one thousand eight hundred and sixty-one, by JAMES CROIL, in the office of the Register in the Province of Canada.

JOHN LOVELL, Printer,
St. Nicholas Street, Montreal.

1315325

Dedication.

To

The Descendants of the United Empire Loyalists

Residing in the

United Counties of Stormont, Dundas, and Glengarry,

Formerly

The Old Eastern District,

This humble effort

To preserve a record of the Settlement of one of the oldest Counties in Upper Canada, is dedicated, in testimony of respect to the memories of the United Empire Loyalists themselves, and with best wishes for the prosperity of their descendants, by

Their obedient Servant,

The Author.

PREFACE.

GENTLE READER, be entreated to revert to a custom somewhat obsolete and read my Preface. The author trusts that no labored apology is required at his hands, for the present humble attempt to gather together, and to present to the inhabitants of Dundas County, a variety of details chiefly connected with its history, many of which are more familiar to individual residents of the district than they are to himself. Yet a word or two of explanation may reasonably be sought for, as to the motives which prompted the attempt, and as to the data upon which the statements are founded. In respect to the motives, it may be asked what has induced *a farmer* to forsake his plough and to venture, an unknown wanderer, into the luckless paths of literature? Reader, a variety of circumstances have induced him for a time to relinquish the arduous but honorable labors of the farm; in prosecuting these, while unfortunately for himself he has lost much that he now ardently wishes he could have retained, he has yet acquired the valuable habit of industry and application. Having been relieved from the toils of farming, and finding time at his disposal, he has looked around him to see how both time and opportunities might be most profitably employed, not however in the vulgar acceptation of Dollars and Cents—he looks for no such remuneration, and certainly he will be none the richer for having written a book—but for the public good. For this an opportunity soon offered.

The Board of Agriculture for Upper Canada having urgently requested the directors of County Societies, to transmit to them more copious and detailed reports of the several counties in the Upper Province than they had been in the habit of doing, and by way of inducement having offered a prize for the best report that should reach them for the year 1859, the author volunteered to report upon Dundas, and this was the origin of the present book. A great deal of what is here submitted in connection with the County was embodied in that report, and the following extract from its introduction is equally applicable here :

"A correct and reliable description of each County, its history, capabilities, and progress, and, as a consequence the comparative inducements which each holds out to emigrants, and others who desire to engage in agricultural pursuits, is a desideratum which even the elaborate Directory of Canada by Mr. Lovell, and the copious and painstaking Census of 1851-2 have not fully supplied. A great deal relating to the several Counties may be gleaned from these sources, but it is a work of time and difficulty to separate what is wanted from the mass of information which they contain. We have long desired to see a full report of each County complete in itself, and we think we cannot better respond to the expressed wish of the Board, than by collecting from reliable public sources all that is known of our County, and adding from local information matters of interest not to be found in the works referred to. The belief that such a report would be particularly acceptable to the inhabitants generally of the County, has induced us to enter freely upon many subjects which would not necessarily have been embraced in a strictly agricultural report." A variety of other matters attracted the attention of the writer in preparing that report, which the limited time did not permit him to include in it. At the solicitation of some esteemed friends, the whole was revised and enlarged, and is now presented to the reader as a history of the County. He has further been induced to prosecute the work from the conviction, that many of the incidents connected with the early history of Dundas would otherwise have been lost, as those from whom authentic information can be had are now few in number, and are one by one in rapid succession disappearing from our midst. This much for the motives.

Piracy has ever been held to be one of the blackest of crimes. Literary piracy is even more despicable still. He who would pawn off the studied compositions of others as his own, may rest assured that in due time " his sin will find him out." In preparing the following pages the author lays very little claim to originality, further than in the selection and arrangement of such subjects as seemed suited to his purpose. This remark applies particularly to the first three chapters. The events therein narrated are presented simply as extracts from the more complete histories of others. "Russel's History of America," a voluminous work published in 1776, and replete with authentic references, has furnished the largest part of that which relates to the discovery of America, and the early history of Canada; "Haliburton's Nova Scotia," all that refers to that Province. From "Hough's History of St. Lawrence County," several interesting statements have been gleaned. The author of that work (a volume of 750 pages) in commenting upon the affairs of Canada, notices us with good feeling, and his remarks are usually characterized by candor and accuracy. From "Allison" and "Montgomery Martin," we are enabled at times to look upon American history, as viewed by British historians, while "Christie," "Smith" and "Morris" have posted us up in local matters. The information respecting the battle of "Crysler's Farm" has been derived chiefly from parties residing in the County or neighborhood, who were eye witnesses of every thing related. It is but justice also to mention, that in comparing their statements with the historical accounts of the above cited authorities, there exists no material discrepancy. Some of the other incidents of the war of 1812 are taken from a history of that war published in the

"Anglo American" Magazine. The "Montreal Gazette" of 1837-8-9 furnished many of the incidents connected with the Rebellion, and a pamphlet published in Prescott, immediately after the battle of the Wind-mill, supplied the facts that transpired there. The narrative of the Prince of Wales' visit is chiefly original, with occasional extracts from the correspondence of the "Montreal Gazette."

These acknowledgements, the author trusts, will be deemed sufficient without having recourse to a display of references altogether inconsistent with the unpretending character of these pages. A host of friends, too numerous to mention, have laid him under particular obligations by the ready manner in which they put themselves to considerable inconvenience to assist in reproducing the details given. Amongst these are Judge Jarvis of Cornwall, Major Clark of Edwardsburgh, Jacob Brouse, Esq., of Matilda, Peter Brouse, Messrs. George Merckley, and Peter Loucks of Williamsburgh; nor should he omit to name the Rev. Herman Hayunga, who rendered valuable assistance in the ecclesiastical department, and the Rev. Alex. F. Kemp of Montreal, to whom the reader is indebted for the notes on Geology and

Natural History contained in the eighth chapter. From him also the author has received much valuable assistance in preparing for the press, which he hereby acknowledges.

If after these frank admissions there be yet room for apology, it can only be in reference to the plan of the work, and the feebleness of its execution. To whatever charges the reader may prefer against him in these respects, the author will unhesitatingly plead "guilty." If at times he has wandered wide of his subject, it has generally been to notice circumstances affecting the Province at large, all of which have a local and particular, as well as a national and general interest; sometimes too the digression has been made in order that prominent events in the history of our whole country may reach those for whose use the narrative has been mainly penned, and who have not access to the historical works in which they are detailed.

If the actions of "Crysler's Farm" and the "Windmill" seem to be too prominently brought out, it is because the one was fought in the County of Dundas, and that in the other the militia of Dundas took a prominent part.

In thus endeavoring to preserve a record of the

history of the County, the author has spared no labour or cost in procuring accurate information, and in making the book worthy of the subject. If this, his first, and in all probability his last literary attempt, be recognized as in any measure an atonement, for thirteen years of his life spent in the County with little or no public benefit to his fellow subjects, his object will have been fully attained, and the time he has devoted to it amply recompensed.

> " If ought of error or intemperate truth,
> Should meet thine ear, think thou that riper age
> Will calm it down, and let thy love forgive it!"
> COLERIDGE.

J. CROIL.

Archerfield, 1st May, 1861.

CONTENTS.

CHAPTER I

(From 1492 to 1549.)

History—Portuguese Mariners—Columbus sails to the West—Land ho! Shipwreck—Return to Spain—Rejoicings—His second voyage—Massacre of Spaniards—Natives rebel, and are reduced to slavery—Third voyage—Further discoveries—Insurrection of colonists—Columbus impeached at Court—Is bound in irons and sent to Spain—His defence—His death—Americus visits the New World—Named America—His death—Discoveries of Cabot and Jacques Cartier...Page 17

CHAPTER II.

(From 1598 to 1713.)

Settlement of the French and English in N. A.—Gilbert occupies Newfoundland—Expedition to Roanoke—Named Virginia—Sir R. Grenville's first settlement—A failure—Sir Walter Raleigh—Disastrous results—Colony abandoned—English Chartered Companies—Smith and Pocahontas.—The Puritans in New England—French occupy Nova Scotia—Dispossessed—N. S. granted to a Scotchman—Ceded to France—Sir David Kirk's exploit—Halifax founded—French in Canada—Quebec founded—War with the Indians... 37

CHAPTER III.

(From 1745 to 1763.)

The Mississippi discovered—La Salle—Louisiana settled—French claims—Fruitless negociations—French war in N.A.—Siege of Louisbourg—Peace—Hostilities between France and England—The fall of Quebec—Amherst descends the St. Lawrence—Sir William Johnston—Conquest of Canada completed...................... 53

CONTENTS.

CHAPTER IV.
(From 1763 to 1815.)

The Revolutionary War—Its origin and results—Character of Washington—Reflections on the war—Causes of the war of 1812—Hull invades Canada—Battle of Queenston—Fall of General Brock—Engagements by sea and land—Wilkinson's Expedition—Battle of Crysler's Farm—Peace concluded—Incidents—Medals and Monuments—Battle of Matilda—The affair at Mariatown—Salmon River raid—The tried Sergeant.................................... 69

CHAPTER V.
(From 1815 to 1860.)

Union of the Provinces—The Rebellion in Lower and Upper Canada—The Hunter's oath—Steamers Caroline and Sir Robert Peel—Bill Johnston—Battle of the Windmill—The sympathizers—Militia of Dundas—Volunteer movement in Canada—The rifleman's song. 105

CHAPTER VI.

The County of Dundas—Situation, extent, population, and first settlement of—The Primeval forest—The U. E. Loyalists—The log shanty—Government grants of lands and implements—Difficulties encountered by first settlers—Hard times—Employments of first settlers—Their character—Dawn of improvement—The first schoolmaster—Brant and his Mohawks—Laws of the early settlers—Captain Duncan—Sir John Johnson—Steichmann—Reflections. 126

CHAPTER VII.

Intermediate History—The soil of Dundas—Cranberry Marshes—Standing timber and building materials—Climate—Meteorological Record—Oldest inhabitant—Eclipse—Earth-quake—Hail Storm—Irrigation—Statute labor and roads of Dundas.................... 151

CHAPTER VIII.
GEOLOGY AND NATURAL HISTORY.

General Geological features—Laurentian formation—Huronian—Lower Silurian—Potsdam Sandstone—Chazy—Trenton Group—Tertiary formation—Post-Tertiary—Composition of surface soil—Forest Trees—shrubs—fruit bearing plants—wild flowers. Animals-mammalia—Birds—Fishes... 165

CHAPTER IX.

Canadian agriculture—Rotation of crops—Systems of farming—Dutch, Scotch, Irish systems—Breeds of domestic animals—Of renting lands—Of the shares system—Of tile draining—Of laborers—Implements of husbandry—&c., &c......................... 192

CHAPTER X.

Social aspect—Character of inhabitants—Territorial divisions—Municipal and legal institutions—Judge Jarvis—Educational statistics—Benevolent and literary societies—Agricultural societies... 215

CHAPTER XI.

Population of Dundas and adjacent Counties—Exports and Imports of the County—Manufactures—Progress...................... 239

CHAPTER XII.

Religious aspects——First Protestant Church in Canada—The Lutheran Church, the Rev. H. Hayunga—Church of England, Rev. Mr Lindsay—Presbyterian Church, Rev. Mr. Broeffle—The Free Church—Methodist Church, Rev. Mr. Pope—Roman Catholic Church—Religious Statistics—Clergy Reserves..................... 247

CHAPTER XIII.

Constitutional changes—First Canadian Parliament—Dundas returns two members—Changes at the Union—Franchise extended—Voter's Qualification, Oath, Registration—Member's qualification and remuneration—Council rendered elective—Representatives of Dundas—Political aspect—Biographical sketches—Lying Campbell, &c.—Col. Crysler—Peter Shaver—George Crawford—Reflections....... 271

CHAPTER XIV.

The St. Lawrence Canals.—The Elliots.—Steam Navigation, History of, on River Lake, and Ocean.—Cunard, Collins, Canadian and other steamers.—The Great Eastern.—Grand Trunk Railroad.—Victoria Bridge.—Benjamin Chaffey............................ 287

CONTENTS.

CHAPTER XV.

Reminiscences.—The mound of Williamsburgh.—Early Methodist Missionaries.—The first Convert.—The luke-warm Lutheran.—Record of the Grave-yard.—Eccentricities.—Perpetual motion.—Novel Windmill.—Early mills in Dundas.—Auld acquaintance....... 306

CHAPTER XVI.

Visit of His Royal Highness the Prince of Wales to Canada....... 319

Index 349

DUNDAS;

OR,

A SKETCH OF CANADIAN HISTORY.

"Lives of great men all remind us,
We can make our lives sublime,
And, departing, leave behind us
Foot prints on the sands of time."
                              LONGFELLOW.

CHAPTER I.

History—Portuguese Mariners—Columbus sails to the West—Land ho! Shipwreck—Return to Spain—Rejoicings—His second voyage—Massacre of Spaniards—Natives rebel, and are reduced to slavery—Third voyage—Further discoveries—Insurrection of colonists—Columbus impeached at Court—Is bound in irons and sent to Spain—His defence—His death—Americus visits the New World—Named America—His death—Discoveries of Cabot and Jacques Cartier.

(From 1492 to 1549.)

" HISTORY is a record of facts and events, relating to the past existence of nations and of the world, handed down from one generation to another." During the first three thousand years of man's existence in the world, little is known of the history of nations, save the brief outline presented to us in the sacred volume. The early history of Europe originates in mythology, and the circumstances attending its first settlement are beyond our knowledge. In tracing the history of any country, the starting-point is usually the period in its existence when the light of lettered civilization first dawns upon it. Beyond that, there may be oral traditions more or less authentic, but these furnish imperfect data for the pen of the historian, whose aim is to set forth nought but the well ascertained facts of the past.

We speak of Europe as the "Old World," with its history stretching into the past two thousand years, we speak of America as the "New World," the existence of which became known to Europeans only three hundred and sixty-eight years ago. How far short does history come of disclosing to us the past, and it may be the stirring events that have transpired in our country during a long series of ages! Who is there amongst the most learned that can with certainty determine the time or the manner in which our aborigines first found their way to this continent? Who can tell how long the red man has held in undisputed possession the territories from which he has been ejected by the white? This much only we do know, that, although recently discovered by Europeans, the whole of this vast continent has, during many ages, been the abode of human beings, endowed with reason, intelligence, and passions like our own.

The Portuguese, who had long been noted as skilful mariners, discovered the island of Madeira in the year 1420, and planted a colony there. Their frequent voyages to this island, and the introduction of the mariner's compass, then newly invented, tended gradually to accustom them to a bolder navigation; and instead of creeping servilely along the shore, they ventured boldly into the open ocean. In a few years the whole eastern coast of Africa was explored, and in the year 1486 the southernmost point of that continent had been reached; and King John, foreseeing that it would lead to the discovery of a passage to India by sea, the great object of all previous explorations, named the promontory "The Cape of Good Hope," in preference to the name given it by the navigator, "Tempestuous Cape."

The fame of the Portuguese discoveries allured into their

service adventurous navigators from all the maritime states of Europe. Among these was Christopher Columbus, a native of Genoa, who had already distinguished himself as a mariner and a scholar. He repaired to Lisbon in the year 1459, and his reputation secured him a favourable reception by the Portuguese. There he married Philippa Perestrello, daughter of an Italian captain of that name, who had the good fortune to discover Madeira. In this way he got possession of the journals and the charts of that able navigator. From them he learned the course which the Portuguese had held in making their discoveries; and he gratified his passion for the sea, by making frequent voyages to Madeira, the Canaries, and Azores.

During the course of these voyages, Columbus formed the great scheme of discovery, which he afterwards carried so happily into execution. As the spherical form of the earth was then known, and its magnitude ascertained with some degree of accuracy, he had early concluded that the continent on the one side of the globe must be balanced by an equal quantity of land on the other. He had observed too, after violent westerly winds, that trees torn up by the roots, were driven on the coasts of the Azores. Pieces of wood artificially carved had also been found floating on the sea to the westward of any known land, and suggested the idea of a vast continent in that direction. From the accounts of travellers from China and Japan, he argued that the further these countries extended to the east, they must, as a matter of course, approach nearer to the islands recently discovered in the west, and that the most direct course to the rich countries of the east might possibly be found by sailing due west across the Atlantic Ocean, instead of winding around the coasts of Africa. His mind was bent upon testing, as soon as an opportunity should offer, the soundness of his conjectures. He repaired to his native country, and laid his scheme before the senate of Genoa. It was rejected as the dream of a visionary projector. Next to his native land, he appealed to the land of his adoption, and made an overture to the King of

Portugal. Unable himself to enter into the merits of the case, the king referred the consideration of the plan to three eminent cosmographers. These men, instead of encouraging, did all they could to divert him from his purpose; and, having extorted from him full particulars of his proposed voyage of discovery, they instigated the king secretly to dispatch a vessel to attempt the discovery, in hopes that they might thus secure for themselves the glory due to another. Full of indignation, Columbus instantly quitted Portugal, and in the year 1484 landed in Spain. Ferdinand and Isabella, being then engaged in war with the Moors of Grenada, had no leisure to listen to the enthusiastic project of the mariner. For five long years he was kept in suspense, and then told, that, until the war was terminated, their majesties could not engage in any new and expensive enterprise. His scheme had in the meantime been submitted to Henry the Seventh of England, and was so favourably received that Columbus resolved to visit the court of England in person. As he was about to start, he received an unexpected summons to the court of Spain, and the conquest of Grenada being soon after completed, an agreement with Columbus was signed on the 17th of April, 1492, by which he was constituted admiral and viceroy over all the lands and seas he should discover, and granting to him and his heirs for ever the tenth part of the clear profits which should result to the crown from the success of his labours.

No time was lost in making preparations. The armament was however ill in keeping with the importance of the service; it consisted of only three vessels, named the Santa Maria, Pinta, and Nigna. The first named was a decked vessel, and was commanded by Columbus in person; the others were open caravels. With this small squadron, carrying only ninety men, and victualled for twelve months, Columbus set sail from the port of Palos, in the province of Andalusia, a little before sun-rising, on the third day of August, 1492. He steered directly for the Canary Islands, which he reached in ten days, without any material occurrence, ave the loss of the Pinta's rudder, which his crew regarded as a bad omen, but which he considered only as a mark of unskilfulness on the part of the ship-builder. After refitting, he again put to sea, and held his course due west, leaving at once the usual track of navigation, and launching boldly into an ocean, with whose extreme shores he was unacquainted and of which he had no chart, in quest of countries which existed perhaps only in his own imagination. No sooner had he lost sight of land, than many of his sailors, already discouraged, began with violent exclamations to beat their breasts and shed tears, notwithstanding all his efforts to animate them. They regarded his enterprise as the desperate project of a rash adventurer, who would soon hurry them to destruction. Columbus happily possessed the courage and presence of mind which triumphed amidst the greatest perils, and never failed to inspire confidence. He appeared always cool and collected, and comforted his crew with assurances of ultimate success, and the prospect of vast wealth in those opulent regions whither he was conducting them. He personally superintended the execution of every order, allowing himself only a few hours for sleep, and was at all other times upon deck. Sensible that the length of the voyage must alarm sailors accustomed to only short excursions, he endeavoured to conceal from them the progress they had made. When two hundred leagues west of the Canaries, the variation of the compass was first observed by them. At this they became greatly alarmed, and refused to continue the voyage. This phenomenon, which is now familiar to every mariner, and the precise amount of which, at any given point, can now be determined by calculation, shook the companions of Columbus with terror. For this, however, he assigned a reason, which, though it did not satisfy himself, seemed plausible to his associates. New fears pressed upon them every day. They continued their course for many weeks, and still there was no appearance of land. His officers now took part with the men, and a general mutiny ensued. They reproached Columbus in the most violent language, and threatened to throw him overboard if he did not instantly alter his course, and return to Spain. He answered their abuse in the mildest and most gentle terms, concluding with a solemn assurance that if land was not discovered within three days he would abandon the enterprise. Before one day out of three had expired, the clouds around the setting sun gave strong presages of land. At midnight of the second night, a light was discovered ahead of the vessel, and the next morning, the 12th of October, 1492, Columbus, who had been all night anxiously watching the light, was the first to utter the joyful cry of " Land ho!" The effect of such an exclamation upon a dispirited and exhausted crew may be easier imagined than described. They instantly began to sing the " Te Deum "; and this done, they fell prostrate at their commander's feet, imploring him to pardon their incredulity and ignorance, and pronounced him to be a man inspired by Heaven. Columbus was as calm in prosperity as he had hitherto been in adversity. He ordered the boats to be manned and armed, and rowed towards the land, with colours flying, martial music, and every kind of warlike pomp. Dressed in a gorgeous robe, he was the first to spring ashore; his men followed; and kneeling down, all kissed the ground. He then took solemn possession of the country in the name of their Catholic Majesties, or, as some say, in the name of Queen Isabella alone, who patronized the expedition. The natives gazed in silent admiration upon their new guests, whom they regarded as a superior order of beings: the dress of the Spaniards, their beards, but more than all their ships, appeared wonderful to those simple people. Nor were the Spaniards less surprised themselves. The inhabitants appeared entirely naked; their faces and bodies were fantastically painted, and their complexion was of that dusky copper-colour peculiar to the New World. They were wholly ignorant of the use of iron and the nature of sharp weapons, innocently rubbing their hands against the sharp edges of the Spanish swords.

The land which Columbus had discovered was an island of fifteen leagues in circumference, in the Bahama group, called by the natives Guanahani. Columbus called it San Salvador, which signifies "being saved": it is now known as Cat Island. He explored the island in search of gold, but finding none, he again put to sea, taking with him seven of the natives, who, when they had acquired the Spanish language, should act as interpreters. Steering east, he next arrived at Hayti, to which he gave the name of Espagnola. In coasting along this island, his ship ran upon a rock, and, but for the timely assistance of boats from the Nigna, and the friendly aid of the natives in their canoes, all on board must have perished. Nothing had been seen of the Pinta since they had left Cuba. There now remained but one vessel, and that an open boat, the smallest of the squadron, to traverse such a vast tract of ocean, and to carry so many men back to Europe.

These were alarming circumstances. Columbus at once resolved to leave part of his crew upon the island, that they might prepare the way for a settlement of the colony. He set them to work to erect a small fort, and placed the great guns saved from the wreck of the Santa Maria upon its ramparts. In ten days it was completed, the simple natives labouring with the greatest alacrity in erecting this, the first monument of their own slavery. He then drew up his men in battle array, in presence of the assembled multitudes, and fired several discharges of musketry, concluding the review with a volley from the great guns, the sudden discharges of which struck them with terror and amazement. They at once concluded that it was impossible to resist men who came armed with thunder and lightning against their enemies. Having taken these precautions for the protection of the infant colony, consisting of 38 men, Columbus left Hispaniola, and steering east was soon out of sight of land. After a dangerous voyage of ten weeks, he arrived at Palos, on the 15th of March, 1493. He was received on landing with royal honours: the bells were rung, cannons fired, and universal joy demonstrated in every possible manner. Ferdinand and Isabella received him, arrayed in their royal robes and seated upon a throne. They loaded him with honors; and what pleased him more than all, they gave orders to prepare without delay a larger armament than the first, that he might return to explore regions more opulent than he had hitherto met with. Seventeen ships were equipped with unusual rapidity, and fifteen hundred persons of all ranks and employments went on board, furnished with seed, plants, domestic animals, and implements;—in fact, with every thing they required for conquest or settlement. On the 25th November, 1493, the fleet sailed from Cadiz, and arrived at Hispaniola after a voyage of seven weeks. Columbus landed at the fort he had erected but a short time before. To his inexpressible grief and consternation, he found it entirely demolished, and not a Spaniard alive to tell the tale: they had been cut off to a man. He found upon enquiry that the Spaniards had brought the calamity on themselves, for no sooner were they freed from his restraints, than they began to perpetrate all manner of cruel and wanton outrages on the unoffending natives. Aroused at last to revenge, these fell upon them in great numbers, burned their fort, and put them all to death. The first act of Columbus now was to provide accommodation for his numerous followers. He traced out the plan of a town, which was quickly reared and strongly fortified, and, leaving most of the Spanish settlers there, he proceeded in quest of further discoveries. In April, 1494, he visited Jamaica, and procured considerable quantities of gold-dust. On returning to Hispaniola, he was greeted with the most heart-rending reports of the insubordination of his own soldiers during his absence. He found the whole island in a state of revolt, and the insulted and inoffensive natives only awaiting the signal of their leaders to rise in a mass and drive their cruel oppressors into the sea. Columbus was forced to have recourse to arms. He assembled his whole force, now reduced to two hundred foot, twenty horse, and *twenty large dogs*. Against him were all the chiefs of the island, save one, together with 100,000 naked savages in arms. Instead of taking advantage of the woods, they assembled in a large open plain, where Columbus attacked them during the night. Filled with consternation, by the noise and havoc of the fire-arms, the force of the cavalry, and the fierce assault of the dogs, they threw down their arms and fled at the first onset; and from that moment relinquishing all thoughts of resistance, they abandoned themselves to despair, and became henceforth the slaves of their opponents. Columbus returned to Spain. In 1498 a third squadron of six vessels was fitted out, and, there being this time no volunteers, the prisons were drained of their malefactors to replenish the numbers of the already wasted colony. This was a fatal mistake to the happiness of all concerned—an unlikely source from which should arise a prosperous and happy colony. In his third voyage Columbus steered more to the south than formerly, and, passing the cluster of the West-India Islands, he arrived at Trinidad, a large island at the mouth of the Orinoco River. Convinced from the magnitude of the river that he had at last discovered an immense continent, he coasted along the shores of the Provinces, now known as Venezuela and Granada, and landed at various points. He was so much pleased with the beauty and fertility of the country, and the intelligence and courage of the natives, that he concluded it to be the paradise described in Scripture. The shattered condition of his ships however prevented him from prosecuting his discoveries further at that time, and he directed his course to Hispaniola once more. Again he found the affairs of the colony in a state of the greatest anarchy and confusion. A serious insurrection had broken out, and threatened its utter annihilation. Columbus saw at once the necessity of prompt measures to quell the rebellion. Some of the malcontents he shipped off to Spain, others he appeased by allotting them extensive tracts of land, and by appointing a certain number of Indians to cultivate the ground for the use of their new masters. Thus, unhappily, were the chains of slavery forged on this hemisphere, and the natives of the New World subjected to the most grievous oppressions. In addition to these calamities, Columbus now became the victim of slander and calumny by the very men whom he had raised from poverty to distinction and influence. He was accused of tyranny, oppression, and avarice, by those who envied his reputation and success. The faith of even his patroness, Queen Isabella, began to give way to suspicion. A resolution fatal to Columbus was taken. Boradilla was appointed to repair to Hispaniola to inquire into the alleged grievances, and, if found to be true, to supersede him in the command. The opportunity thus afforded to aggrandize himself, though it should prove the destruction of a great and good man, was more than the Spanish adventurer could resist. In the most arbitrary manner he condemned him without a hearing, ordered him to be instantly arrested and hurried on board ship. Columbus submitted with composure, and even dignity, to this reverse of fortune. Touched with sentiments of pity due to the rank, age, and merit of his prisoner, the captain of the vessel on board of which he was confined offered, as soon as he was clear of land, to release him from his fetters. "No, Vallejo!" replied Columbus. " I wear these chains in obedience to the orders of my sovereigns; they shall find me as obedient to this as to all their other injunctions. By their command I have been confined, and their command alone shall set me at liberty." The voyage to Spain was fortunately short, Ferdinand and Isabella, ashamed of their own conduct, instantly ordered his fetters to be struck off. He threw himself at the feet of his sovereigns, where he remained some time unable to utter a word, so deep was his emotion. At length he recovered himself, and, in a pathetic speech, completely vindicated his conduct, producing the most satisfactory proof of his own integrity, and of the base malevolence of his enemies. Their majesties affected regret for all that had occurred, but did not evidence their sincerity by reinstating him to his former command. They fitted out however another expedition for the aged adventurer, who in the year 1502 set out on his fourth and last voyage, with all the ardour and buoyancy of youth. It resulted in a series of disappointments and disasters. At Hispaniola he met with an inhospitable reception. He penetrated the Gulf of Darien in search of some strait through which he might emerge on another ocean, which he conjectured extended to the East Indies; but he sought in vain. In attempting to establish a colony on the main land, he was frustrated by the determined opposition of the natives;—and this, the first repulse that the Spaniards had met with in the New World, was the commencement of a series of calamities that pursued Columbus to his grave. His feeble squadron was assailed by a furious hurricane in which two of his vessels were lost. With the remaining two he had great difficulty in reaching Jamaica, where he ran them aground to prevent them from sinking, and took refuge in a cave, which is still shown as the cave of Columbus. Worn out with fatigue and privations, he returned to Spain, where he did not long survive his misfortunes. He died at Valladolid on the 20th of May, 1506, in the 69th year of his age. By orders of Philip the First, then king of Spain, these words were inscribed on his tomb; 'To Castile and Leon Columbus has given a new world."

His conspicuous services undervalued and unrequited by his king—the glory of his achievements envied by his fellow mariners—his unostentatious worth unappreciated by the nations of Christendom,—the star of Columbus set obscurely under the dark cloud of a distant horizon. Another star arose in meridian splendor and attracted the gaze of Europe, once more aroused to a sense of the vast importance which these discoveries in the New World would be to the inhabitants of the Old—another mariner, skilled in astronomy and nautical science, endowed with virtues equalled only by those of Columbus, engraved his name on the tablet of the world's history—a name destined to be had in remembrance while the world endures—Americus entered the field of discovery, and clearly unfolded what his great precursor had but dimly shadowed forth.

That Columbus did not reach the main land of the New World until his third voyage is certain, and it is equally certain that Americus *did* reach it on *his first voyage*, but while there is no disputing the day and date of the landing of Columbus there, unfortunately public opinion is divided as to the year in which Americus first landed. Reputed, not only as a man of science, but a ready writer, Americus gave to the world an interesting account of his discoveries, addressed to Soderini, president of the Florentine republic, of which Americus was a native. He thus commences his letter, "In the year 1497, on the 10th day of May, we left the port of Cadiz, with four ships in company. The first land we made was that of the Fortunate Island, situated in the western ocean, distant from Lisbon 280 leagues. We tarried here eight days, taking in wood and water, when, having offered up our prayers, we weighed anchor and set sail. We sailed so rapidly that at the end of twenty-seven days we came in sight of land, which we judged to be a continent being about 1000 leagues west of the Grand Canaries." A long epistle follows, giving the most minute details of his landing at various points, of his reception by the natives, their appearance, manners, and customs, his battles with them, and his excursions into their country, extending to a distance of eighteen leagues from the sea. In conclusion he says: "we set sail for Spain with 222 prisoners (slaves) and arrived in the port of Cadiz on the 15th day of October, 1498, where we were all well received, and found a market for our slaves."

The circumstance of his having written an account of his travels is ungenerously used by those who would detract from his fame, as an evidence that he himself was desirous of giving his own name to the new continent. His enemies even go so far as to assign a fictitious character to the whole narrative; while others hold that a mistake occurred in the date of it, and maintain that the voyage narrated was identical with his second voyage, by which he reached the continent in 1499. They say, "The near resemblance of the incidents, the similarity of dates of arrival and departure, and the direct testimony of Ojeda, the captain of the vessel in which he sailed, render it almost certain that the first voyage of Ojeda and the second voyage of Americus are identical."

As to the authenticity of the letter, we can offer no opinion, and in so far as the name "America" is concerned, it matters little. Americus was highly skilled in the construction of maps and charts, and it is quite likely that in depicting the coast of Brazil, on which he made his first landing, he gave to that part of the continent, the name of America. If he did so, he did no more than what many another mariner has done since then ; and he is no more to be blamed for this, than is Henry Hudson, who gave his own name at once to Hudson River, and to Hudson Bay. The error, for an error doubtless it was, lay with those who, unintentionally it may be, came to designate a whole continent by the name which Americus had given to a very small portion of it. The distinct origin of the name, cannot it appears, be traced. It was not until the year 1550, or thirty-eight years after the death of Americus, that the name of America came to be generally accepted ; at all events, it is quite certain that while Americus was to some extent indebted to Columbus for his success, Columbus in his voyage of 1498 was in no wise indebted to Americus. If the supposition seems conclusive that Americus did not reach the continent till 1499, unquestionably the honor is due to Columbus who landed in 1498. If on the other hand Americus did land in 1497, it is equally clear that the previous voyages of Columbus to Hispaniola had fired his ambition, and that he was piloted to these shores by Ojeda, who had been an attentive observer of the journals and charts of Columbus during his voyage with him. Little more need be said of Americus here than that he performed his third voyage, said by his enemies to be only his second, under the auspices of the king of Portugal, sailing from Lisbon on the 13th of May, 1501. After sailing along the western coast of Africa, he made for the shores of the New World, which he reached after a tempestuous voyage of ninety-seven days, and coasted along the shores of South America a distance of 750 leagues. His return to Lisbon was celebrated with great magnificence, and the accounts of his discoveries were received with universal enthusiasm by his countrymen. His ship, which had become unseaworthy was broken up, and portions of it carried in solemn procession to a church, where they were suspended as valuable relics.

He returned from his fourth and last voyage in 1504, and very soon after published a full and highly interesting account of all his voyages. He died at Seville in Spain, on the 22nd of February, 1512.

Simultaneously with Americus, another mariner accidentally stumbles on the shores of the western continent. The possibility of finding a short western passage to the East Indies was still uppermost in the minds of scientific and adventurous men, and the recent successes of Columbus encouraged others to enter the field of investigation. John Cabot, a scientific and fearless mariner, a native of Venice, though for a long time residing in England, arrived at the conclusion, that, from the known shape of the globe, if a direct passage did exist, the nearer they approached to the north, the shorter must the passage be. Confident too in his own mind that such a passage did exist, he communicated to Henry VII, King of England, his willingness to sail in search of it. Henry, though in no wise of an enterprising turn of mind, readily assented to the proposal, in hopes that, in some way or another, the adventure might prove so far successful as to be a kind of offset to the lustre shed upon the crown of Spain by the recent voyage of Columbus. The renown that accrued to Spain was felt to be more galling to Henry, because he himself had refused the services of the man who had done so much for Spain, and had repented of that refusal just when it was too late; and now that another opportunity occurred, he resolved to avail himself of it, if perchance it might add to his fame, and the extent of his dominions. Accordingly a commission was issued to John Cabot and his three sons, and their heirs, "with full powers to sail to all countries of the east, west, and north, under English colors, with five ships of such burden and force as they should think proper, *on their own cost and charges*, to seek and to discover all the isles, regions, and provinces of Heathens, unknown to Christians."

The king reserved to himself the dominion of all the towns, castles, and lands they should discover, and expressly required them to return to Bristol, and to pay him one-fifth of all the gains after the expenses of the voyage were deducted. Two vessels were, however, fitted out and provisioned at the public expense, to assist in the enterprise; the adventurers themselves fitted out four. With this fleet, carrying 300 men, John Cabot and his son Sebastian set sail from Bristol in the month of May, 1497, and to his great surprise came in sight of land on the 24th of June. This happened to be the Island of Newfoundland, and being the first land they had seen, he named it Prima Vista, since changed to Bona Vista. A few days afterwards they discovered another island which they called St. John, (now Prince Edward.) Here they found inhabitants, clothed with skins, who made use of darts, bows and arrows. Three of them they took on board that they might have some certain proof to show for the statements they might make of their discoveries. Cabot did not discover the Gulf of St. Lawrence: had he done so, undoubtedly he would have penetrated it, in hopes that it would lead to the much-desired channel to the Indies. Continuing a northerly course, he next came upon the coast of Labrador, which he explored for nearly a thousand miles, reaching the latitude of $67\frac{1}{2}$ degrees. Here his progress was much impeded with ice; and, as the land appeared still to stretch to the northward, without any indidation of the expected opening, they put about, and cruised to the south along the whole coast of North America, until they reached the most southern point of that tract now known as Florida, where, his provisions failing, and his crew becoming disaffected, he returned to England, with the fame of a discoverer, but neither bringing gold, nor having fulfilled the great purpose of his voyage, namely, the discovery of a north-west passage to India. Since the time of Cabot this favorite theory has never been lost sight of, and has enlisted the energies of the most scientific and daring navigators in the world. It was this that tempted Hudson in 1610, when he discovered, entered, and explored the bay that bears his name, and which, for various strong reasons, he felt confident must be connected with a passage to the east. He perished in a future attempt to realise his expectations; and many a brave mariner and gallant ship have since perished in the same cause.

In 1818, a series of voyages was commenced by Ross, Parry, and others, which terminated by verifying the predictions of the wise men of old;—in fact, by actually discovering a channel and passing through from the Atlantic to the Pacific, round the northern promontories of America. But the fearful dangers attending navigation in these Arctic seas, even under the most favorable circumstances, are now known to be such as to render the channel of no practical value. It is almost impossible to speak of Arctic explorations without calling to mind the tragic fate of our own Sir John Franklin and his gallant companions. The mind is at a loss whether most to mourn their untimely end, or to admire that heroism, which, regardless of dangers and privations, endured through years of fruitless search, and never for an instant flagged, until every vestige of a doubt was removed as to their fate. In connection with these icy regions, too, the name of Lady Franklin will be had in everlasting remembrance, as manifesting the most extraordinary development of genuine devotion, of hope inextinguishable, and of Christian resignation.

The splendid results of Cabot's voyage were not immediately apparent; yet this very voyage was the foundation of the claim that England subsequently made to all her American possessions, from the Gulf of Mexico to the North Pole. "Seventy-two years passed away before England bestowed any attention upon that distant land, destined to be a chief source of British opulence and power."

In the year 1513, Balboa first beheld from the Isthmus of Darien that great Pacific Ocean which so many adventurous mariners had longed to see. Seven years later, Magellan sailed from the Atlantic into the Pacific, passing through the straits that bear his name, and thus removed all doubts as to the extent of the continent to the south. His ship was the first to circumnavigate the Globe, though he did not live to see it consummated;—and thus too was conclusively set at rest the long-disputed theory of the sphericity of the Earth.

In consequence of these various explorations, the situation and extent, as well as the prominent features of the New World, had been rendered somewhat familiar to all the nations of Europe; and in the meantime, the fisheries had early attracted the attention of all, to the far-famed Banks of Newfoundland. As early as 1517 at least fifty sail were engaged in the fisheries there. Jacques Cartier, a native of St. Malo, who had long been engaged in the fishery, had taken the lead in exploring at his own risk the northern parts of the new hemisphere.

In the year 1534, Francis the First of France fitted out an expedition for the purpose of establishing a colony in the New World, which he entrusted to the command of Cartier. He set sail from St. Malo on the 20th of April, 1534, and with a fair wind in twenty days arrived at Newfoundland. At this time he explored a large portion of the Gulf of St. Lawrence, and sailed into a bay, which, from the heat experienced there, he named the "Bay of Chaleurs." He also landed on the shore of Gaspé Bay, took possession of it in the name of the French King, and erected a large cross with a shield bearing the arms of France. Having seized two of the natives, he returned to St. Malo without having attempted any settlement. He sailed again the following year with three vessels in company, the largest being only of 120 tons. Many adventurers, including young men of good families, joined the expedition as volunteers. After a boisterous passage, during which they parted company, they all arrived safely at Newfoundland. Some of them had been nine weeks at sea. Having supplied themselves with water and fuel, they again set out to explore the Gulf. After cruising about for ten days, during which time they encountered a violent storm, the vessels entered the mouth of a great river, which Cartier named the St. Lawrence, because they first entered it on the tenth of August, a day held sacred to the memory of St. Lawrence, or Laurentius, (a deacon at Rome, who in the year 258, under the Emperor Valerian, was roasted before a slow fire). He leizurely explored both shores of the river, and came to anchor, on the 7th September, 1535, at an island abounding in vines, which he called Isle de Bachus, now known as the Island of Orleans, where an Indian Chief, named Donnaconna, came with twelve canoes to visit their ships.

Jacques Cartier had with him the two Indians whom he had carried off on his former voyage, and who now acted as interpreters. The good account which they gave of their captors, and the description of the wonders they had seen in France, interested the natives, and secured for Cartier a favorable reception. He thence proceeded up the river to an Indian village, the residence of Donnaconna, called Stadacona, on the site of the Lower Town of Quebec. Here they were hospitably received, and learned from the inhabitants that a larger town existed much further up the stream. Regardless of the danger which he incurred by exposing himself and his handful of men to the treachery of thousands of savages, he left two of his ships at Stadacona, and, with the smallest vessel and three row-boats, manned by thirty-five men, boldly ascended the river, greatly against the wishes of the Indians of Stadacona, who began to suspect that no good could result to themselves from the explorations of these strangers. Before leaving, Cartier fired a volley of ball-cartridge from his cannons, which so overawed the natives that no further resistance was offered to his wishes to ascend the river. On the second of October they reached Hochelaga, consisting of about fifty Indian huts, and surrounded with fields of Indian corn. The appearance of the village was thus described: "It was of circular form, each hut fifty paces long, and from fourteen to fifteen wide, all built in the shape of tunnels, formed of wood, and covered with birch-bark. The dwellings were divided into several rooms, surrounding an open court in the centre, where the fire burned. Three rows of palisades encircled the town, with only one entrance above the gate, and over the whole length of the outer ring of defence there was a gallery, approached by flights of steps, and plentifully provided with stones and other missiles to resist attack."

The inhabitants spoke the language of the Huron nation, and were more advanced in civilization than any of their neighbors; they cultivated the ground, and remained stationary. Here too Cartier met with a friendly reception, and explored the surrounding country without any molestation from the Indians. He ascended the hill, or mountain, near the village of Hochelaga, which he named Mont Royale, since corrupted into Montreal, and which gave its name to the city at its base. The season being too far advanced for further researches, he returned to Stadacona, where he passed the winter. Himself and his whole crew were attacked with scurvy, of which disease twenty-five of them died. Most probably all would have perished, had not the Indians supplied them with a remedy. In April following he took his departure from Quebec. "On the eve of his departure he was guilty of a shameful act of treachery toward his kind entertainers, in seizing the Chief Donnaconna, the intrepreter, and two other Indians, whom he carried with him to France, and presented to the king." In 1541, Cartier again visited the St. Lawrence, and explored the river some distance above Hochelaga. He also distinctly surveyed the coast of Nova Scotia, and called at Newfoundland on his way back to France. Here he met La Roque, Lord of Roberval, who had also been despatched to the St. Lawrence by the king, with the title of Viceroy, and to whom Cartier was deputed to act as lieutenant. Cartier would not listen to the entreaties of Roberval to return to Hochelaga: the state of matters there had greatly changed. The Chief whom Cartier had shamefully betrayed and carried captive to France, had died there, and the Indians looked upon the strangers now with well-founded suspicions, and by their threatening attitude had compelled them to retire ; hence Cartier's objection to return, " but, that he might not quarrel outright with Roberval, he left him unobserved in the night for France, where he arrived disappointed in his bright hopes, ruined in health and fortune, and neglected by his fickle countrymen." He died there in 1549. Roberval prosecuted his voyage, but returned to France without having effected any permanent settlement.

CHAPTER II.

Settlement of the French and English in N. A.—Gilbert occupies Newfoundland—Expedition to Roanoke—Named Virginia—Sir R. Grenville's first settlement—A failure—Sir Walter Raleigh—Disastrous results—Colony abandoned—English Chartered Companies—Smith and Pocahontas.—The Puritans in New England—French occupy Nova Scotia—Dispossessed—N. S. granted to a Scotchman—Ceded to France—Sir David Kirk's exploit—Halifax founded—French in Canada—Quebec founded—War with the Indians.

(From 1598 to 1713.)

The quotations given in the previous chapter may serve to illustrate the discovery of America, which, as we have seen, was explored from the Arctic circle to the parallel of 54° south latitude, embracing an area of 15,000,000 square miles. The subsequent settlement of this great continent partakes more of romance than of sober history. We shall notice in this chapter a few of the earliest attempts at settlement, giving prominence to the English and French, who however made no successful effort to colonize, until the Spanish, Portuguese, and Dutch had for some time been settled.

The first formal act of occupation by the English was at the hands of Sir Humphrey Gilbert, a half-brother to Sir Walter Raleigh, who received a patent from Queen Elizabeth "for discovering, occupying, and peopling such remote, heathen, and barbarous countries, as were not already possessed by any Christian people."

On the 5th of August, 1583, he landed in state on the Island of Newfoundland, and, having summoned around him all the traders and captains of vessels there, he pitched his tent upon a conspicuous part of the shore, ordered his commission to be read in different languages, and issued a proclamation that in virtue thereof he took possession, for the Crown of England, of the harbor of St. John, and two hundred leagues every way around it. A turf and a twig, with a hazel wand were then delivered to him, which he received. Assent and obedience were signified by loud acclamations, and a pillar was erected, bearing a plate of lead, on which the Queen's arms were engraved. A tax was also levied on the ships, and laws promulgated for the government of the colony.* This nominal occupation however did not imply actual settlement. The first attempt to form a colony by the English in America was projected by Mr. Raleigh, afterwards the famous Sir Walter. At his instigation, two ships were sent out in the year 1584 under a patent from Elizabeth, commanded by Philip Amidas and Arthur Barlow. They came to anchor in the Bay of Roanoke in North Carolina, and took formal possession of the country in the name of the Queen, as Gilbert had done in Newfoundland. They returned home without effecting a settlement, but with a very favorable report of the land, and the kindness of the natives. Raleigh lent his powerful influence to heighten their glowing descriptions of the fertility of the country, and salubrity of the climate they had visited. "The English nation was all on fire at the prospect which was offered to its avidity; even the Queen was so delighted with it, that she promised to support the adventurers. She knighted Raleigh, and consented that the country should be called Virginia, in honor of one of her most suspected virtues."†

Next Spring, Sir Richard Grenville, Raleigh's principal associate,

---

* Haliburton.   † Russel.

sailed from Plymouth with a fleet of seven ships, well provided with arms and stores, and landed at Roanoke. After making some experiments upon the soil with a view to settlement, he left 108 men under the command of one Ralph Lane, and then returned to England. Instead of contenting themselves with the goodly land before them, and exerting their industry to cultivate it, Lane became impatient for further discoveries; and ere long, he and all his band became entangled in warfare with the natives, their provisions became exhausted, and a ship that had been left by Sir Richard, to facilitate their retreat to England in case of need, had been wrecked. Fatigued with their wanderings, enervated by disappointment, and constantly harrassed by the Indians, they had well nigh abandoned themselves to despair, when Admiral Drake, who had been dispatched to annoy the Spaniards in the New World, fortunately arrived off the coast, took them all on board, and reconveyed them to England.

In the meantime the company in England, still sanguine of the success of their new colony, were busy fitting out another expedition of four ships to proceed to Virginia, for so the whole country was now called from the borders of Florida to the river St. Lawrence. This time, Sir Walter Raleigh resolved on seeing the country himself, and took command of one of the ships. His vessel being the first ready, and himself impatient to be off, he proceeded at once to sea in advance of the others, and arrived safely at Roanoke in 1586, where he expected to find the much-talked-of settlement. After a fruitless search, without being able to find one Englishman, he returned to England chagrined with the failure of his hopes. It is said that it was during his short stay in Virginia, at this time, that he acquired the habit of smoking,—at all events he had the notoriety of being the first Englishman who smoked tobacco.

Sir Richard Grenville who had sailed a fortnight after him with the three other ships, also arrived safely at Roanoke, but could learn nothing of the colony he had planted there the year before.

He left fifty of his men to make another attempt, and returned to England. In 1587, Captain John White was sent out with a reinforcement of settlers, and with provisions and stores for the colony, and was also invested with the authority of Governor. To his extreme surprise and mortification, all that he found on arriving at Roanoke, was the bones of one of his countrymen; the fifty men left by Grenville had all been slaughtered. Nothing daunted, White landed with his men and took up his abode on the very spot where his countrymen had been butchered a short time before. He conciliated the Indians by presents, and other kind offices, and everything seemed to promise prosperity; but his provisions failing, he was obliged to return to England for supplies. A variety of causes detained him there nearly three years, and when he did return, his fleet on nearing the shore, was assailed by violent storms which drove them out to sea again. White cruelly abandoned the colonists to their fate, and steered straight for England. The unfortunate settlers all perished, either by famine or the arrows of the Indians; not one survived to tell the tragic tale, and Virginia was as completely forgotten as if it had never been discovered.

During the next twenty years, no Englishman seems to have visited the luckless shores of Virginia, except for the purpose of bartering with the natives for fur, or in connection with the fisheries, which were very prolific in all the northern parts of the coast. In 1606, the spirit of adventure revived, and a systematic plan of settlement commenced. Two joint-stock companies were organized, and a grant made to them, under one charter, of the whole coast of America from the 34th to the 45th degree of N. latitude. The one company consisted of parties in London, who wished to settle the southern tract, or Virginia proper. The other company, hailing from Bristol and Plymouth, preferred the north, or as they called it Nova Anglia—now New England. Both had to contend with many difficulties before a permanent footing was obtained. The natives were suspicious of the motives of their white brethren, and their previous success in cutting off the first settlers made them both daring and dangerous: in truth, they were upon the eve of again being annihilated. John Smith, the Governor of the emaciated colony, seeing no other alternative than starvation before them, ventured out in person among the Indians, to traffic with them, if it were possible, for provisions. They took him prisoner at once, and Powhattan the most powerful chief in the country, exulting over his prize, gave orders that his brains should be beaten out with a club. While the sentence was about to be put into execution, Pocahontas, daughter of the chief, interposed, and, clasping Smith's head in her arms, laid her own upon the block. Upon seeing this the savage chief relented. Smith regained his liberty and was abundantly supplied with provisions by this noble Indian heroine. Some years after this, Pocahontas was married to a young Englishman of respectability; and from that time forth, all difficulty with the Indians was at an end, and the colony increased with great rapidity. In the year 1619, a Governor General arrived from England, with instructions to convoke a Legislature. This, the first American Legislature, consisted of eleven representatives, who sat along with the Governor and Council.

In 1620, the Puritans who had fled to Holland to escape the rage of persecution, applied to the Plymouth Company for a part of the country included in their grant. As evidence of their good faith, they added to their request the following statement: "We are well weaned from the delicate milk of our native country, and inured to the difficulties of a strange land. We are knit together in a strict and sacred bond, by virtue of which, we hold ourselves bound to take care of the good of each other and of the whole. Nor is it with us as with other men, whom small obstacles may discourage, or small discontents cause to wish themselves home again: we have properly no home, and will therefore struggle hard to find one."

Preliminaries being arranged, the pious adventurers embarked in one ship, to the number of 120 souls, and landed in the neighborhood of Cape Cod, in what is now called Massachusetts, on the 22nd of December, 1620. They called the name of this place New Plymouth, which it still bears, and chose as their Governor, one John Carver. The Puritans made good their promises: instead of restlessly roaming about in search of gold, as others had done, they immediately applied themselves to agricultural pursuits, and very soon earned for themselves a comfortable subsistence.

New York was settled by the Dutch as early as 1609, and was held by them until 1664, when the Duke of York sent out a powerful force to dispossess them. The Dutch submitted, and the New Netherlands, as it was called, became an English Province; the name of "New Amsterdam" was changed to "New York," and the town of "Orange" took the name of Albany, one of the Duke's titles.

In 1623 the first settlements were made in New Hampshire.
1624. New Jersey was settled by the Dutch and Danes.
1627. Delaware was settled by a number of Danes and Fins.
1628. John Endicot and others colonized Massachusetts.
1632. Maryland was granted to Lord Baltimore and settled next year.
1633. The first house was erected in Connecticut.
1639. Colony of New Haven formed, and charter granted for the Province of Maine.
1663. Rhode Island chartered. Carolina granted to Lord Clarendon and others.
1681. Penn, the Quaker, obtained a grant of the Province of Pennsylvania.
1782. New Brunswick became a Province.

We have described a variety of unsuccessful efforts, on the part of the English, before they secured a permanent footing on the shores of America. We shall now see how it fared with our rivals the French. " They were not inattentive spectators of the enterprises of the other European powers, and at an early period several French navigators visited Canada, for the purpose of annexing it to the Crown of France. Although their first attempts at settlement were equally unfortunate with those of other nations, yet the trade with the Indians and the fisheries on the coast proved so lucrative, that the number of annual adventurers to that country was very great." It is not precisely known by whom the coast of Nova Scotia was first seen, after the voyage of Cabot. The Marquis de la Roche was the first however who visited it with an intention to colonize. He sailed from France in the year 1598, carrying with him a number of convicts from the prisons, and landed on the Isle of Sable, which lies about two hundred miles to the east of Nova Scotia. This desert island, since rendered notorious from the number of ships that have been wrecked on its treacherous shores, was absurdly deemed by the Marquis, a fit place for a settlement. He here landed forty persons, and proceeded to explore the main land. Unfavorable weather compelled him to return to France, without the miserable outcasts whom he had set ashore. Destitute of shelter and all the necessaries of life, they were soon reduced to the greatest distress. Providentially for them, a ship was wrecked upon the island, and a few sheep driven on shore. They constructed huts with the fragments of the wreck, which served to shelter them from the inclemency of the weather. The sheep being soon consumed, they were compelled to live wholly on fish, and their worn-out garments were replaced by clothes made of seal-skin. In this miserable condition they spent seven years, when the King of France sent out a vessel to rescue them from their gloomy exile. Only twelve of the forty were found alive; and their appearance was so squalid and distressing, that he ordered them a general pardon for their offences, and gave to each of the survivors a gratuity of fifty crowns.

No further progress was made by the French in Nova Scotia until the year 1603. At that time De Monts, a French gentleman, was appointed Governor General of that part of North America lying between the 40th and 46th degrees of north latitude, that is, from Virginia to the head of Hudson's Bay, and which was named in his commission "Cadie." It was afterwards variously styled "L'Acadie," "Acadia," and "Arcadia."

De Monts was a Calvinist, and, strange to say, he was allowed the free exercise of his religion personally, upon conditions that he should convert the savages to the Roman Catholic faith. He sailed from Havre in March, 1604, with four ships in company. His destination was Canseau, but being carried to the west, he landed on the south-east coast of Nova Scotia. He remained there for a month waiting for the other vessels that had sailed with him, having on board their supplies for the winter, as well as their implements of husbandry and building materials. At the end of that time, his companions began to be much dispirited; they could neither undertake a settlement without their materielle, nor much longer wait on the arrival of their comrades. Luckily however, when they were upon the point of leaving, intelligence reached them, by a party of Indians, of the arrival of the missing ships at Canseau.

The stores were transported over land, and, cheered by this seasonable relief, their drooping spirits revived. De Monts who was accompanied by Champlain and others, now rounded Cape Sable, and explored the bay separating L'Acadie from the mainland. This they called La Baye François; it is now called the Bay of Fundy. In course of their explorations, they came upon a large river, called by the natives Oungandy, but which they named St. John. Thence they came to an island which was named by them St. Croix. Here they erected a fort and established themselves for the winter.

They soon discovered however that they had made a very injudicious choice of a location; for on the approach of winter they found themselves without the means of obtaining either fuel or fresh water. They were reduced to salt provisions, and had to drink melted snow; the consequence was, that thirty six died of scurvy, and only forty remained. The following Spring they moved to Port Royale, now Annapolis; and, as soon as they were comfortably settled, De Monts returned to France. During his absence they suffered a variety of hardships and calamities, and were only prevented from returning to France by the shipwreck of their only sailing craft.

De Monts on his return found the colony abandoned: they had all left twelve days before. Luckily however they were not yet far off, and, in a harbor where they had taken refuge, receiving intelligence of their leader's arrival, they returned immediately and joined him, and abandoned the idea of seeking to regain France. They now set to work with good courage, to cultivate portions of the soil, and their labours were amply recompensed by the bountiful returns which rewarded their exertions. It happened so far fortunately for them, that their lot had been cast on the richest part of a peninsula, elsewhere sterile and inhospitable. But although this handful of settlers had made a tolerably good beginning, although they had in many respects bright prospects for their future prosperity, the originators of the settlement in France failed to back them up. Suffering from the indifference of those who should naturally have upheld and strengthened it, the colony did not improve as it would otherwise have done. It remained in a languishing state, undisturbed however, by the Indians and others, until the year 1613. At that time the English settlers of Virginia, hearing of the French occupation, and considering them intruders upon their chartered limits, dispatched a force, under one Captain Argall, to dispossess them. He accordingly sailed for Acadia in a ship of war mounting fourteen guns, accompanied by two smaller vessels, entered the Bay of Fundy, and came to anchor abreast of the battery of Port Royale, and proceeded to land a party of forty men. A gun was fired from the battery as a signal for the scattered settlers to assemble; but Argall advanced with such rapidity, that he found the fort abandoned, and immediately took possession of it. The French, completely taken by surprise, offered but little resistance. "Some fled to the woods and mixed with the savages; others went to the St. Lawrence and strengthened the French settlements there, the rest were carried to England, and were reclaimed by the French ambassador." Thus terminated the first French settlement in North America, after an existence of eight years.

Eight years more elapsed before the English appear to have turned their attention to the settlement of the territory from which they had expelled the French. In 1621, King James the First of England made a grant to Sir William Alexander, then Secretary of State for Scotland, of the whole of Acadia, which included part of New Brunswick, the islands of Cape Breton and Prince Edward, and the district of Gaspe. This tract was named for the first time in the patent, *Nova Scotia*. Two years after this, a ship was sent from England with settlers. On landing, they met with a few of the scattered French: hastily forming the opinion that they had resumed possession of the country, and, esteeming discretion to be the better part of valor, they returned whence they had come, without even making an attempt to form a colony. In 1625, Charles quit-claimed Nova Scotia to the French king; but hostilities soon after commencing between the two powers, an opportunity occurred of restoring it to its rightful owners. There was at that time a French colonist by the name of David Kirtck, who had sought an asylum in England, from religious persecution in his native land. This extraordinary man, assisted by Sir William Alexander, fitted out a private expedition, with a view of restoring Nova Scotia to the English. In 1629 Sir David Kirk, for he was familiarly known by that name, arrived in Nova Scotia with an armament of three vessels. With this inconsiderable force he reduced all the settlements of his countrymen, both in Nova Scotia and in Canada. As a reward for these services, he received a grant of the whole of the lands called Canada, upon the north side of the River St. Lawrence; while Nova Scotia and all to the south were confirmed to Sir Wm. Alexander.

The grant to Sir William was probably a type of all the grants of lands in America made about that time. There were no restricting clauses, but on the contrary, an unconditional surrender, for reasons conveyed in the following extract: "James, by the Grace of God, King, &c., &c. To all the clergy and laity of his Dominions,—Greeting,—Be it known that we have ever been careful to embrace every opportunity that offered for the honor and advantage of our kingdom of Scotland, and that we think there are no acquisitions more easy and more innocent than those that can be made by carrying new colonies into foreign and uncultivated countries, where are the necessaries of life; especially if such lands are either inhabited or occupied by unbelievers, whom to convert to the Christian Faith is a duty of great importance to the Glory of God, &c., &c. For these causes, as well as in consideration of the good, faithful, and acceptable services which have been already, and are to be hereafter, performed to us, by our trusty and well beloved counsellor, Sir Wm. Alexander, knight, who is the first of our subjects of Scotland that undertook to carry over this foreign colony at his own expense, and has desired leave to cultivate the lands and countries included within the limits undermentioned: We therefore, from our Royal attention to extend the Christian Religion, and to promote the wealth, prosperity, and peace of the natural subjects of our said kingdom, have given, granted, and transferred to the said Sir William and his heirs, all and singular, the lands of the continent and islands, situate in America, as follows, &c., &c., together with all the mines of iron, lead, copper, pewter, brass, &c., &c."

Very little value appears to have been set upon these countries, by either government, for, by the treaty of St. Germains in 1632, they were all restored to France. In 1654, Nova Scotia again became English, and in 1662 French, and so continued every few years to be alternately English and French until 1713, when, by the treaty of Utrecht, peace was restored between the two countries; Canada was retained by France; Nova Scotia and Newfoundland became British Provinces, and have so continued ever since. Nearly half a century however elapsed, before any progress was made by the English in settling the country, and, during the interval, the French inhabitants began to renew their claim to a portion of it. "They contended that the name of Acadia applied only to the peninsula; that they had yielded that, and nothing more to England, and that the rest of the country lying between New England and the Bay of Fundy was a part of 'New France' which still belonged to them." The New Englanders loudly remonstrated against this claim, and the subject was closely investigated by the Home Government. The importance of the position in a mercantile light, became so apparent, that active measures were soon taken for confirming and extending the dominions of the Crown of Great Britain in this Province. A systematic and extensive plan of settlement was resolved upon, and its execution referred to the Board of Trade and Plantations, over which the Earl of Halifax presided. Lands were granted gratuitously to intending settlers, and an offer was made to convey them and their families to Nova Scotia, to maintain them twelve months after their arrival at the expense of Government, and to supply them with arms and ammunition for their defence, as well as with implements of husbandry and building materials. Attracted by these liberal terms, 3,760 adventurers set sail in May, 1749, under the command of the Hon. Edward Cornwallis, whom the king had appointed as Governor of Nova Scotia. They landed in Chebucto Harbor, and immediately began to build a town for their occupation, to which they gave the name of Halifax. This was the first English settlement in what are now called the British Provinces. We need not add that it proved a permanent and a prosperous one, in many ways advantageous to the mother country.

Having dwelt, perhaps unduly, upon the settlement of Nova Scotia, we shall bring this chapter to a close by stating, in as few words as practicable, the circumstances attending the first settlements of the French in Canada.

De Monts after, having established a small colony in Acadia, returned to France. "During his absence many complaints had been made of the injustice of the exclusive privileges that had been bestowed upon him. In consequence of these remonstrances, his patent was revoked, nevertheless he continued his efforts for the promotion of the settlement of Canada, and succeeded in obtaining a renewal of his privileges for twelve months, upon condition that he should establish a settlement on the banks of the St. Lawrence." With the assistance of the trading company, De Monts fitted out two vessels, the command of which was intrusted to Samuel Champlain and Pontgrave. On the 3rd of July, 1608, Champlain reached Stadacona, where Jacques Cartier had wintered seventy-three years before. The Indian town had in the meantime dwindled away, and only a few miserable huts marked the spot. "This magnificent site was at once chosen by Champlain as the place for a future city, and centuries of experience have confirmed the wisdom of the choice." Here he erected huts for shelter, magazines for stores and provisions, and crowned the summit of the precipice with barracks for the officers and men. He then gave to the future capital of the country the name of Quebec; and it is now just one of the very few old towns in Canada that retains its original name.

During the first winter, in addition to the ravages of scurvy, these pioneers suffered severely from the extremities of famine. Early in spring, Champlain ascended the St. Lawrence till he reached the River Richelieu. Following up this stream, he emerged upon the beautiful lake that now bears his name. He passed through the entire length of it, and thence into Lake George. Having accomplished the object of his visit, he returned to France, where he was well received by Henry the Fourth, who, about that time gave the name of *New France* to Canada. Champlain devoted the remainder of his life to the advancement of the colony, which he had been instrumental in planting on the St. Lawrence. It was mainly at his instigation that New France was restored in 1632 to the French crown, after it had been subdued by Sir David Kirk. At this time he was reinstated as Governor of the colony. He died in Quebec in December, 1635.

The death of the master-spirit of the colony was felt to be a severe blow to its prosperity. " The company in France, deprived of his advice, instead of sending out troops and traders to protect and extend the colony, sent out only monks and nuns," and their possession was by no means so peaceable as to warrant this procedure. The settlers had become entangled in a harrassing war with the Indians; an inveterate feud of long standing, was still raging between the Huron and Iroquois tribes, when the French came to settle in Canada. The latter imprudently allied themselves with the Hurons, and thus subjected themselves to the deadly attacks of the Iroquois, who were the most warlike and powerful of all the Indian tribes. Their territory was nearly eighty leagues in length, and more than forty in width, it included the countries bordering upon Lake Erie, Ontario, and the River St. Lawrence, the greater part of New York, and also of Pennsylvania. This vast space was inhabited by five nations, that could bring twenty thousand effective warriors into the field. " They had learned to approach like foxes, to attack like lions, and to fly like birds." They were not prepared however for the new mode of warfare introduced by the strangers, and they fled in disorder at the first discharge of the French muskets. The English, who had in 1664 dispossessed the Dutch from New Amsterdam, and who remained in possession of the conquered territory, which they had named New York, ingratiated themselves with the Iroquois, already giving way before the combined machinations of their double enemy. They were invited to bring their beaver and other furs to Albany, and in exchange were supplied with fire-arms and ammunition. This tended to widen the breach between them and the French, who, having failed to subdue the Iroquois by force, next had recourse to stratagem. Under pretext of a friendly negotiation they decoyed a number of the Iroquois chiefs to Quebec, and dishonored the French name by a most infamous perfidy. No sooner had the unsuspecting Indian chiefs arrived than they were placed in irons, and sent to France to be condemned to the gallies. The Iroquois, in retalliation, committed the most frightful ravages on the French. About the year 1690, the governor of New York openly espoused the cause of the Iroquois, and, as a consequence, hostilities became general between the English and French residents in America. In the year 1710, a formal alliance was entered into between the English and the Iroquois, and the entire conquest of Canada was resolved upon, and now for the first time openly acknowledged. No sooner however were hostilities commenced, than the wily Iroquois began to reason among themselves, that in the event of the English proving victorious, they themselves would, in all likelihood soon be annihilated—that their glorious hunting-grounds would be forfeited to the cupidity of their new allies—and they themselves be ignominiously expelled from "*their own, their native land.*" They saw in short, that their very existence depended upon a continuance of hostilities between the rival combatants, either of whom would tolerate them for the sake of their alliance, until they had accomplished their own purposes of self aggrandizement, *and no longer;* and now that the Indian race has melted away " like snow before the sun, " we need not express surprise at the language used by Sir Francis Bond Head, in a dispatch to the Colonial office, dated from Toronto, 20th November, 1836. "The fate of the red inhabitants of America, the real proprietors of its soil, is, without any exception, the most sinful story recorded in the history of the human race; and when one reflects upon the anguish they have suffered from our hands, and the cruelties and injustice they have endured, the mind, accustomed to its own vices, is lost in utter astonishment at finding, that in the red man's heart, their exists no sentiment of animosity against us, no feeling of revenge; on the contrary, that our appearance at the humble portal of his wigwam is, to this hour, a subject of unusual joy." Neither can we wonder, that, at that particular time, yielding to the forebodings of their intuitive instinct, they deserted the English, who, deprived of their aid, failed to reduce Canada.

A second attempt was rendered fruitless from similar causes; shortly after which, by the treaty of Utrecht, peace was restored, and Canada remained a French Province. How it eventually became annexed to the British Crown, must be reserved for another chapter.

CHAPTER III.

The Mississippi discovered—La Salle—Louisiana settled—French claims—Fruitless negociations—French war in N A.—Siege of Louisbourg—Peace—Hostilities between France and England—The fall of Quebec—Amherst descends the St. Lawrence—Sir William Johnston—Conquest of Canada completed.

(From 1745 to 1763.)

As early as 1675, the French in Canada had learned in their intercourse with the Indians, of the existence of a great river much further westward than they had yet penetrated, and, from the description given of its course, they justly considered that it must empty itself into the Gulf of Mexico. No sooner was this made known, than a small band of daring adventurers volunteered their services to proceed to that distant region, and to ascertain what truth there might be in the announcement. The party consisted of Marquette, a Jesuit priest, whose virtues were known and respected by nearly all the Indians of Canada, Jolyet, a merchant of Quebec, and six boatmen. They set out in high spirits, and, yielding to neither fears nor dangers, reached the head of Lake Michigan, entered the river of the Foxes, and ascended that stream to the Lake Winibago. A short portage brought them to the River Ouisconsing, flowing in a westerly direction. Here they obtained the services of two Indian pilots, and, swiftly descending the river, in a short time found themselves on the bosom of the great Mississippi, which they descended for a long distance, and became satisfied that it did empty itself into the Gulf of Mexico. Their provisions failing, and having so far accomplished their mission, Jolyet returned in safety to Quebec, leaving Marquette amongst the Miami Indians, to minister ghostly counsel, as well probably as to conciliate them, in order the better to secure their trade with them for furs.

Some years after this, La Salle, a Frenchman of family and of enterprise, perceiving that the Canadians had neglected to follow up the discovery of the Mississippi by settlement, determined to add to his fortune, or at least to earn for himself a brilliant reputation. He proceeded to France, where he was assisted in fitting out an expedition. He returned to Quebec, and, taking with him Father Hennipin, proceeded to the Falls of Niagara. During the winter they constructed a vessel of 60 tons burthen, at a distance of about four miles above the Falls. In the Spring they set sail, and, traversing the great lakes, landed in Green Bay, and pursued their journey thence in canoes to the Mississippi. Having spent some time in exploring the river and its shores, he returned to Quebec, and thence to France, for the purpose of urging the Government to send out a colony. His plan was approved of, and a party of about 250 sailed for the mouth of the Mississippi; but the precise whereabouts of the mouth of that river not having as yet been determined, they spent a considerable time in a fruitless search for it, and eventually landed about 200 miles beyond it. La Salle, naturally of a haughty disposition, irritated by this disappointment, quarreled outright with the commander of his fleet, and so exasperated his followers that they fell upon him unawares and murdered him; and with him perished the success of the enterprise.

Another attempt was made in 1699, by M. Iberville, a Canadian. A feeble and dispirited band of emigrants was left by him upon the most barren part of the whole country. During forty years they dragged out a miserable existence, and at the end of that time twenty-eight wretched families constituted the colony.

After a time their numbers were replenished by convicts and felons from the prisons of France.* Two years rolled on, and the sickly colony in Louisiana proved of no value to France, further than by a nominal possession, establishing her claim to the territory. In the meantime the French fortified a few trading-posts on the Ohio, in addition to those they already had along the frontiers of Canada, including strong fortresses at Niagara, Frontenac, and La Présentation, (Ogdensburg) for the purpose of keeping the English within the range of the Alleghany Mountains. Pursuant to this, they asserted their right to the whole of the western and northern parts of America, and this the English were not prepared to concede.

In the year 1750, commissioners met at Paris for the purpose of adjusting the rival claims of the French and English to the American Provinces; but no satisfactory terms could be arrived at. The negotiations were broken off, and for a time the colonists were left to fight their own battles.

Although Newfoundland and Nova Scotia had been relinquished to the English in 1713, unfortunately, the Island of Cape Breton, closely adjoining Nova Scotia, was still held by the French, and long remained a thorn in the side of the New Englanders. The French were fully alive to the importance of this post in connection with the fisheries and the fur-trade, and they spent twenty-five years in fortifying it, at an expense of thirty millions of livres. The fort at Louisbourg, the chief harbor on the island, was surrounded by a rampart of stone two and a half miles in circumference, and thirty-six feet in height, with a ditch eighty feet wide. One hundred and five pieces of cannon, mostly 42-pounders, were mounted on its bastions, besides sixteen mortars. Jealous of so formidable a fortification within sight of their shores, the New Englanders resolved to demolish this Gibraltar of the New World. In the year 1745, they dispatched a force of six thousand

---

* Russel.

volunteers for that purpose, under the command of one Mr. Pepperal, a colonel of Militia, who, although bred a lawyer, displayed all the tact and bravery of a veteran soldier. Having landed upon the island, they immediately invested the city of Louisbourg, saluted its inhabitants with three hearty cheers, and thereafter plied them with shot and shell for forty-nine days. At the end of that time a general assault was resolved upon, and preparations were making to carry it into effect, when the French commander surrendered, and the Provincials took possession of the fort, on the 16th of June. It was only then that they became aware of the vast strength of the place, and of the impossibility of carrying it by assault if properly defended. It was garrisoned by regulars, militia, and citizens, to the number of 4130 men, who having engaged that they would not bear arms against Great Britain or her allies, for twelve months, were all transported to Rochfort in France. "In no one instance of history," says Haliburton, "is there to be found such a combination of fortunate occurrences; had any one of which been awanting, the object of the expedition must have been defeated. There was no reason to expect any aid from the navy; but several fortuitous circumstances brought together every British ship of war, from the ports of the American continent, till they had a formidable fleet of four ships of the line, and six frigates, under Admiral Warren, mounting in all 514 guns; but this did not lessen the merit of the man who planned, nor of the people who effected the conquest of this regularly-constructed fortress, considering that they were but a body of husbandmen, and merchants, wholly destitute of professional skill." The Island of St. John (Prince Edward) fell into the hands of the English at the same time, and its inhabitants were also sent to France. Pepperal and Admiral Warren were both preferred to the dignity of Baronets of the United Kingdom, in acknowledgment of their gallant services; but to the great annoyance of the New Englanders, who were bent upon the demolition of this fort, it was restored to the French with all its fortifications entire, in terms of the treaty of Aix la Chapelle, on the 12th of July, 1749.

The tranquillity which Canada had enjoyed for some time previous to this period, served to recover it from that state of languor, into which it had been so long plunged. The varied resources of the country, and its unequalled geographical features for sustaining a prosperous colony, had at last become apparent to the French; emigration began to be encouraged by them, and strong bodies of regular troops were sent to protect them from the attacks of the Iroquois Indians, as well as from the designs of their more formidable rivals in New England. In the year 1753 the population of Canada had reached 70,000, exclusive of the troops, and the Indians, whose numbers in the neighbourhood of the French settlements were estimated at 66,000. The French remained clustered thickly together, in the vicinity of Quebec, Three Rivers, and Montreal. A few straggling traders were also to be found at Detroit, and the other fortified posts we have named.

While England and France were nominally at peace, a series of vexatious skirmishes, and even some considerable engagements took place, between the New Englanders and the French of Canada, in reference to projected settlements on the Ohio. Major Washington took a conspicuous part on the side of the English. The formidable settlements effected in 1749 by the English in Nova Scotia, and the large sums of money which were expended by them in fortifying the city of Halifax, suggested to the French, precautionary measures for their own safety in America. Accordingly in 1755, they dispatched a fleet of twenty-five ships of the line, besides frigates and transports, with abundance of stores, and 4,000 troops. Aroused by this unusual demonstration directed to the shores of America, the English also sent out a fleet of eleven sail of the line and a frigate, under Admiral Boscawen with some land-forces, to watch the French movements. The English fleet steered for the Banks of Newfoundland. A few days after reaching their destination, the French ships also arrived there; but as there was a thick fog, neither fleet saw their antagonist, and the French ships entered the St. Lawrence unperceived, with the exception of two which had parted company from the squadron. As bad luck would have it, they came in contact with two English ships of nearly equal strength: the two Frenchmen mounting 118 guns, the English 120. A sharp conflict ensued, which ended in the capture of the French vessels; and by this act were the two nations again plunged into a state of open warfare. Reinforcements of regular troops arrived from England, and the New Englanders armed themselves for their own defence. The tranquillity of Nova Scotia was secured, by driving the French from the posts they had usurped in that country, with little or no loss on the part of the English. They were less fortunate on the Ohio; there, General Braddock with an army of two thousand men was totally routed. About the same time Sir William Johnston was entrusted with the command of an expedition against Crown Point, on Lake Champlain, where the French were strongly posted. With a force of 6,000 men under him, he not only failed to carry out his designs against the French, but narrowly escaped being defeated himself; for the French having already routed part of his army, came down upon him unawares. Fortunately for Johnston, the surprise was mutual, and the French supposing that he was all ready for action, halted at 150 yards from his front. Advantage was promptly taken of this to open fire upon them from the great guns. The fortunes of the day were reversed; great numbers of the French were slaughtered, and the Baron Dieskau, their commander, with many others, taken prisoners. This success however was followed by no important result, and upon the whole rather detracted from than added to Johnston's military reputation.

General Shirley was in the same year compelled to abandon the attack upon Niagara with which he had been entrusted, without striking a blow. So that upon the whole the result of the opening campaign of the French war was disastrous indeed to the British arms.

It would far exceed our limits to attempt even an outline of the desperate struggle that was maintained, during eight years, between the two powers, for the possession of Canada. But the closing scenes of this memorable period in the history of the country are so full of interest to every Canadian, that they will bear repetition, even though they may be already familiar to the reader.

The importance of Canada as a colony had already become apparent to the statesmen of England, and although they had for the most part hitherto allowed the New Englanders to fight their own battles with the French in Canada, the time had now come when the dormant claim of England should be renewed to the whole of North America, in virtue of its discovery by John Cabot. Canada, so long undervalued, was now considered worth fighting for, and the preparations made for its conquest were entered into with a vigor and alacrity which augured well for the final result.

In the year 1758, Admiral Boscawen left Halifax harbor with a fleet of one hundred and fifty sail, having on board fourteen thousand troops, under General Amherst and General Wolfe. On the 2nd of June they arrived off Louisbourg, on Cape Breton Island, which the French had spared no means to render impregnable, looking upon it as the key to the St. Lawrence; for the same reason the British regarded its destruction, as the first step towards the conquest of Canada. Six days elapsed before the troops could land, on account of the heavy surf which broke with prodigious violence along the whole shore. On the seventh day, the sea having moderated, a landing was effected, several strong batteries were erected, and the fortress was regularly besieged. After a determined resistance of forty-eight days, during which Wolfe covered himself with glory, the beleagured garrison were forced, unconditionally, to surrender themselves prisoners of war. The articles of capitulation were signed on the 26th of July; in terms of which the inhabitants were transported to France in English vessels. The regular troops, the marines, and mariners, in all 5,637 men, were sent prisoners of war to England. Two hundred and thirty-one pieces of cannon, eighteen mortars, and a large quantity of stores and ammunition, fell to the victors. " Intelligence of this affair was immediately dispatched to England, accompanied by eleven pairs of colors. These were, by his Majesty's orders, carried in pompous parade from Kensington Palace to St. Paul's, where they were deposited as trophies, under a discharge of cannon, and other expressions of exultation; and public rejoicings were held all over the kingdom."

The effect of this important victory upon the spirit of the troops was exhilirating in the extreme, and it was at once resolved to follow it up by a simultaneous attack upon all the strong positions of the French in Canada. It was arranged that General Wolfe should proceed up the St. Lawrence with 8,000 men, and a considerable fleet, and undertake the siege of Quebec. General Amherst with 12,000 was to reduce Ticonderoga and Crown Point, cross Lake Champlain and proceeding by the Richelieu River to unite with Wolfe at Quebec. General Prideaux, with a third army, was to invest Niagara, and, having secured possession of that important point, was to descend the St. Lawrence to Montreal.

On the 26th of June, 1659, Wolfe with his armament came to anchor at the Isle of Orleans, a short distance below Quebec. He immediately issued a proclamation to the inhabitants of Canada, informing them, that "He had come to conquer the province, and that he had an ample force at his disposal to effect this. He implored them, by a prompt submission, to avert from themselves the calamities of war. He guaranteed them safety in person and property, and assured them the free exercise of their religion." This earnest appeal, however, had no effect beyond arousing the French general to the most energetic measures of defence. The priests urged the populace to resist the heretical invaders, telling them it were better for them to die in defence of their country, than that they should fall alive into the hands of the cruel and perfidious English. Quebec was in every way prepared for a siege:

the citadel was strongly garrisoned with veteran French troops. The Marquis de Montcalm, who conducted the defence, took up a position along the shore, from the city to the falls of Montmorenci, and was entrenched there, while another force was strongly posted at Point Lévi, opposite the city. "The Canadians placed considerable reliance on the supposed difficulties of the river navigation; but when the crowding sails were seen rounding the Isle of Orleans, the people in despair flew to the churches, to offer up their prayers for the preservation of their country." So admirable were the dispositions of the defenders, that their position seemed even to an experienced eye to be impregnable, and Wolfe, sanguine and intrepid though he was, began to despair as to the result of his mission. His first step was to dispatch a force to Point Levi, which soon fell into his hands, and its batteries were turned against the adamantine walls of the city. A part of the fleet was stationed above the town, to protect Point Levi, and to guard the river. Wolfe hesitated to commence the attack. For five weeks he had lain before the fortress, many lives had been lost, and but little accomplished. The season too was advancing, and he was little encouraged to hazard an encounter so dubious, as must result from an attempt to force the strong position of Montcalm. He felt that by each day's delay his own army was suffering severely, while the position of the enemy was daily becoming more unassailable. "He resolved to attack them where they lay, in their intrenchments above the falls of Montmorenci. The result confirmed his worst fears; the English grenadiers, who led the attack, instead of forming themselves into column, as they had been ordered to do, impetuously rushed upon the enemy's intrenchments, which they failed to carry. By this hasty movement they were thrown into confusion, and forced to retire, leaving five hundred men dead upon the field."* The camp which the British had formed below the Falls, was now broken up, and the army crossed over to the south shore of the St. Lawrence. A council of war was held, and

---

* Russel.

it was determined to make a night attack, to scale the heights, and to approach Quebec from the Plains of Abraham, which, being the least suspected point of attack, was also the weakest in fortifications.

On the evening of the 12th of September, a part of the fleet was ordered to make a feint below the town; and in the meantime the whole of the army was hastily embarked on board the remaining ships, which proceeded about eight miles up the river. This *ruse de guerre* had the desired effect of diverting the attention of the enemy, and effectually concealed the real design. As soon as it was dark, the first division of the army was placed in boats, and silently floated down the river with the tide, until they reached the point they had chosen to land at. General Wolfe accompanied them himself, and was among the first to spring ashore. The 78th Highlanders were in the foremost boats. Headed by their Captain, McDonald, they scrambled up the tangled precipice with amazing activity, and ere long reached the summit. Here they were met by a small party of the enemy, who were soon overpowered, and fled immediately to the city with the astounding intelligence, that the British had landed at their very gates. By the break of day, the whole of Wolfe's army had gained the plateau, and were drawn up in battle array. The right wing was commanded by Brigadier Monkton, the left by Brigadier Murray, and Colonel Howe, with the light infantry, secured the rear; in all the British numbered 4,828 regular troops. The French force, exclusive of the Indians, amounted to 7,520 men, not more than half of whom, however, were regular soldiers, the remainder, militia and peasantry. "When Montcalm was informed that the English had gained the heights, he could not credit the report: the ascent of an army, by such a precipice, exceeded the idea of any enterprise that either reading or experience had ever suggested to him; but when convinced of its reality, he no longer hesitated; when he found that a battle could not be prudently avoided, like a true hero he resolved to hazard it, and immediately put his troops in motion."

At eight o'clock, the heads of French columns began to appear, ascending the hill from the St Charles river, towards the heights in rear of the city, now occupied by the British army. At nine, Montcalm moved some distance to the front, and developed his line of battle. At about ten o'clock, a crowd of Canadians and Indians emerged from the slope which falls towards the north east. As they advanced, they opened fire upon the English piquets of the extreme left, and drove them in to their supports. Fifteen hundred marksmen were concealed in the bushes and corn fields, who maintained a withering fire upon the British lines, and which proved fatal to many a brave officer. Under cover of the smoke of these skirmishes, the centre and left of the French army rapidly advanced. Wolfe was wounded in the wrist, but wrapping a handkerchief round the wound, he calmly awaited the attack. When the head of the French columns had arrived within forty yards, he gave the word to fire, and a volley from the whole British line told with terrible effect. A desperate struggle ensued. The Highlanders drew their broadswords, and completed the impression they had made; they fell upon the French with their characteristic impetuosity, and drove them before them into the citadel and the fortifications at St. Charles.

Wolfe was a second time wounded, still he persevered; and now that the fortunes of war had turned in his favor, he placed himself at the head of the grenadiers, to lead them on to a final charge, when unfortunately he received a bullet in his breast. He was carried a little to the rear, and the command devolved upon Monkton, who was immediately afterwards severely wounded. Townshend the next in command, hastened to the centre, and, finding the troops disordered in the pursuit, reformed them as quickly as possible. The victory was indeed already complete. The French General, Montcalm, and his second in command, were both mortally wounded; about a thousand of the enemy were made prisoners, and an equal number killed. The loss of the English in regard to numbers, was very inconsiderable, amounting only to forty-five killed, and 617 wounded. But the death of Wolfe was truly a national misfortune. "At the age of thirty-five he united the ardor, the humanity, and enlarged views of the hero, to the presence of mind, and military skill of the commander."

Even under all the agonies of approaching dissolution, he continued to encourage and animate his troops. When told that they were routed, and fled on all sides, his eyes, then closing in death, for a moment brightened up; "Who run?" he exclaimed, "The French," was the reply. "Then," said he, "I am satisfied," and immediately expired. His remains were conveyed to England, and interred at Greenwich. "Montcalm was scarcely his inferior. Though less fortunate in the last scene of his life, he made the most perfect dispositions that human prudence could suggest, both before and during the engagement." Some years afterwards, when Lord Dalhousie was governor in Canada, he erected a monument on the citadel of Quebec, which still remains, a graceful tribute to the memory of the two equally brave and beloved commanders.

The taking of Quebec was an important point gained towards the entire reduction of Canada. Much however still remained to be done. During the ensuing winter, the French troops retired into the heart of the country, and were reinforced to the number of ten thousand men. With these M. De Levi proposed to attempt the recovery of the capital early in spring. In the meantime, General Murray had omitted no step that could be taken by the most consummate officer, for maintaining the important conquest committed to his care; but the garrison had suffered severely during the winter from cold and scurvy. One thousand soldiers had died, and twice that number were unfit for service, when the French arrived before Quebec in the month of April following. In order to avoid the hardships of a siege in a place, which to him seemed hardly tenable, General Murray at once led out his troops to the plains of Abraham, to give them battle. After an obstinate encounter, which lasted an hour and three quarters, he was obliged to quit the field and shut himself up in the citadel, having sustained a loss of a thousand men killed or wounded, as well as the greater part of his artillery. At the same time the French lost upwards of two thousand men in the action, without deriving any real advantage from it. Having driven the British into their stronghold, the French opened trenches before the city walls on the very evening of the battle, and vigorously prosecuted the siege. In all probability Quebec would have reverted to its former owners, but for the opportune arrival of a considerable fleet from England in the month of May. Cheered by the prospect of assistance, Murray again marched out at the head of his garrison. The French, overawed by the appearance of the fleet, did not wait his attack, but fled in disorder, and afterwards retired to Montreal, where Vaudreuil, the Governor of Canada, had fixed his head quarters, and was resolved to make a last stand.

In the meantime, General Amherst was diligently employed in carrying out the pre-concerted measures for the conquest of New France. His own progress, however, through Lake Champlain, had been resolutely disputed by the French, and, although he had succeeded in driving them from Ticonderoga and Crown Point, the French were still posted in great strength, at the northern extremity of the lake, on the Isle aux Noix. The advanced season of the year obliged Amherst to return to Crown Point for winter quarters, which he did in the month of October. At this time he was still in ignorance of the result of Wolfe's operations at Quebec, and was thus completely frustrated in his efforts to join him. The third division of the army, directed against the Niagara frontier, was more successful. In 1759, General Prideaux appeared before Niagara, but was unfortunately killed while reconnoitering the fort, to which he had been suffered to advance without the least opposition. The conduct of the expedition now fell temporarily upon Sir Wm. Johnston. Amherst had dispatched General Gage to replace Prideaux; but before he could arrive, Johnston had already achieved wonders. He vigorously pushed on the siege of Niagara. A party of French and Indians 1700 strong, had been dispatched from Detroit to relieve the beleagured garrison; but before they could unite, Johnston forced them to an engagement, and, after a determined battle near the Falls, he completely routed them. The pursuit was hot and bloody, and continued for several miles. "This was the second important military service performed by Sir William Johnston; and it is recorded to his honor, that, though not regularly bred a soldier, the most consummate general could not have made more excellent dispositions for battle, or conducted the siege, from beginning to end, with more cool and steady resolution."

The capture of Louisbourg, of Quebec, and lastly of Niagara, had reduced the French sway in Canada to very circumscribed limits, and the time was evidently not far off when it was destined to be totally extinguished. In 1760, General Amherst sent instructions to General Murray to prepare for an advance upon Montreal, with all the troops that could be spared from the garrison of Quebec. Colonel Haviland was ordered to sail from Crown Point, take possession of Isle aux Noix, and then proceed to the same destination; while he himself, with an army of ten thousand men, left the frontiers of New York, on the 21st of June, passed up the Mohawk river, and down that of the Oneidoes to Oswego, where he was joined by a thousand Indians of the Six Nations, under Sir William Johnston; and then set out upon that memorable expedition down the St. Lawrence, which terminated in the bloodless conquest of Canada.

At that time the difficulty of transporting an army of eleven thousand men in safety through the dangerous rapids of the St. Lawrence, was considered more formidable by far, than even the capture of Montreal, for which it was undertaken. In fact, without French pilots, not easily to be had, it was deemed impracticable. Having set sail, the expedition met with no obstruction until they reached Isle Royale, an island below Prescott (now known as Chimney Island), where they found the French so strongly posted, that it required two days of sharp firing to dislodge them. Having made themselves masters of the place, they now commenced a war with the elements: they had reached the first of the famed rapids of the St. Lawrence, and the river as it became swifter, became also more contracted in width, and afforded less sea room for the numerous fleet of boats which were now crowded together on its surface. They passed safely down the Galouse, and Rapid du Plat, and halted for the night at Isle aux Châts (opposite Aultsville). In passing the Longue Soult Rapids, which are very swift, narrow, and full of short turns, with numerous dangerous shoals and eddies, several of their boats were jammed to pieces. There are still said to exist, opposite Massena, the wrecks of several vessels, supposed to have belonged to this English fleet, and to have perished at that time. Before reaching the Island of Montreal, twenty-nine boats belonging to the regiments, seventeen whale-boats, seventeen artillery-boats, and one row-galley, were dashed to pieces, with the loss of eighty-eight men. After a tedious, dangerous, and most harassing voyage of two months and seventeen days, from the time they had left New York, the gallant Amherst and his brave followers reached the Island of Montreal, having performed a feat, accompanied doubtless with less stratagem, but even more hazardous, than the scaling of the heights of Abraham at midnight by General Wolfe.

Generals Murray and Haviland reached Montreal within two days of the arrival of Amherst's army. By this singular and happy coincidence, the conquest of Canada was completed without further bloodshed. Montreal soon after capitulated, the old French war was brought to a close, and, by the treaty of Paris in 1763, Canada was formally ceded to the English, and became a British Province.

We had intended at this point to have abandoned the history of Canada, and to have restricted ourselves to the subject more immediately in hand, and to some of our readers, perhaps, we should apologize before proceeding further. The original intention was simply to have presented a narrative of the action of Crysler's Farm, which occurred in the county of Dundas and upon the Author's farm. Some reference to previous as well as subsequent movements seemed necessary, in order that it should assume its relative place and importance in the eventful war of 1812. It shall be our object in the following chapter, briefly to trace the causes of that war, and to glance cursorily at some of the leading events in it, and their results.

CHAPTER IV.

The Revolutionary War—Its origin and results—Character of Washington—Reflections on the war—Causes of the war of 1812—Hull invades Canada—Battle of Queenston—Fall of General Brock—Engagements by sea and land—Wilkinson's Expedition—Battle of Crysler's Farm—Peace concluded—Incidents—Medals and Monuments—Battle of Matilda—The affair at Mariatown—Salmon River raid—The tried Sergeant.

(From 1763 to 1815.)

From the year 1610, when the English, French, and Dutch Colonies were first formed in North America, up to the treaty of Paris in 1763, the progress and prosperity of the British Provinces in numbers and in wealth, far exceeded even the most sanguine expectations of the adventurous pioneers themselves.

It will be remembered that at this period, Old England was undergoing all the miseries of a civil war, and of a political despotism, which closely followed in the wake of the ever memorable religious Reformation. One innovation and act of despotism had followed another, until the outraged people rose in riot, the riot rapidly became a revolution, and ambition—patriotism—fanaticism, were mingled in one headlong torrent—the whole nation was in arms—an interval of eleven years had elapsed without the semblance of a Parliament being convoked. The king fled from London, never to return, till the day of a terrible and memorable reckoning had arrived. In 1649, a revolutionary tribunal was formed, Charles the first, the lawful king of England, was pronounced a tyrant, a traitor, a murderer, and a public enemy, and his head was severed from his shoulders before thousands of spectators, in front of the banqueting hall of his own palace.*

In Scotland, the Presbyterians fought to the death, in defence of their rights, civil and sacred. The Protector Cromwell, with an iron hand, subjugated Ireland, and annihilated the military force of Scotland. Thousands of Britain's inhabitants were, in such circumstances, glad to seek an asylum in the wild woods of America, where they had a wide field of enterprise, and the full right accorded to them of worshipping God, and governing themselves as they pleased; reserving only the political connection of the same sovereign, strengthened by the ties of mutual commercial interests. "At this time nothing could exceed the loyalty of the British colonists, and, by the treaty concluded in 1763, England's sway extended over the whole of North America, from the Gulf of Mexico to the North Pole. Unfortunately for Britain, her short-sighted ministers commenced the persecution of these loyal colonists, by needless interference with their foreign commerce, a series of unpopular restrictions and taxations were imposed upon them, and the climax of colonial resentment and discontent was reached by the imposition of the Stamp Act." This act was all but unanimously assented to, by both Houses of Parliament, and ratified by the king (George the 3rd), in the year 1765, and its promulgation in America roused the feelings of the colonists to the highest pitch of indignation. Not that the particular mode of taxation was in itself more obnoxious than any other, but because they repudiated the right of the mother country to tax them at all, excepting for their local benefit and improvement. The English government justified themselves in this course, as being the only method in which the colonists could indemnify them for the expense incurred in their protection. The Stamp Act was repealed the following year, but

---

* Macaulay I. 99.

was followed by no healing balm to the deeply wounded feelings of the refractory colonists. They refused to be comforted, nor would listen to any terms, short of absolute freedom. From remonstrances they proceeded to threats, and from threats to open defiance. The several provinces appointed delegates to meet annually in a general congress, to deliberate on measures for their common guidance. This at once brought them in collision with the Government authorities. The cry, To Arms! resounded throughout the thirteen Provinces, and slight skirmishes were succeeded by pitched battles in the field. The first considerable engagement was fought at Bunker's Hill, near Boston, in the month of June, 1775, where 500 provincials were killed or wounded, and double that number of British. The result, as is known to all, was the "Declaration of Independence," which was formally signed on the fourth of July, 1776, and which was followed by the bloody revolutionary war. Not till 1783, did this war terminate, by Great Britain recognizing the American Independence, and withdrawing from the unnatural contest. "The Americans nobly fought for, and secured their independence, which, while it reflects glory on the American, covers the British statesmen with irretrievable infamy."*

There are still amongst us men who regard Washington as no better than a successful rebel, and who cannot speak of American institutions or American men but with scorn and opprobrium. We can express no sympathy with such; and without committing ourselves to the question whether the American Colonies did right or wrong in throwing off their allegiance and declaring their independence, we have no hesitation in saying, that it is the duty now, of every British subject, and especially of every Canadian, to consign all past animosities to oblivion, and to cultivate, by every legitimate means, a spirit of forbearance and amity towards our neighbors. This course is necessary, alike for our own comfort,

---

* Martin III. Intro. 9.

safety, and prosperity, and for continuing and fostering those commercial relations which are alike indispensable to both.

The unbiassed student of history will, we doubt not, endorse the eulogium of England's greatest historian, who thus sums up the character of Washington. " Modern history has not so spotless a character to commemorate. Invincible in resolution, firm in conduct, incorruptible in integrity, he brought to the helm of a victorious republic the simplicity and innocence of rural life. A soldier from necessity and patriotism, rather than disposition, he was the first to recommend a return to pacific counsels when the independence of his country was secured, and bequeathed to his countrymen an address, when leaving their government, to which there is no composition of uninspired wisdom, which can bear a comparison. Having signalized his life by successful resistance to English oppression, he closed it by the warmest advice to cultivate the friendship of Great Britain, and, by his casting vote, ratified a treaty of friendly and commercial intercourse between the mother country and its emancipated offspring. It is the highest glory of England to have given birth, even amid transatlantic wilds, to such a man, and that, amid the convulsions and revolutions of other states, real liberty has arisen in that country alone, which inherited in its veins the genuine principles of British freedom."*

Nations are not, any more than individuals, exempt from errors in judgment. We imagine there are few who will commend the policy of Lord Grenville in 1764, which irritated and estranged the feelings of a loyal and attached colony. Still later, the constitution which was conferred upon our own Province in 1791, under Mr. Pitt's administration, unwisely divided in twain the Province of Canada, which should ever have remained one and indivisable. This blunder has bequeathed to Canada a seemingly irreconcilable antagonism of race against race, of which it is impossible for the most far-seeing to predict the issue.

---

* Allison I. 445.

The treaty of peace which followed the American war, was the result of no amicable feeling towards Britain, or respect for British institutions, in the minds of American statesmen, but rather a matter of expediency, nay of necessity. It had become apparent to the most warlike, that the commercial relations then existing between the now United States and Britain, demanded peace for their prosperity, the very existence also of the republic required peace.

The war left behind it a dormant feeling of animosity, and a disinclination on the part of either to forbear with the other, which thirty years of peace did not allay. During this period the Americans were "nursing their wrath to keep it warm," and we cannot conceal our impression, that the war of 1812 was an unnatural and aggressive demonstration. As such, it was, we believe, destined by Providence to teach future ages the folly of rushing unprovoked and unprepared into hostilities, that might easily and honorably be settled by diplomatic negotiations.

"There is little doubt that America was influenced in provoking this war, by the temporary ascendancy and flattering representations of Napoleon I. Had they delayed their belligerent demonstrations until after his final overthrow at Waterloo, the unnatural war of 1812 would never have been recorded in the historian's page." As it was, various were the excuses urged for the commencement of the war. Prominent amongst these, was the right of search claimed by Great Britain for the recovery of British seamen on board of neutral ships. An unfortunate, and by the British Government unwarranted application of this right to ships of war in the year 1807, brought about a collision between the American frigate "Chesapeake," and the English ship "Leopard," 74. The former was known to have on board some deserters from the British navy, whom her captain refused to surrender; upon which the British captain fired a broadside, killing and wounding a number of Americans. The Chesapeake struck her colors, the deserters were arrested, and the ships parted. The Leopard proceeded to Halifax, where the deserters were tried by court-martial on board the "Belleisle." One of them, John Wilson, a British-born subject, was sentenced to death, and executed four days thereafter; the others were liberated. The English Government disavowed the act, recalled their captain, and offered reparation; but the American mind was too much exasperated to listen to reasonable terms, and a proclamation followed forthwith, forbidding all British ships of war to enter the ports of the United States.

"The subsequent policy of the American Government, betrayed a manifest disinclination to meet the honorable advances of Britain, to establish the basis of a permanent peace between the two countries, already united by bonds of common origin and identity of interest." A second naval engagement, the real cause of which has never been satisfactorily explained, ended in a very different result from the affair of the Chesapeake. The American frigate "President," fell in with the British ship-of-war "Little Belt," of 18 guns, off Cape Charles, in May, 1811, and, after a sanguinary encounter maintained by the British for half an hour, against such fearful odds, the ships withdrew, and retired to their respective harbors. While the former engagement may well be supposed to have exasperated the Americans, the latter might naturally enough have been considered as an offset. A variety of unsatisfactory negotiations, resulted in a recommendation by the President to place the United States army on a war-footing, by raising 10,000 regulars, and 50,000 militia. Congress, more enthusiastic than the president, raised the levy to 25,000 regulars, and voted a loan of ten million of dollars to prosecute the war.

On the 18th of June, 1812, by a vote of 79 to 49, a bill declaring war against Great Britain, passed the House of Representatives, James Madison being President. For some time previous to this, General Hull had been concentrating a large force at Detroit, and was in readiness to invade Canada. On the 12th of

July, 1812, he crossed over to Sandwich, with 2,500 men and 33 pieces of cannon, and issued a ludicrous proclamation, "that he had come not to wage war, but to emancipate the inhabitants of Canada from tyranny and oppression, and to restore them to the dignified station of freemen." Little did he dream of the warm reception that awaited him. His first attempt showed him the temper of the British steel, and he lost little time in beating a retreat to his stronghold in Detroit, where, strongly entrenched, a humiliating retribution awaited him. No sooner did the tidings of an invasion reach York, the capital of Upper Canada, than General Brock, then Lieutenant Governor, set out in person in quest of the foe. Nowise intimidated by the strength of his position, he boldly followed him up, determined to punish him for his temerity. With only 300 regulars, 400 militia, and 600 Indians, he invested Detroit, and before preparations could be made for an assault, on the 16th of August, the American general sent in a flag of truce, and, without drawing a trigger, surrendered himself and all his host, prisoners of war. This ungallant conduct of General Hull was suitably recognized by his superiors: he was tried by court martial, and, for his unheard of cowardice, was sentenced to be shot, though he was subsequently pardoned. By his surrender, not only Detroit, but the whole of the Michigan territory, fell into the hands of the British.

On the 13th of October following, the Americans, under General Van Ranselaer, met with a signal defeat at Queenston Heights. General Brock was again waiting to receive them, and, placing himself at the head of his men, bravely led them on to the charge, but soon fell mortally wounded. "*Revenge the General!*" shouted the soldiers, who still pressed on, and literally drove a superior force up the mountain side. The Americans were, however, at this juncture reinforced, and the British, dispirited by the fall of their beloved general, and overpowered by superior numbers, were forced to retire. At this critical moment, General Sheaffe arrived at the scene of action with 400 fresh troops, and immediately determined to renew the combat. Having gained the heights by a circuitous march, the British troops, thirsting to avenge the fall of their general, charged the enemy with irresistable determination. Many of the invaders were driven over the precipice into the Niagara River, and were drowned, whilst their general Wadsworth, and 900 men, were made prisoners. "The fall of General Brock, the idol of the army, and of the people of Upper Canada, was an irreparable loss, and cast a shade over the glory of this dear-bought victory."

Irritated rather than discouraged, by these two successive failures, to possess themselves of Canada, the Americans resolved upon renewing the attempt, and a combined attack upon Upper and Lower Canada simultaneously, was determined upon.

General Smyth, with 5,000 men, having the command on the Niagara frontier, and General Dearborn, at the head of 10,000 men, on the Lower Canada confines, took the field. Again were they repulsed in Upper Canada, while in Lower Canada, nothing of any importance was achieved. This, the third invasion of Canada having been frustrated, the troops of both the contending parties were sent to winter quarters.

In the meantime the American navy had in some measure atoned for the disastrous attempts of the army, and a series of maritime engagements ensued in favour of the Americans. Britain had now to learn with surprise, that even on the element of which she claimed the sovereignty, she was not invincible. The enthusiasm of the Americans was raised to the highest pitch by these successes, in a quarter the most unexpected, and the war was prosecuted with redoubled energy. The capture of Montreal, the commercial capital and key of Canada, was consequently entertained, as being highly desirable and apparently practicable.

During the campaign of 1813, a number of engagements took place with varied success. In the month of January, after a stout resistance, the British captured Ogdensburgh; and on the 27th of April, York, the capital of Upper Canada, fell into the hands of the Americans. About the same time a strong demonstration against Sackett's Harbor, by the British, ended in a miserable disappointment. In May, Fort George, at the mouth of the Niagara River, was invested by the Americans by land and water, and was battered to pieces by their cannon, and evacuated by its gallant defenders. In June, the British regained their ascendancy, and thrice in succession defeated the enemy, namely, at Stony Creek, Beaver Dam, and Blackrock. In September, the whole British squadron was swept from Lake Erie; and General Proctor, no longer able to obtain supplies and ammunition, dismantled Detroit and Amherstburgh, and commenced a retreat. He was quickly overtaken by the American General, Harrison, and nearly the whole British force was annihilated.

Elated with these successes, the Americans openly announced their intention of at once taking possession of Montreal. Harrison, with 8,000 men, was to complete the capture of Upper Canada. Wilkinson, with 10,000 men, at Sackett's Harbor, was in readiness to act as circumstances might indicate; and General Hampton lay at Chateauguay, prepared at a day's notice to march upon Montreal. It was arranged that Wilkinson should descend the St. Lawrence, and, being joined by Hampton at the Lake St. Louis, that they two should close the campaign by a triumphal entry into Montreal, and establish themselves there in comfortable, winter quarters.

The season being far advanced and all things now ready, Wilkinson moved his army to Grenadier Island, nearly opposite Kingston, with a view of first reducing that post, and then in succession demolishing all the minor forts between that and Montreal. Finding, however, a powerful British fleet and land force there ready to receive him, under General De Rottenburgh, on the fifth of November, he skilfully shifted his plan of attack, and, while appearing to menace Kingston, suddenly changed his course down stream, and swiftly glided down the river, towards Prescott and Ogdensburgh. Lieutenant-Colonel Pearson was in command at Prescott, and kept a vigilant look out. On the first of November he had dispatched Lieutenant Duncan Clark to Elliott's point, five miles above Brockville, with instructions to observe the movements of all vessels navigating the river, and at the first appearance of the enemy, to endeavor to ascertain their number. "You will," so read his instructions, "upon the appearance of an enemy, instantly take horse, and repair to Prescott, with all possible diligence, alarming the country as you pass down." On the evening of the 5th November, Lieutenant Clark, in obedience to the command, *took* the first *farmer's horse* he could lay hands on, and hastily returned to Prescott, reporting the approach of the American army in great force, on board of a flotilla of some three hundred of every description of craft, including several gun-boats.

Upon this announcement, the most active preparations were made in Prescott, to resist a landing, and to prevent them from passing down. Wilkinson, however, again dodged the British. Unwilling to expose his troops to the guns of Prescott, he landed them on the American shore, two miles above, and marched them, by a circuitous route, about the same distance below Ogdensburgh. The boats, manned by only a few hands, hugged the American shore, and under cover of night passed the fort. An active bombardment was kept up on them the whole night, without however doing much damage. Having dropped down beyond gun-shot reach, the troops again embarked, and soon glided down the Galops rapids, meeting with no obstruction until they reached Point Iroquois. There, the river is reduced in width to about five hundred yards, and is very rapid. A piquet of about a dozen men, amongst whom were Jacob and Peter Brouse, were posted at this point, which commands an extensive view of the river. On Sunday afternoon the 8th, they discovered the flotilla of boats and barges rapidly approaching; the river seemed literally covered by them. The advanced boats were soon abreast of the piquet, who fired a volley at them by way of welcome. The report of their pieces aroused their comrades of the Dundas militia, two hundred in number, who lay in the hollow in rear of the point, under captain Monroe: they were quickly on the spot, and gave them another volley. The enemy were thrown into some confusion by this surprise, and, being in ignorance of the number of their opponents, did not attempt a landing, but instantly struck across the river, and brought to in the bay opposite. Wilkinson observing this movement, and determined to ascertain the cause of it, as well as the strength of his opponents, ordered the main body of the flotilla, still nearly a mile above the point, to draw in to the Canada shore. Accordingly they landed at Jacob Brouse's farm and disembarked the troops, who, without losing a moment, proceeded by land in quest of a foe. Monroe, and his gallant little band, were now in turn taken aback, and, perceiving resistance to be hopeless, quickly relinquished their post, and made the best of their way to the woods, allowing the invading host to pass down unmolested. As the day was now far spent, the Americans continued their march only about one mile below the present village of Iroquois, and encamped there by the river side, within sight of their comrades, who still kept to their boats in the bay opposite. These now put into the stream, and, crossing the river, landed at the same place. They remained there till Tuesday about noon, meanwhile making themselves quite at home, and receiving from the farmers, such stores as they could supply. Their officers, strictly enjoined them to pay for every thing that they took; and in justice to them it must be allowed, that the household stuff of the farmers was respected. The hay and grain in the barns were, however, seemingly considered lawful booty, and much more was wasted and trodden under foot than was actually consumed. The British government, however, subsequently, with characteristic honor, amply compensated the farmers for their losses in this way.

Wilkinson, suddenly alarmed by the report of an armed force coming down upon him from above, and rightly judging that he had tarried long enough, early on Tuesday the 10th embarked his forces, and, passing without molestation the Rapid du Plat, proceeded to the lower limit of Williamsburgh. He there halted for the purpose of obtaining pilots, lightening his boats, and making other necessary arrangements for descending the dangerous rapids of the Longue Sault. He was on the same day reinforced by General Brown's brigade of 3000 men, and a body of dragoons from the American side. These, with a portion of Wilkinson's troops, were sent in advance by land, to clear the way of all obstructions, and to take possession of the Government stores and ammunition at Cornwall. By noon of the same day, Wilkinson was apprized, by the booming of cannon, that Brown was already engaged, some distance below. It appears that Brown, on his march to Cornwall, was intercepted by the Glengarry militia, 1300 strong, under Major Dennis, near Hoople's Creek. He accordingly placed a gun in position, on the elevated ground there, and prepared to force his way. The militia being undisciplined, and indifferently armed, Major Dennis did not venture an engagement, and, after firing a few volleys of musketry, retired into the interior. Brown, pushed on to Cornwall. His boats meantime having run the rapids, lay at Barnhart's at the foot of the Sault.

Great was the consternation in Cornwall, and throughout Glengarry, when it was announced that a powerful American army had landed, and was even now at their very doors. The country lads, who had been summoned to fight for their king and country, and " their ain fire sides," and who had frequently been seen to mount guard, armed with an axe or a pitch-fork, began to feel some uneasiness as to the result of a conflict, in which their rude implements would be met by the musket and bayonet in the hands of disciplined troops. As soon therefore as the enemy's landing had been reported, all the waggons that could be found in the surrounding country were despatched to Cornwall, where a large amount of Government stores destined for Upper Canada had been detained. One hundred and fifty waggons were loaded with the stuff, and before Brown arrived at Cornwall they were beyond his reach at St. Andrews, five miles in rear of the town. The cavalcade rested here for an hour, and then pushed on through mud and mire, till they arrived at Martintown, where they passed the night. The next evening they reached the river de Lisle, and encamped for the night, indulging in all kind of surmises as to the result of the engagement in Williamsburgh—the whereabouts of Brown, and more especially as to the comparative safety or danger of their own precious carcases. How far they would have fled, or what would have become of them had the enemy overtaken them, it is difficult to imagine; but their further retreat was arrested by the arrival of Colonel Crysler direct from the battle-field, with news of the enemy's defeat. The Highlanders swung their blue bonnets in the air, and made the neighboring forest to resound with their vociferous cheering. They immediately proceeded to Coteau du Lac, where they left the stores, and returned to their homes.

But to return to Wilkinson, whom we left at Williamsburgh. He effected a landing at Cook's Point, and from that place to Charlesville, a distance of about three miles, the shore was lined with his boats. Cook's tavern, a large and substantial building, was made his head quarters, and all the farmers' houses around were filled with his men. The Americans were in excellent spirits; they appeared to be quite enchanted with the appearance of the country, and assured the farmers that they might consider themselves perfectly safe under their protection—that they had not the slightest intention of molesting them, or injuring their property—for in a very short time they would return, to share their farms with them. Here, as in Matilda, they paid in Spanish dollars for all the provisions the farmers had to sell, and the conduct of their officers is never spoken of by those of the farmers who still survive, without the remark, that "they behaved themselves like gentlemen."

At the commencement of this expedition Wilkinson had issued the following pompous proclamation: "The army of the United

"States, which I have the honor to command, invades the Pro-"vince to conquer, not to destroy; to subdue the forces of his "Britannic Majesty, not to war against unoffending subjects. "Those therefore amongst you who remain quiet at home, should "victory incline to the American standard, shall be protected in "their persons and property; but those who are found in arms "must necessarily be treated as avowed enemies. To menace is "unmanly—to seduce dishonorable—yet it is just and humane, to "place these alternatives before you." In the mean time, Lieutenant-Colonel Morrison, of the 89th regiment, lost no time in setting out in pursuit of the enemy who had so dexterously given him the slip at Kingston, and hastily embarked the small body of troops that could be spared from that important point, on board of several ships of war and a flotilla of gun boats. These were necessarily slower in their motion and less easily managed in the intricate channel of the river, than the light boats and batteaux of his opponent Wilkinson, and it was not until the evening of the eighth, that the squadron reached Prescott. The troops were immediately transferred to smaller craft, and, being reinforced by detachments of the Canadian Fencibles and Voltigeur corps, under Lieutenant-Colonel Pearson, and accompanied by the gun-boats under Captain Mulcaster, amounting in all to 850 men, left Prescott at sun-down on the 9th, in pursuit of the enemy. They landed at Saver's in Matilda and halted there for the night, where intelligence reached them that the enemy had landed a short distance further down the river. Early next morning Morrison marched to Point Iroquois, from whence the American army, nearly two miles distant, was distinctly visible. He continued to advance until he came within half a mile of his adversary, and, having ascertained his numbers and position, decided that he would not *there* hazard an engagement, and returned to Point Iroquois. No sooner had he done so, than the Americans took to their boats and were off again. Morrison likewise embarked and cautiously followed, well aware that Wilkinson must land again ere he run the rapids of he Longue Sault; and he hoped to meet him on more favorable ground than that which they had abandoned. During a halt, two American soldiers were observed, on the opposite side of the river, shouting at the top of their voices, and waving their caps in the air, evidently mistaking the British vessels for their own. A small boat was run across, and the *green uns* brought off, prisoners of war, the victims of misplaced confidence. Another halt of two hours ensued at Stata's bay, near the Williamsburgh stage-house, during which time a gun-boat with fifty men was sent across to Hamilton (now Waddington). There they found a considerable quantity of ammunition and some stores, which they seized, and, having burned the barracks, they quickly embarked and rejoined the flotilla.

The same evening, having learned that the Americans were landing in force at Cook's, Morrison dropped down to Monroe's bay and there landed his troops, at a distance of about two miles above them. That very evening the enemy's piquet approached the British, but was quickly driven in, and a strong patrol was set for the night. Crysler's house was made the head quarters of the gallant little army, and a council of war was held there, to which all the commissioned officers were admitted, and, notwithstanding the fearful odds, it was then determined to give the enemy battle.

All that Morrison asked for his handful of troops was " a fair field and no favor," and in the level and open fields of the " old Crysler farm," he saw at a glance, just such a battle-ground as he desired. And if he could only entice the Americans to meet him *there*, he felt perfectly confident that their raw recruits, even though their number might be legion, must eventually yield to the steady and resolute charge of the British bayonet. Upon this weapon and the discipline of his troops, he based all his calculations for success. From the old Crysler house, still standing by the way-side, the road leading to the woods extended a distance of about half a mile from the river St. Lawrence, and at right angles to it. This road, forty feet in width, was lined on either side by fences constructed of heavy cedar logs and of about five feet in height. Throughout its entire length they afforded considerable cover, and formed the western boundary of the battle-field elect. On the north was a swamp densely covered with timber and impassable for troops. On the south it was bounded by the king's highway running contiguous and parallel to the river. This field, covered at the time with a luxuriant crop of fall wheat, stretched away to the east, a distance of quarter of a mile, unobstructed by tree, fence, or ditch, and extended northwards to the woods half a mile. This plateau is elevated some twenty-five feet above the level of the river. To have been of much service, the gun-boats should have anchored about mid-channel; but as the current is here very rapid, and of great depth, this arrangement could not be carried out, so that they proved of less service in the action than they otherwise might have done. In the centre of the river lies an island circular in form, of about 100 acres in extent and covered with a dense growth of maple trees; and at the foot of it, a large bay or expanse of still water, extending about a quarter of a mile below, where the two branches of the river again converge. This bay is some distance above Cook's point, where the American gun-boats were lying, and was rendered inaccessible to the enemy by the rapid current flowing between, and was sufficiently distant to be out of reach of their small arms. One of Morrison's gun boats was directed to anchor in this bay. Another was anchored immediately opposite Crysler's house, while the third was stationed at the head of the rush-bed some distance above.

Early in the morning of the 11th November, 1813, Wilkinson was preparing to take his departure for Montreal, but Morrison was determined that he should not do so, until he had first paid for his night's lodging, and a vigorous and galling fire from the gun-boats was the significant intimation to that effect.

Shortly after day-break, the British troops were formed on the nine-mile road leading to the woods, as already described, their right resting on the King's road, under the command of Lieutenant-Colonel Pearson, consisting of a skeleton of the 49th regiment, under Captain Nairn. A company of Canadian Fencibles under Lieutenant De Lorimier, and part of a troop of Provincial dragoons under Captain R. D. Frazer, with the companies of the Voltigeurs, extended a little in advance under Major Herriot. The left wing was commanded by Lieut. Colonel Morrison, consisting of the 89th regiment of the line, and a party of militia, under Lieut. Samuel Adams, with about thirty Indian warriors, posted along the skirts of the woods under Lieut. Anderson.

Observing the determined attitude of the British, the American army was quickly drawn up in battle array on Cook's farm, distant about one mile and a quarter, under the command of General Boyd, Wilkinson being confined to his barge by indisposition, induced it is said by intemperance.

Thus arranged, the adverse armies, each confident of victory, yet neither seemingly inclined to begin the conflict, rested on their arms, ready to march at the word of command. With a view of bringing the Americans to the ground he had selected, Morrison, about noon detached a small force to proceed within range and open fire upon their opponents; they were met by a similar party of Americans, before whom they retired, their pursuers following them up to within ten or twelve yards of the nine-mile road, where the main body were concealed by the fence. The first intimation they had of their presence was a well-directed volley of musketry. They immediately *took to their heels* (so says our informant) and lost no time in rejoining their comrades at Cook's, leaving however three or four of the party dead on the field.

Now that American blood had been drawn, the American General could no longer honorably remain inactive, and a strong movement was made in advance. The British moved down in force, about a quarter of a mile, to the edge of a deep ravine, and there calmly awaited the attack.

A strong body of the enemy's cavalry having made a rapid

advance, gallantly dashed up the side of the ravine, but met with such a warm reception at the summit, that they were forced to wheel about, and retire in disorder, in their downward retreat over-riding many of their comrades who were pressing on behind. A strong reinforcement of infantry however coming up to their support, they rallied and made another desperate charge. This time they succeeded in gaining the level ground, and a sanguinary contest was maintained for some time, till the British, with a steady and irresistible charge, drove them at the point of the bayonet once more into the ravine, but not until Captain Nairn, and ensign Clause of the 49th, and Lieut. De Lorimier of the Canadian Fencibles, were killed.

About the same time the enemy's columns under General Covington, who rode a white horse, were advancing on the right and centre of the British line in double quick time, with a view of turning their flank. Colonel Morrison, observing this, formed the 89th in *echelon;* the enemy then gave a cheer, and commenced a determined and very destructive fire, which the British troops returned with deadly effect. This checked his advance, and at the same time a considerable number of the enemy were captured by the militia, under Lieut. Adams. They were also thrown into some confusion by the fall of General Covington, who was at this time mortally wounded while in the act of pointing out to his troops the mode of attack. A thirty yard sharpnell shell fired immediately after, from one of the gun-boats, by Captain Jackson, added to their confusion, and caused a wavering in their ranks. Morrison now closed his columns with the enemy, and, together with the troops under Colonel Pearson, kept up such a destructive fire by platoons, that the enemy was driven from his position, and compelled to retire from the field, with the loss of one gun, 200 prisoners, most of his cavalry horses, and a stand of colors which were found chained to a stump. "This," remarked a corporal of the 49th "is liberty chained to a stump."

Major Henry Merckley of the Dundas militia, and Captain Kerr of the incorporated militia, attended with the troops, and were of great service in the field during the engagement. The gun-boats also kept up a brisk fire and "scratched" the enemy severely while they lay at Cook's, and though their situation was somewhat unfavorable, they contributed very materially to the success of the day. They were three in number. The two smaller ones were armed each with a six-pounder brass gun. The third one, named the "Nelson," was a very large and cumbrous galley, mounting a thirty-two pounder and a twenty-four pounder, and was propelled by eighty rowers, forty on a side. This one was stationed at the head of the rush-bed, and it was from it that the shell was discharged which was noticed as assisting to turn the fate of the battle.

The action lasted till half past four in the afternoon, and was fought with the most resolute bravery by both combatants. Morrison, aware that the enemy had a large force in reserve, was unwilling to risk his small force in pursuit; he therefore contented himself with occupying for the night, the ground from which the enemy had been driven. The Americans repaired to their boats precipitately, and a scene of indescribable confusion followed. The east wind having sprung up, and the water in the river considerably subsided, their boats were left high and dry. The affrighted soldiers as they arrived in hot haste from the battle, threw their arms and ammunition, and finally themselves into the boats, and in the general scramble, the attempts of the officers to restore order were of no avail. After much delay in launching, they were once more afloat in great disorder, and the whole flotilla moved down the river to Barnhart's Island, where they were joined by Brown's brigade, and by the dragoons, who brought with them five pieces of artillery from the field of action by land, in order to lighten the crafts, while descending the rapids.

To his unspeakable mortification, Wilkinson there received a letter from General Hampton, informing him of his (Hampton's) repulse by General De Salaberry, near Chateauguay, and his subsequent retreat to Lake Champlain. A council of war was hurriedly convened, when it was resolved that the attack upon Montreal should be abandoned for that season, and that the army should cross to the American shore for winter quarters. On the following morning, the combined forces made the best of their way to Salmon River, where they laid up all their boats, erecting with extraordinary celerity, extensive barracks for the whole army, and having fortified their position by a strong abattis, they there passed the winter.

The British loss was three officers and twenty-one rank and file killed, eight officers and 137 men wounded, and twelve missing. Wilkinson acknowledged to three officers and ninety men killed, sixteen officers and 221 men wounded. In General Covington the Americans lost a brave and able officer.

Thus terminated the battle of "Crysler's Farm," and with the defeat of the American army here, vanished all hopes, during that campaign at least, of carrying out their designs upon Lower Canada.

The conduct of the British troops, regulars and militia, was beyond all praise, and elicited the encomiums even of their opponents. The devoted loyalty of the militia is thus noticed by Wilkinson in his report from Salmon River, dated the 16th of November, 1813: "The enemy deserve great credit for their zeal and intelligence, which the active universal hostility of the male inhabitants of the country, enabled them to employ to the greatest advantage." Ingersoll, the American historian, speaks in terms of the highest praise, of the conduct of the British and Canadian troops, "for the persevering and invincible spirit in which they met a formidable invasion, and forced Wilkinson to a dishonored retreat, when, had they been well led, there was every pledge of victory." Morrison, in his report of the battle to head-quarters, testified to the "distinguished bravery of the regulars and militia" under his command.

The numbers in this engagement are variously estimated. Of the British there were, as already said, but 850 regulars, including the men on the gun-boats, a handful of militia, and 30 Indians.

The American force engaged, is stated by Wilkinson to have been, from 1600 to 1800 men, while British authorities place it at 2900. Our information from local sources confirm us in the belief that the larger figures are the more correct, nor have we the slightest hesitation in disbelieving the general, who at the same time cooly states the British force to have been " from 1200 to 2000 ;—at least," says he " there were 1800."

Allison alludes to the battle thus : " The glorious defeat of an invasion so confidently announced, and so strongly supported, diffused the most heartfelt joy in Lower Canada, and terminated the campaign there, in the most triumphant manner." Christie says of it : " This, called the battle of Crysler's Farm, is, in the estimation of military men, considered the most scientific military affair during the late war, from the professional skill displayed in the action, by the adverse commanders, and when we consider the prodigious preparations of the American Government for that expedition, with the failure of which, their hopes of conquest vanished, the battle of Crysler's Farm may probably be classed as the most important, and the best fought, that took place during the war."

The avowed abandonment of their projects by the American Generals, having removed every appearance of danger, the commander of the forces, by a general order of the 17th November, dismissed the sedentary militia, with due acknowledgment of the loyalty and zeal which they had manifested. The following is an extract —

" His Excellency the Governor in chief and commander of the forces, in dispensing for the present with the further services of the militia, feels the greatest satisfaction in acknowledging the cheerful alacrity with which they have repaired to their respective posts, and the loyalty and zeal they have manifested at the prospect of encountering the enemy. Although he has been checked in his career by the bravery and discipline of his Majesty's troops in the Upper Province, and thus frustrated in his avowed intention of landing on this island (Montreal), his excellency feels confident, that, had he been enabled to reach it, whatever might have been his force, he would have met with that steady and determined resistance, from the militia of the provinces, which would have terminated his third attempt for its invasion, like those which preceded it, in defeat and disgrace."

The above extracts suffice to shew that the services of the militia were duly appreciated, that the battle of Crysler's Farm was an important one, and its results highly satisfactory. In the face of the well-authenticated facts adduced, it will scarcely be credited, that Wilkinson had the audacity, and that American historians have since had the imbecility, to claim the victory in the action of Crysler's Farm. Listen to the General's modest account, in the following extract of his report of the 16th November: "It would be presumptuous in me to attempt to give you a detailed account of this affair, which certainly reflects high honor on the valor of the American soldiers, as no example can be produced of undisciplined men, with inexperienced officers, braving a fire of two hours and a half without quitting the field, or yielding to their antagonists. But, sir, the information I now give you, is derived from officers in my confidence, who took active part in the conflict; for although I was enabled to order the attack, it was my hard fortune not to be able to lead the troops I commanded, the disease with which I was assailed on the 2nd September, having, with a few short intervals of convalescence, preyed on me ever since. At the moment of the action I was confined to my bed, unable to sit on a horse, or to move ten paces without assistance. I must however be pardoned for trespassing on your time by a few remarks in relation to this affair. The objects of the British and American commanders were precisely opposed, the latter being bound by the instructions of his government, and the most solemn obligations of duty, to precipitate his descent of the St. Lawrence by every practicable means; because this being effected, one of the greatest difficulties opposed to the American army would be surmounted; and the former by duties equally imperious to retard it, and if possible to prevent such a descent. The British commander having failed to gain either of the objects, can lay no claim to the honors of the day...... The battle fluctuated, and the victory seemed at different times inclined to the contending corps. The front of the enemy was at first forced back more than a mile, and though they never regained the ground they lost, their *stand was permanent*, and *their charges resolute*. Amidst these charges, and near the close of the contest, we lost a field-piece, by the fall of the officer who was serving it with the same coolness as if he had been at parade, or at a review...... The enemy having halted, and our troops having again formed in battalion, front to front, and the fire having ceased on both sides, we resumed our position on the bank of the river, and *the infantry being much fatigued*, the whole were re-embarked, and proceeded down the river, without further annoyance from the enemy or their gun-boats...... The dead rest in honor, and the wounded bleed for their country, and deserve its gratitude." On the 18th he adds a supplementary report from which we quote: "I last evening received the enclosed information, the result of the examination of sundry prisoners taken on the field of battle, which justifies the opinion of the general officers who were in the engagement. This goes to prove that although the imperious obligations of duty did not allow me time to rout the enemy, they were beaten; the accidental loss of one field-piece notwithstanding, after it had been discharged 15 or 20 times. I have also learned from what has been considered good authority, but I will not vouch for the correctness of it, that the enemy's loss exceeded 500 killed and wounded...... Having received information late in the day that the contest had become somewhat dubious, I ordered up a reserve of some 500 men, whom I had ordered to stand by their arms, under Lieut. Upham, who gallantly led them into the action, which terminated a few minutes after his arrival on the ground."

The United States government, however, took a different view of the matter, and called General James Wilkinson to account for his deliquencies upon this and other occasions, before a court martial held at Utica, in January, 1815. In addition to general incompetency to command, he was charged with four distinct counts. First, "neglect of duty, and un-officer like conduct, in eight particulars. Second, drunkenness on duty, with two particulars. Third, conduct unbecoming an officer and a gentleman in six instances. Fourth, countenancing and encouraging disobedience to orders." After a protracted trial, and very severe animadversion from the court, he was discharged.

Our limits will not permit us to follow out the particular incidents of the war, during the eventful campaign of 1814. Several determined attempts at invasion by way of the Niagara Frontier were resolutely repulsed, not however without severe loss on both sides. The battle of Lundy's Lane was perhaps one of the most extraordinary ever recorded; the more so from the romantic ground on which it took place, it being close by the falls of Niagara, and the time the dead hour of night. "Nothing," says Christie, "could have been more awful and impressive than this midnight contest. The desperate charges of the enemy were succeeded by a death-like silence, interrupted only by the groans of the dying, and the dull sound of the falls of Niagara, while the adverse lines were now and then dimly discerned through the moonlight, by the gleam of their arms. These anxious pauses were succeeded by a blaze of musketry along the lines, and by a repetition of the most desperate charges from the enemy, which the British regulars and militia received with the most unshaken firmness." This memorable action was fought on the 25th July, 1814. Both parties claimed the victory,—at midnight, however, the Americans sounded a retreat, and regained their camp near Chippewa, which they abandoned the following day. In their haste to be off, they threw the greater part of their baggage, camp equipage, and provisions into the rapids, and continued their retreat in great disorder towards Fort Erie. Surely the victory remained with those who occupied the field.

In August, the British made a descent upon Washington, the capital of the United States, and, after a short and decisive engagement, dispersed its defenders, and thereafter applied the torch to all the public buildings in the place. In a short time, the Capitol, the arsenal, dockyard, treasury, war-office, the President's palace, a well as the great bridge across the Potomac, were consumed by the flames. The Americans as they retired, aided the conflagration, by firing their magazines, containing immense quantities of powder, as well as twenty thousand stand of arms. Two hundred and six pieces of cannon, and one hundred thousand round of ball-cartridge were taken by the British, and all the warlike establishments in the place were levelled with the ground.

On the other hand, the British, under Sir George Prevost, were most disgracefully beaten, on land and water, at Plattsburgh on Lake Champlain. Their ships were compelled to strike their colors, their gun-boats to seek safety in ignominious flight, and the veteran heroes, who had marched under the standard of the invincible Wellington, were forced to retire in confusion and disgrace, leaving behind them an immense amount of stores. With the exception of some minor engagements on the Niagara Frontier, this terminated hostilities in Canada. But in January, 1815, the British experienced a severe repulse at New Orleans, upon which they had made an attack, and which was bravely defended by General Jackson.

In the meantime a treaty of peace had been concluded at Ghent, on the 24th of December, 1814. This was not formally announced in Canada until the 1st of March, 1815. The militia were consequently disbanded and sent to their homes, having throughout the war been characterized by the most devoted loyalty, and unflinching courage.

We shall close this part of our subject with a few fragmentary incidents connected with the battle of Crysler's farm, and the county of Dundas, as communicated to us by men of the time, and which we consider reliable.

There was one Samuel Adams of Edwardsburgh, who, with his father, acted as a bearer of dispatches from Montreal to Kingston. He was a tall, handsome, active, and very powerful young man, and withal, as brave as he was powerful. On the day of the battle at Crysler's, he happened that way, where, although duty urged him to proceed, he nevertheless resolved to tarry awhile, intending to make himself useful if possible, and at all events, to see the fun. Having no particular duty assigned to him by the officer in command, he resolved to have a foray on his *own hook;* accordingly in the morning early, he left the British lines, and, making a detour through the second concession, came out upon the river at Ranney's farm, in rear of the American army. Just as he reached the King's road, which at that time followed the margin of the river, a troop of the enemy's cavalry, who had been quartered at Louck's inn, dashed up at full speed. Resistance and flight being alike out of the question, he threw himself down behind an old log, which barely served to conceal him from the horsemen, who, in their hurry, passed within a few feet without observing him. He had not time to congratulate himself on his narrow escape, before the noise of accoutrements warned him of the approach of a party on foot, and caused him to repent the rashness of his adventure. He kept to his lair closely, until he should ascertain their numbers, and soon discovered that his alarm was caused by a brace of American officers, in dashing uniform, who were leizurely sauntering up the road, their swords dangling on the ground, and a pair of pistols in each of their belts. Adams felt quite relieved, that the odds were no more than two to one, and at once made up his mind that he would *bag* them. Leaving his ambuscade, he planted himself in front of them, and, levelling his musket, with an air of determination summoned them to surrender their arms, or their lives. To his surprise they did surrender at discretion, and, arming himself with their pistols, for his own musket was unloaded, he marched them back to the woods, and reached head-quarters by the same route he had left, with his prize, in time to take a part with the militia in the battle. His exploit was rewarded with a pair of cavalry horses branded U. S., which he retained for many years afterwards.

Previous to the battle of Crysler's Farm, the American soldiers had imprudently been feasting to excess upon honey, which they found plentifully in Matilda and Williamsburg. The consequence was, that hundreds of them were so weakened and enervated by dysentery, that they reeled and staggered like drunken men, as they were marched up through the mud, anckle deep, to face the resolute charge of the British bayonet. Even in the field of battle they could not be restrained from repeating the imprudence, for in passing Bouck's farm, where stood nearly one hundred bee-hives, many of them so literally surfeited themselves that they died in consequence, before the battle was over; their bloated corpses presenting a disgusting aspect, as the honey with which they were gorged, oosed from their mouths, their noses, and even from their ears.

The Indians present on the field, though only thirty in number, so yelled like demons, during the engagement, that many of the raw American recruits were terrified beyond measure, and, not knowing whither they went, plunged into the woods, to escape the dreaded horrors of the scalping-knife. On the evening of the battle, fourteen prisoners, more dead than alive with fright, were captured in *a pile* in the Nudle Bush, two miles distant from the field of battle, by Ensign Snyder, George Cook, and others of the militia.

The battle being done, Crysler's house, which had hitherto been Morrison's head-quarters, was now converted into an hospital, and was literally filled throughout with the wounded; and suffering friends and foes, were indiscriminately tended with unremitting care and sympathy, by the members of the household. The day following the engagement was devoted to burying the dead. Fifty were buried in one huge grave, on a sand knoll close by the nine-mile road, fifteen in another grave in the orchard by the river side, thirty on Soprenus Casselman's farm, and the rest, chiefly where they fell. Their hurried sepulture is attested, by many of their skeletons having been turned up by the plough. During the past year, two entire skeletons were thus rudely disinterred, at a depth of not more than nine or ten inches from the surface of the ground.

Medals commemorative of our Canadian battles were struck by the British Government in 1848, and the same year were distributed amongst those who were present on the different fields. There are however several who were in the action of Crysler's farm, that did not receive a medal, simply because they did not take the trouble to apply for it. Amongst these is Major Merkley, whose name appears in the report of the battle. The medals are of silver, very chaste and beautifully finished; they are held in high estimation by their owners, and a medal-man is considered as only inferior to a genuine old U. E. Loyalist. On the one side of the medal, are the Queen's head, with the features particularly well defined, "Victoria Regina" in raised letters on either side, and the date "1848" below. On the reverse is a representation of Her Majesty, standing on a dais carved with a lion couchant, and in the act of crowning a kneeling warrior, with a wreath of victory and the inscription " To the British army 1793–1814." On the clasp is the name of the action (mispelt) " Chrystler's Farm," and on the outer perimeter, the soldier's name, and " Canadian Militia " engraved. At the time of issuing the medals, something was said in regard to the erection of suitable stone monuments, on each battle-field, by the Canadian government. This would indeed be a graceful acknowledgement of the services of the militia in conjunction with the Queen's troops: but as we have heard no more of the matter, the inference is that the pious purpose has been abandoned. Though it may be a matter of questionable policy with the government, there is nothing to hinder the inhabitants of each county where the battles were fought, from rearing a monument, that might indicate to future ages the hallowed spot where Britain's sons rallied round her standard, and shed their blood to perpetuate British institutions. It may be argued by some, that it were more in accordance with the Christian precept which tells us to love our enemies, that we should endeavour to efface from memory all recollections of the past,—that we should forgive and forget. It is to be hoped we have long ago forgiven our enemy, and that even now we *love our neighbors* as ourselves. But *forget* we never can the heroic deeds of our forefathers. Most sincerely do we trust that the friendly relations now happily subsisting betwixt us and the people of the United States, may be as perpetual as the flow of the mighty river that laves the shores of the great republic and our own. At the same time, if we are ever to take a place among the nations of the earth, we must cultivate sentiments of nationality NOW. And should the time ever come, which may God forbid, that our descendants, should be called upon to arm themselves in defence of their country, such monuments as these we speak of would recall to their minds the bravery of their ancestors, inflame their patriotism, and inspire them with devotion to their sovereign. The expense of carrying out the idea would be quite inconsiderable and whether it were done by municipalities, or by private subcription, or by both, it would scarcely be felt; and while doing honor to those to whom honor is due, they would at the same reflect credit on themselves.

The whole of the stores and ammunition for the troops, as well as merchandize for the inhabitants of Upper Canada, were at this time, of necessity, conveyed up the St. Lawrence in boats, which were constantly exposed to the depredations of the Americans, throughout a distance of 150 miles. In view of this everlasting annoyance to the transport of troops and ammunition in time of war, the British Government in 1819 commenced the Rideau Canal, which following the river and lake of that name, extends from Kingston, by Smiths' Falls to Ottawa City, formerly called Bytown, (in honor of Colonel By the engineer who superintended the construction of the works). At that time this was considered a stupendous undertaking, and, when completed, it afforded a safe and secluded water communication, between Lake Ontario and Montreal, by way of the Ottawa River. The canal is about 150 miles in length, has forty-seven locks, and passes through some very wild and romantic scenery. The masonry of the locks, and other stone work, is of the most substantial and expensive description ever adopted in similar works, and, though somewhat cast in the shade by the gigantic St. Lawrence Canals, the Rideau Canal must ever be accounted a great and a valuable undertaking. It was constructed by the Imperial Government, as a military work.

In connection with the transport service during the war of 1812, we subjoin the accounts of two skirmishes which took place in the county of Dundas, as related to us by Major Clarke and Captain McMillan, and of which we are not aware that any notice has previously appeared in print.

A brigade of batteaux laden with military stores, on route from Montreal to Kingston, under the escort of a detachment of the Newfoundland regiment, commanded by Major Heathecoate, and a flank company of the Dundas militia, under Captain Ault, were suddenly attacked at Van Kamp's point, a short distance above point Iroquois in Matilda, on the morning of the 16th September, 1812, by about 500 American Militia. This force had taken up a position on Toussant's Island, under the command of Captain Griffin, and had a gun-boat stationed at the foot of the island commanded by one Lieut. Church.

Major Heathcoate had made preparations to defend the boats, in case the enemy should attempt to dispute their passage. Ensign Clark and a part of Captain Ault's company, were ferried across to Presqu'isle, and reached the south side of this small island, just as two American vessels filled with troops were preparing to land. Clark's party, covered by trees and bushes, immediately opened fire upon them, and with such effect, that they hastily retreated to Toussant's Island, where they took shelter in the woods. In the confusion, one of their small boats got adrift, and was picked up by our militia; it contained seven muskets, two swords, and a quantity of provisions. In a short time, a large number of the inhabitants from different parts of the county were assembled on Presqu'isle, amongst them were Captain Ault, Captain Shaver, with Colonel Allan McDonnell, commanding the Dundas militia, at their head. The news that blood had been drawn, and that too in their own county, fired the dormant enthusiasm of the old warriors, who had served under Sir William Johnston and his son Sir John, in the revolutionary war. Many of them tottering under a load of years, seemed now to renew their youth, at the prospect of meeting the descendants of their ancient foe in combat, and hurrying to the scene were soon foremost in the fight.

Two companies of the Grenville Militia, under Captains Monroe and Dulmage, arrived in the course of the day, and a nine-pounder which had been captured from the French at Chimney Island in 1760, was brought from Prescott by Lieut. R. D. Frazer. The attack having commenced, the shots of this gun, directed into King Peter's bay, together with the well sustained fire of the militia, compelled the Americans to evacuate the island on which they were posted, and retire to their own side of the St. Lawrence, with considerable loss, the precise numbers could not however be ascertained. The loss on the Canadian side was only one killed and several wounded.

In October of 1813, a brigade of boats, twelve in number, were dispatched from Cornwall for the west, under charge of an escort, and, having reached the head of the Rapid-du-Plat, halted for the night. Their midnight slumbers were disturbed by a party of Americans, who, crossing the river, caught them napping, and, in the absence of any effectual resistance on the part of the escort or their crews, seized the boats, and conveyed them bag and baggage to their own side.

A second brigade arrived at Cornwall in November of the same year, consisting of 36 boats, averaging about three tons each. This was the last trip of the season, and they had on board a large and valuable winter's supply for the troops in Upper Canada, besides general merchandize. To capture stores so seasonable, would indeed be a happy wind-fall to the enemy, who stood much in need of them; and the loss of them to the British would be correspondingly severe, as it would be next to impossible to replace these supplies by land carriage, until the winter was far advanced. These considerations, added to the mishaps attending the former flotilla, indicated the necessity of a strong escort from Cornwall upwards, in addition to the ten or twelve regulars who had accompanied them from Montreal. This service was entrusted to Captain Alex. McMillan, (now of Edwardsburgh,) commanding the first company of the Glengarry militia, and Captain Merckley of Williamsburgh, with 120 men.

The convoy reached the foot of the Rapid-du-Plat, without any molestation, and laid up for the night. Early next morning the Americans were observed to be posted in force upon Ogden's Island, immediately opposite, evidently meditating an attack. The boats were towed up the rapids in full view of the enemy, who then assured themselves of the value of their freight, and formed the resolution to make them their own. In the meantime Lieut. Colonel Pearson having been apprised that several attempts would likely be made by the enemy to capture the boats, had sent Captain Skinner with orders, that such part of their cargo as was destined for Prescott should immediately be landed, and conveyed thither in waggons, and that the boats with the rest of the stuff should return to Cornwall. Waggons were accordingly impressed, and by eleven o'clock p. m., every thing was ready for a start. At this moment a report reached them that 500 American (dismounted) dragoons had landed, and were advancing to attack them. Captains Merckley and McMillan at once resolved to meet them half way. The loaded waggons were removed to some distance from the river, and instructions left with the boatmen to get under way as soon as the report of firearms should announce to them that the attention of the enemy was diverted by the attack of the militia on shore, and to drop down the river to Hoople's Creek, and there await the arrival of the escort. With these arrangements, they proceeded towards Mariatown. The night was cold, and the roads in a fearful state of mud, while the moon shone fitfully through the lowering clouds, at times lighting up their path, and anon leaving them in darkness. When near Doran's, a glimpse of moonlight disclosed to them a formidable party approaching, recognized to be the enemy by their white trousers, and the tuft of white horse-hair which surmounted their brass helmets. Placing themselves in ambush, they allowed them to come within pistol shot, when they opened a well directed fire upon them. Unable to see their foe, the invaders were seized with a sudden panic, and retired with the loss of eleven killed and wounded, and several prisoners. The militia pursued them beyond Mariatown, when a report that another party had landed above, caused them to return. The Americans took to their boats and quickly regained their own side of the river, having been completely frustrated in their avaricious design, and having received a sound drubbing to boot.

At two in the morning, the militia set out on their weary march of eighteen miles over bad roads, in total darkness, and reached Hoople's bridge just as the rising sun gilded the horizon. There they found the boats snugly moored, and, having all embarked, proceeded to Cornwall, and the following day joined the cavalcade in their retreat through Glengarry, elsewhere described.

The Salmon River Raid.—On the 9th of February, 1814, the American army began to leave their cantonments at Malone, General Brown with one division going to Sackett's Harbor, and Wilkinson with the other retiring to Plattsburgh. On the 18th,

Lieut. Colonel Pearson despatched a force of about 500 regulars from Prescott, with instructions to proceed to Salmon River and Malone, to harass the enemy in their movements, and possess themselves of any stores that might come in their way. Through the exertions of the militia, over 100 double sleighs were impressed, many of them from Dundas county, and at a few hours' notice were assembled at Edwardsburgh. The party set out in high spirits at 9 o'clock on the morning of the 19th, and, the roads being good, they reached Salmon River, distant 56 miles, the same evening. Here they set fire to all the boats and barracks of the enemy, and utterly consumed them. They then proceeded to Malone, where they ascertained that the last detachment of the enemy had just decamped hurriedly, leaving behind them a considerable quantity of stores and ammunition. Of pork, beef, flour, and whiskey, our troops took with them as much as they could carry. The remainder they destroyed, and the following afternoon recrossed the river on the ice to Summer's. Here they were ordered, each man, to leave his loaded sleigh on the ice in view of the hotel, and a strong guard was set for the night. This precaution was considered necessary, lest, *by mistake,* some of the teamsters who had been indulging in Yankee whiskey rather freely, might drive their loads to their own doors, instead of to the Government depôt at Cornwall. Some confusion, and a great deal of merriment was connected with this midnight raid into hostile ground, and it required all the efforts of the officers in command, to preserve even the semblance of discipline as they returned home. While crossing the river, one sleigh, heavily loaded, suddenly broke through: the passengers had barely time to spring out on each side, when, in a moment, the horses, sleigh, and load, disappeared from their view, and were swept underneath the ice, leaving not a trace behind them.

One of the teamsters had for his load a hogshead of whiskey, which served to enliven the whole company. Frequently the soldiers ran up unobserved behind his sleigh, and bored a hole in the cask with their bayonet, using it as a brace, and then darted off to their comrades with a gallon jug full: in this way the old man's load was reduced to very small compass before he reached his journey's end, and he himself narrowly escaped punishment for the defalcation.

In referring to this little expedition, Hough, in his history of St. Lawrence County, bestows the following complimentary epithets upon our gallant militia. " On Saturday, the enemy hearing that our troops had marched, ventured to cross the St. Lawrence with a *motley tribe* of regulars, provincials, and a detachment of *the Devil's own*, sedentary militia, and *their brethren a band of savages*, and carried off 200 barrels of provisions, scouring the country for a week." So far as our information goes, there were neither provincials, militia, nor Indians of the party, beyond the militia men who had charge of the teams, and, as they were paid four dollars per day for their services, the presumption is, they were there in a *civil* capacity.

Having said all that seems necessary to render intelligible the battle of Crysler's Farm, it may seem wicked in us any further to *persecute* the memory of poor Wilkinson. We cannot refrain, however, from following him yet another step, in order to initiate the reader into the improvements of modern American warfare, no doubt suggested by dear bought experience. It is well known that Wilkinson opened the campaign of 1814 by an unsuccessful attack upon Lacolle Mill, with a force of 3999 men, against 1400 British. The following extract of a general order to the American army, dated the 29th of March, 1814, requires no comment: " The army will enter Canada to-morrow, to meet the enemy. On the march, when approaching the enemy, or during an action, the men are to be profoundly silent, and will resolutely execute the commands they may receive from the officers. In every movement which may be made, the ranks are to be unbroken, and there must be *no running forward or shouting.* An officer will be posted on the right of each platoon, and *a tried sergeant* will form a supernumerary rank, *and will instantly put to death any man who goes back.*" Was ever sergeant's duty rendered so honorable and meritorious as this? Was ever incentive to glory so powerful? This was a practical and *forcible* illustration, of a man being "brought up to the scratch," those who were inwardly comforting themselves, that "they who fight and run away, may live to fight another day," must have been taken somewhat aback by the unexpected announcement.

CHAPTER V.

Union of the Provinces—The Rebellion in Lower and Upper Canada—
The Hunter's oath—Steamers Caroline and Sir Robert Peel—Bill
Johnston—Battle of the Windmill—The sympathizers—Militia of
Dundas—Volunteer movement in Canada—The rifleman's song.

(From 1815 to 1860.)

According to Bouchette, the population of Upper Canada in 1811 was 77,000. In 1838 it had reached 385,824. This extraordinary increase in population was accompanied by a corresponding increase in wealth and commerce; but it was also attended with yearly increasing difficulties in directing its Government, which up to this time remained strictly under the control of the colonial department in Britain. Dissatisfaction not only began to appear amongst the people, but also pervaded every branch of the Canadian Legislatures. The Colonial office in Downing street was besieged by delegates from Canada, armed with petitions and remonstances against the conduct of the Canadian Government, and the consideration given to their statements in England was loudly protested against by Sir Francis Bond Head, the Governor of Upper Canada. Numerous dispatches passed between him and the Colonial Secretary, in respect to the grievances of the inhabitants. Shortly after his arrival in Canada, he made a tour of the Upper Province, to satisfy himself as to the real sentiments of the people, and summed up the conclusion he had come to, in a memorandum addressed to Lord Glenelg, in October,

1836. He strenuously deprecated the proposed union of the two Provinces, and suggested the policy of *killing* the French influence, by annexing Montreal to Upper Canada, Gaspé to New Brunswick, and making the north branch of the Ottawa the boundary of Lower Canada, giving the waters of that river, and the St. Lawrence, together with the expense of making them navigable, to Upper Canada. Lower Canada having the free right to use them, upon paying the same tolls as Upper Canada.

The British Government did not however act upon the suggestion, but, instead, sent Lord Durham to Canada in 1838 as governor in chief, and high commissioner, to enquire into the workings of the institutions of the country, to examine the nature of the alledged grievances, and to suggest reforms for the future. The result of his observations and enquiries, was conveyed to the British Government, in an elaborate "Report" on the affairs of all the British North American Colonies. He represented the state of matters in both Upper and Lower Canada to be in a deplorable condition, demanding immediate and vigorous remedial measures. As a remedy for the griefs of Canada, Earl Durham recommended a federal Union of all the British North American Provinces, or if that was not approved of, at least a Legislative Union of Upper and Lower Canada. He brought many cogent reasons to the support of his views, and concluded by a variety of suggestions for consummating his plans. He strongly objected to the principle of giving equal representation to Upper and Lower Canada, and clearly pointed out the advantages that would accrue to the country, by the introduction of municipal institutions and the principle of responsible Government. His report displayed great research, and was ably compiled. By many it was admired, and by some censured. By all, it was conceded to have advanced many excellent suggestions for the future peace and prosperity of Canada. The British Government so far acquiesced in this report, by introducing a bill into the House of Commons for uniting Upper and Lower Canada, which passed in 1839 and became law. Mr. Poulett Thompson was sent out as Governor General, in room of Lord Durham, who had resigned. The terms of Union were laid before the Council of Lower Canada, and the Legislature of the Upper Province, and after some discussion were agreed to. In 1840 the Union was consummated; and from that time, the two Provinces have been governed by one Legislative Council, and one Assembly. Among other provisions of this reunion, it was agreed that Upper and Lower Canada should each send an equal number of representatives to the Parliament of United Canada; that all duties and revenues from either province, were to form one fund for the public service; and that all debts owing by either Province should be borne by the United Provinces.

Need we remind our reader of the unhappy events which preceded this change, and indeed forced it upon the British Government? It is true that they are too recent to excite particular interest, but their importance forbid us to pass them unnoticed: we shall therefore glance at them very briefly.

The redress of a few real grievances, and a great many imaginary ones, was the ostensible cause of the unhappy rebellion of 1837. Amongst these were the extension of the elective franchise, that the judges should be independent of the Crown, and that an elective Legislative Council should be substituted for that which was then nominated by the crown. But to those who had discernment enough to penetrate beyond the surface, to the under current of popular feeling, it was evident that other causes were at work, and that, no matter how many grievances were redressed, there were factious and designing men ever on the alert to conjure up new grievances as quickly as the Imperial Government endeavored to alleviate the old ones. In Lower Canada, the real cause was, neither more nor less, than the determination of the French portion of the House of Assembly to throw off the British authority, and to erect the Province into an independent Republic, after the manner and model of the United States.*

---

* London Quarterly, 1838.

Thwarted in their designs to undermine the fundamental principles of the constitution conferred upon the Province in 1791, they had recourse to popular agitation. Public meetings were held in almost every parish, at which the people were harangued in the most inflammatory terms. Upon this the Governor dismissed eighteen magistrates, and thirty-five militia officers. The seditious meetings still went on, and their proceedings increased in violence. They elected magistrates and officers themselves, in room of those who had been dismissed, and otherwise set the laws of the land at defiance. On the other hand, a numerous meeting of the loyal inhabitants of Montreal, was held in the Place d'Armes, having for its object " the maintenance of good order, the protection of life and property, and the connection now happily existing between this Colony and the United Kingdom, at present put in jeopardy, by the machinations of a disorganizing and revolutionary faction within this Province, professedly bent on its destruction."

A reinforcement of troops was sent for from Nova Scotia, as well as from Upper Canada. Sir Francis Bond Head, the Lieutenant Governor of Upper Canada, confiding in the loyalty of the Upper Canadians, immediately sent the whole of the regular troops in that Province to Lower Canada. The insurgents having committed themselves by several instances of resistance to the local authorities, assembled, to the number of fifteen hundred, at St. Denis, under the command of one General Brown, assisted by Papineau, Wolfred Nelson, and others. General Gore with a party of regulars and militia attacked them there; many of them were killed or made prisoners, while the ringleaders escaped to the States. Soon after this, another formidable party met at St. Eustache: Sir John Colborne proceeded in person, at the head of a force of infantry and artillery, and inflicted a fearful punishment upon them; nearly 200 of them fell victims to their folly, 105 were made prisoners, the church in which they had taken refuge was burned over their heads, and sixty houses in the village reduced to ashes. The example was severe, but salutary: many of the armed peasantry hastened to surrender their arms, and were dismissed in peace to their homes.

In Upper Canada, a few discontented and ambitious politicians aroused a bitter feeling amongst a portion of the inhabitants there. The much vexed question of the Clergy Reserves, and the establishment of the fifty-seven Rectories of the Church of England by Sir John Colborne in 1835, added fuel to the flame.

Without organization or any definite plan of operations, these infatuated leaders of the blind instigated their misguided followers to assume an attitude of hostility to the constituted authorities. Distrustful of the propriety of their own proposals, and of their ability to carry them out, they used every means in their power to arouse the sympathies of the republicans of the neighboring States. "The pretext was seized," says Hough, an American historian, "as a favorable opportunity to push forward their private schemes of personal aggradizement, and pecuniary speculation, and the planning of enterprises which they had neither the honor nor the courage to sustain, when their support involved personal danger; the masses who acted in these movements, were doubtless actuated by sincere motives, but were blinded and misled by a few designing villians." The American Government affected to discountenance the treasonable acts of their citizens who sought to interfere with the disturbances of a people, with whose Government they were at peace. There is no doubt however that this *Patriot War*, as it was significantly termed by them, was winked at by American officials in high places.

All along the Frontiers, secret associations under the name of "Hunters' Lodges," were organized. Members of the American Senate and Congress, Governors of States, Generals in the United States Army, and many leading citizens, there and in Canada, were enrolled as office-bearers of the associations, under the name of "Grand Eagles." According to the "Brother Jonathan" newspaper, 60,000 members were sworn "to devote life and property for the extirpation of Royal Dominion in North America, and to relieve nations from the absurdities of Monarchy." The Montreal Gazette of 1838 states the number of these lodges to be 1174, the number of members 80,000, and the funds at their disposal $300,-000. The following was the Hunter's oath, by which they were solemnly bound to each other. "I swear to do my utmost to promote republican institutions and ideas throughout the World, to cherish them and defend them, and especially to devote myself to the perpetuation, protection, and defence of these institutions in North America. I pledge my life, my property, and my honor to the Association. I bind myself to its interests, and I promise until death that I will attack, combat, and help to destroy by all means that my superiors may think proper, every power or authorities of Royal origin, upon this continent; and especially, never to rest till the British tyrants cease to have any possession or footing whatever in North America. SO HELP ME GOD."

In a moment of profound peace, in the month of December, 1837, the city of Toronto was invested by a band of armed rebels, and Sir Francis Bond Head had an opportunity presented, sooner perhaps than he had expected, of testing the loyalty and bravery of the Militia of Upper Canada, who now alone remained to defend it. McKenzie and his infatuated followers were posted near Gallows hill, four miles in rear of the city. On the approach of the Militia they fled in a state of great agitation; their leaders succeeding in gaining the States, where they related in excited language their version of the movements, and induced many to believe that the Canadians were really sighing for an independent republican existence. The happiest refutation of such assertions was found in the fact, that, within three days of the first alarm, from ten to twelve thousand Volunteers had simultaneously marched toward the capital, to aid in maintaining for the people of Upper Canada, the British Constitution.

So great was the enthusiasm of the inhabitants, that His Excellency found it necessary to print and circulate notices that there existed no further occasion for the resort of Militia to Toronto, and a general order was issued for the whole of the Militia in the Bathurst, Johnstown, Ottawa, and Eastern Districts, to go and lend their assistance to Lower Canada.

The destruction of the American Steamer Caroline on the 29th of December, 1837, excited the feelings of the Americans along the lines to an extraordinary degree. This vessel had been seized by a party of scoundrels from the States, who styled themselves sympathizers with the disaffected Canadians. They had taken up a position on Navy Island in the Niagara River, and were using this steamer in transporting arms and ammunition for the use of the rebels, when she was seized by the militia of Canada, set fire to, and precipitated over the falls of Niagara. Again, on the night of the 29th May, 1838, the British steamer Sir Robert Peel, on her passage from Prescott, while lying at an American wharf in the Lake of the Thousand Islands, was boarded by a force of thirty or forty men, armed with guns and bayonets, and painted and dressed in Indian costume; the passengers were driven ashore in their night clothes, the vessel plundered and set fire to, and the pirates then took to their boats and decamped. The British Government offered a reward of one thousand pounds, and the Governor of the State of New York, as promptly, a reward of five hundred dollars, for the arrest of the perpetrators of this act. All doubts as to the guilty party were set aside by the following proclamation of Bill Johnston, the terror of all the inhabitants on these shores of the St. Lawrence: "To all whom it may concern: I, William Johnston, a natural-born citizen of Upper Canada, certify that I hold a commission in the Patriot service of Upper Canada, as commander in chief of the naval forces and flotilla. I commanded the expedition that attacked and destroyed the Sir Robert Peel. My head-quarters were on an Island in the St. Lawrence, without the jurisdiction of the United States, at a place called by me Fort Wallace. I am well acquainted with the boundary line, and know which of the Islands do, and which do not belong to the United States, and in the selection I wished to be positive and not to locate within the jurisdiction of the States......I yet hold possession of that Station, and we also occupy a station some twenty or more miles from the boundary-line of the States, in what was his Majesty's dominions until it was occupied by us. I act under orders. The object of my movements is *the Independance of Canada*. I am not at war with the commerce or property of citizens of the United States.—Signed this 10th day of June in the year of our Lord 1838.   WILLIAM JOHNSTON."

In consequence of this occurrence, an American steamer with fifty armed troops was sent to cruise among the Thousand Islands, and discovered the head-quarters of the bandit upon a small island. His home was found to be a spacious cave, partly natural, and partly excavated by human labor. The captain of the steamer entered it to a distance of 85 feet, and found that it contained several apartments, which had been recently occupied. But Bill Johnston and his gang had disappeared. He was arrested in November following by a party from the States, and was found armed with a Cochrane rifle with twelve discharges, two rifled pistols, and a bowie-knife, but, in his extremity, his craven heart failed him, and he yielded without resistance.

Early in November, 1838, the brigands, who had previously rallied in clubs and secret lodges, began to give symptoms of fresh demonstrations upon Canada. Unusual numbers of strangers were congregated about Syracuse, Oswego, Sackett's Harbor, and Watertown, and large quantities of arms and warlike stores were collected and concealed about these towns. Floating rumours had been in circulation for several days that an attack might shortly be expected in the vicinity of Prescott; but rumours of that kind had lately been so rife, that little attention was paid to them. On the night of Sunday the 11th, however, information was obtained that a large number of armed men had embarked on board the steamer *United States*, and also on two schooners, the *Charlotte* of Oswego, and the *Charlotte* of Toronto, and that the convoy was rapidly approaching Prescott.

The news proved to be true, for about two o'clock on Monday morning, the schooners, lashed side by side, were observed by some of the inhabitants, dropping down the stream, in close proximity, to the wharves at the upper end of the town of Prescott. Twenty or thirty men hastened to the river bank, and hailed the mysterious strangers, who represented that one of their vessels was in a sinking condition, and that they had put in, in distress. As no one was seen on deck, but the necessary hands, no opposition was offered to their landing at the time. but after several ineffectual attempts to make fast to the wharf, the lashings were cut, and the vessels parted company; one of them crossed over to Ogdensburgh, and grounded on the flat at the mouth of the harbour, the other dropped down the river, and anchored about mid stream, opposite the Wind-mill. This building, which has attained a world-wide celebrity from the occurrences which we are about to relate, stands upon a bluff rocky point, one mile and a half below Prescott. Its prominent position, large dimensions, and glittering tin dome, render it conspicuous at a considerable distance. It is of circular form, massively constructed of stone; its walls are three and a half feet in thickness and eighty feet high, and its interior divided into several stories, the small windows of which admirably served the purpose of loop-holes. Around it stood a number of stone houses, and nearly all the fences in the neighborhood were of the same material; while the margin of the river above and below was over-grown by a thicket of low scrubby cedars, highly favorable for concealment. Upon the whole the spot was well chosen, and was indeed worthy of a better cause. The banditti, concealed under the hatches of the schooner, effected a lodgment here on Monday evening, and were soon joined by numbers who crossed from Ogdensburgh in small boats. The night was spent in fortifying the Wind-mill and adjacent premises, under the direction of Von Schoultz, a Polish exile.

As might be supposed, great excitement prevailed in Prescott and the neighborhood on the commencement of these warlike demonstrations. Early on Monday morning a little steamer, the *Experiment*, was dispatched from Brockville for the assistance of their neighbors in Prescott. This vessel was armed with two small cannon, and continued during the day to ply up and down within the compass of a mile, and in a very spirited manner peppered the the boats of the sympathizers, as they crossed and recrossed from Ogdensburgh. The American steamer *United States* played a conspicuous part in aiding the so-called patriots. A crowd of excited ruffians had, in the morning, assembled at the dock where she was lying, took possession of her by force, for the purpose of carrying out their lawless designs, and used her during the day in carrying arms, ammunition, and men, to the Wind-mill. As she was returning from her last trip a shot from the *Experiment* entered the wheel-house, and instantly beheaded the pilot who was steering. The U. S. Marshal arrived in the evening at Ogdensburgh, and made a formal seizure of the vessel. Late at night the British steamers *Queen* and *Cobourg*, arrived, having on board a party of marines and regulars, amounting in all to 70 men. The same night, a detachment of the Glengarry militia, under captain McDonald, lay on the ground during a heavy rain, covered only with their blankets, and every moment expecting an attack from the pirates. Lieut. Colonel Gowan with a detachment of the 9th Provincial Battalion, numbering 140 men, also arrived at Prescott. On Tuesday morning early, a battalion of Dundas militia, consisting of 300 men, commanded by Colonel John Crysler, made their appearance, and were soon after joined by a part of the 1st Grenville militia, when the following dispositions were made. The left wing, consisting of 30 marines under Lieut. Parker, part of Captain McDonald's Glengarry volunteers, and a portion of the Grenville and Dundas militia under Colonel R. D. Fraser, took up a position along the edge of the woods, where the enemy had posted their piquets, and drove them in in gallant style. The right wing, consisting of 40 men of the 83rd regiment of the line, part of Colonel Gowan's battalion, 60 men under Edmonston, and part of the

Dundas militia, the whole under the command of Colonel Young, proceeded along the bank of the river, and, having advanced to within a few rods of the Wind-mill, encountered a sharp fire from the enemy. The action on the left commenced by a galling fire from the brigands posted behind the stone walls in rear of the mill. The British being upon the rising ground, were placed at great disadvantage from their exposed situation, nevertheless they advanced steadily, in double quick time, loading and firing with great precision, "a long line of fire blazed along the summit of the hill in rear of the mill for about eighty or a hundred rods, and the report of small arms made an incessant roar. As the morning was dark and lowering, the gleam of the discharges became the more observable, and tended to heighten the horrors of the dramatic events that were transpiring. At the time the action commenced, the patriot forces are supposed to have numbered from 200 to 300, but, during the engagement, a party consisting of fifty-two, who had pursued the retreating militia over the hill, were separated from their comrades, scattered, pursued, and captured in detail." The enemy were now driven from their shelter in great confusion, and, retreating some distance, took up a position behind another stone wall. From this they were dislodged in like manner, and finally were driven into their citadel the wind-mill, and the adjacent stone buildings, from which they maintained a vigorous fire upon their assailants, who suffered severely from the sharp-shooters that were posted in the upper stories of the mill. About 3 o'clock in the afternoon, a barn which had afforded shelter to the British was burned by the patriots. During the remainder of the day, both parties kept up an irregular discharge of musketry without coming to close quarters. The dead and wounded lay on the field till next morning, when the British sent a flag of truce to bury their dead, and both parties were engaged for a short time in performing this duty.

While these matters were transpiring on the north shore of the St. Lawrence, our neighbors opposite were not inattentive spectators. Immense crowds lined the south shore below Ogdensburgh, and rent the air with their cheers at the supposed success of the Patriots, whose cause many of them eagerly connived at, but which they dare not openly espouse. "Even at that distance (about a mile and a half) the officers on horseback were distinctly seen to fall, and the ranks of the soldiers to waste away under the unequal contest." The Board of Supervisors were in session at Canton at the time, and even these, twenty miles off, heard the cannonade of the battle distinctly. That some members of that board were warm sympathisers in the movement, may be gathered from the following resolution, moved by Isaac Ellwood, one of its number. "Whereas the members of the board of supervisors of St. Lawrence county having received information, and believing the same to be authentic, that the patriots have made a noble stand at Wind-Mill Point, near Prescott in Upper Conada, and have had a severe engagement with the advocates and minions of British tyranny and oppression, on the 13th instant; and having every reason to believe, from said information, unless the said patriots are reinforced in the perilous situation in which they are placed, that they will meet with defeat, and sacrifice their lives in contending with a merciless and cruel foe: and whereas this board feel a deep interest in the success of that patriotic struggle, which would spread the light of liberty over our oppressed brethren in Canada, and for the preservation of the lives of those patriots who are contending for the rights of men born free, and for the republican principles for which our venerable forefathers shed their blood—*Resolved,* that this board adjourn to meet again at the court house in the said county, on the last Monday of the present month, a one o'clock, p. m., in order to enable the members thereof to rescue that Spartan band of patriotic friends, and preserve their lives from the hands of their enemies, the tyrants and advocates of the British Crown."

It was resolved that the above resolution lie on the table until the same be again drawn up: and it is but justice to state, that this was never done.

In Ogdensburgh, crowded meetings were addressed by excited orators, who, in similar language, sought to induce the Americans to go over to the assistance of the rebels. General Winfred Scott, who had been sent to the Frontiers by the American Government, was present at one of these meetings, and exerted himself to allay their ill-directed enthusiasm. He told them, says one who was present, that if they wanted to bring disgrace upon the name, and arms of the United States, they would go over to the Wind-mill, and join themselves to the rebel rabble there; " the greater your numbers, the more complete will be your humiliation, it will only be the more credit to the handful of British; your confusion will be indescribable. I tell you plainly, that no body of undisciplined citizens, however numerous, can stand for ten minutes the charge of a single regiment of British regulars." He concluded by pointing out to them the folly of attempting to force upon the Canadians, measures, which their own acts proved they did not desire.

Wednesday and Thursday were passed at the Wind-mill, in comparative inaction, the British waiting for reinforcements and for guns of sufficient calibre to reduce the place; the brigands remained locked up in their prison, and kept up a desultory fire from the windows of the buildings. On Friday, at half-past twelve, the Canadians were relieved from their anxiety; three steamers hove in sight, which proved to be the *William IV*, the *Brockville*, and the *Cobourg*, having on board the 83rd regiment of the line, and a detachment of the Royal Artillery, with three 24-pounders. The 83rd, with the heavy cannon, took up a position in rear of the Wind-mill, and immediately opened up a heavy fire upon the rebels, which dislodged them from the stone houses, and drove them all into the mill. At the same time the three steamers assailed them from the river side.

Within half an hour after the cannonade commenced, a white

flag was seen to wave from the top of the tower, but it waved in vain, and was at last nailed to the outside of it. The exasperated British continued to pour in deadly volleys upon them, and every building in the vicinity of the mill was set fire to, in order to concentrate their attack upon the enemy's main fortress. "The flames raging in the gloom of night, showed at a great distance the position of the combatants and, shedding a lurid light upon all around, had an effect at once awful and sublime." At length the firing ceased, when the severely chastised rebels marched out, and surrendered at discretion. Von Schoultz, and many others, were found concealed among the bushes, and dragged from their hiding places. The number of prisoners who surrendered was 110, besides those who had been taken during the siege. In the mill, were found several hundred kegs of powder, a large quantity of cartridges, pistols, and swords, and 200 stand of arms, most of which were of costly and very superior workmanship; many of the swords and dirks were silver mounted, and their handles ornamented with elaborate carving. A flag, composed of the finest texture, valued at $100, was also taken, on which was exhibited a full spread eagle, beautifully executed, surmounted by *one* star, and beneath were the words wrought in silk, " Liberated by the Onondaga Hunters." The total loss of the rebels in killed and wounded was never accurately ascertained, as numbers of them were taken across the river; not less than forty, however, are known to have been killed, among these was a young officer, a son of General Brown, and two other officers, in the pocket of one of them was found a list of proscribed persons in Prescott, who were to have suffered death. The official return of the British loss was 2 officers, 11 rank and file killed, 4 officers and 63 men wounded. The officers killed were, W. S. Johnston, lieutenant 83rd regiment; and ——— Dulmage, lieutenant 2nd Grenville Militia. The officers wounded were, Ogle R. Gowan, lieut.-col. 9th Provisional Battalion, slightly; lieutenant Parker, Royal Marines, slightly; John Parlow, lieutenant 2nd Dundas Militia, severely; and Angus McDonald, lieutenant Glengarry Highlanders, slightly. Of the Dundas Militia four were killed and seven wounded.*

Not content with their overthrow at Prescott, a similar attempt was made by another gang, who crossed over from Detroit to Windsor, on the 4th of December following. This incursion terminated in similar results, which were thus laconically summed up in a military dispatch, by Colonel Prince, the officer in command: "Of the brigands and pirates twenty-one were killed, besides four who were brought in just at the close, and immediately after the engagement, all of whom I ordered to be shot on the spot, and which was done accordingly." The prisoners taken during these engagements in Upper Canada, were nearly all Americans. 180 of them were tried before general courts martial, held at Fort Henry and London, in the spring of 1839, on the charge "of having been unlawfully and treasonably in arms against our Lady the Queen." The whole of them were condemned to be hung, at such times and places as the Lieutenant Governor might appoint. 24 of them were recommended to the merciful consideration of the Governor. A number were pardoned in consideration of their youth, and other extenuating circumstances. The greater part had their sentence commuted, and were transported to Van Dieman's Land, where numbers of them died. After several years,

---

* Each of the wounded received a life pension of £20 a year, from the Canadian Government. A certain militia-man, who was returned as severely wounded, applied to the British Government for an additional allowance. He was referred to the staff surgeon at Brockville. A musket ball had passed through his wrist. He exhibited the wound and solicited the Doctor's kind offices to aid him in getting the addition.— "I perceive," said the latter, "your wound is severe, but the service regulations require that a wound must be equal to the loss of the limb, otherwise, no pension. I fear your application will be rejected." "It might as well be off for all the good it will do me," quoth the wounded man, somewhat indignantly. "The simplest thing in world, Mr. ——; let me take off the hand, and I will guarantee the pension." The application was not renewed, and the wound thereafter healed up rapidly.

the remainder were pardoned and mostly returned to their homes. Ten only of the whole number were hung at Fort Henry; amongst these was Von Schoultz, whose miserable end excited universal sympathy. He pleaded guilty to the charges preferred against him, and died the deluded victim of the designing traitors who urged him into the enterprize, and then cruelly abandoned him in the hour of danger.

The Lieutenant Governor, in a general order of the 24th November, 1838, while deploring the unhappy events that had transpired, expressed his admiration of the prompt and loyal exertions of the militia in the Eastern section of Upper Canada in the destruction and capture of the piratical force in the neighborhood of Prescott. "Her Majesty's regular troops and the gallant militia have proved each as brothers in arms. They have once more fought side by side, they have bled and died together; their patriotic example will not be forgotten in Upper Canada, and their blood is not, and shall not be shed in vain on the ground which they have so nobly defended; that blood will extinguish every unkindly feeling, and will rouse to arms every loyal Canadian."

The Queen thus gracefully acknowledged the services of the militia, in a general order from Head Quarters: "Her Majesty has contemplated with the greatest satisfaction the zeal, promptitude, and gallantry with which her loyal subjects in both Provinces have come forward for the suppression of the insurrection and the defence of their country; the steadiness and valor displayed by the militia and volunteers in Lower and Upper Canada are deserving of the highest praise." Internal quiet having been completely restored throughout the Province, that portion of the militia which had been enrolled for six months active service, including the two regiments of Dundas, was discharged, and, on their retirement to their homes, again received the warmest thanks of the Lieutenant Governor.

While the American Government succeeded in restraining its citizens from openly espousing the cause of the rebels, a circumstance arose in connection with it, which had well nigh plunged the two nations again into war. Alexander McLeod, a British subject, while engaged in business in the United States, was in 1841 arrested by the American authorities, upon the charge of having been concerned in the destruction of the steamer *Caroline*, and the alleged murder of one Durfee, an American citizen on board. The British Government held that the *Caroline* was a piratical vessel, unlawfully employed, and demanded the release of McLeod: this the Americans refused to accede to, and retained him a prisoner for nine months. At last he was tried at Utica, in October, 1841, and, as it was then proven that he was not near the scene of action when the *Caroline* was attacked, the jury returned a verdict of "*not guilty*." From this time forth was obliterated every vestige of the unhappy rebellion in Canada, and nothing has since occurred to distuib the tranquillity of the Province, or to endanger our friendly relations with the citizens of the neighboring Union.

Previous to 1837, the militia of the county of Dundas was organized as one body, known as the Dundas Militia. In that year it was divided by a militia general-order into two regiments, to be styled the 1st and 2nd Regiments of Dundas Militia, the militia residing in Williamsburgh and Winchester to compose the 1st Regiment, and those residing in Matilda and Mountain the 2nd. When also the following appointments were made.—1st Regiment: To be Colonel, Major John Crysler, 29th April 1837, 2nd Regiment: To be Colonel, Captain George Merkley, 29th April, 1837. In 1842, the Townships of Mountain and Winchester were separated from the front townships, and constituted the third battalion, and in 1852 these two were divided, Mountain being styled the 3rd, and Winchester the 4th battalion.

In terms of the Militia Act of 1855, the Province of Canada was divided into eighteen military districts, whereof nine were in Upper Canada, and nine in Lower Canada. All colonels commanding militia regiments were reduced in rank to Lieutenant

Colonels, and one officer only, in each military district, was invested with the rank of full Colonel. Dundas County lies in military division No. 2, which comprises Glengarry, Stormont, Dundas, Leeds, and Grenville, and the colonel commanding the district, is Alexander McLean, Esq., of Cornwall.

The sedentary militia of the Province is divided into two classes, called respectively, *service* men, and *reserve* men, and includes all the male inhabitants of the Province between eighteen and sixty years of age. All doctors, lawyers, postmasters, mail carriers, school teachers, ferrymen, one miller for each run of stones in every grist mill, toll keepers, jailors, with all quakers, mennonists, and tunkers, and others who from the doctrines of their religion may be averse to bearing arms, are exempt therefrom, except in case of war, invasion, or insurrection. The service men, are those from 18 years of age and upwards to 45; the reserve men, those from 45 to 60. The service men are again subdivided into two classes, respectively styled first and second class. The first class consists of bachelors, and widowers without children; the second class consists of married men and widowers with children. No part of the second class of service men are to be called out, until the whole of the first class have been drafted. The service men are required to muster once in each year, at such place as the commanding officer of each battalion shall direct, and all disobedience to orders lawfully given under the act, is punishable by penalties to be imposed by one or more Justices of the Peace in a summary manner. The Queen's birth-day (the 24th of May) is the day appointed for muster in Upper Canada, or if that day fall on a Sunday, then the next day thereafter. Every militia-man drafted for actual service must either serve, find a substitute of the same class, or forthwith forfeit a penalty of $40. The penalty for refusing to attend muster, at the place and hour appointed therefor, or refusing to obey orders at such muster, is $5 for each offence.

The above cited act, authorizes the forming of volunteer companies to be styled the active militia force, to consist of volunteer troops of cavalry, field batteries, foot companies of artillery, and companies of infantry armed as riflemen: the whole not to exceed five thousand men for the Province, and to be found with suitable arms and ammunition, by the government, but to find their own uniforms. The Militia Act was amended in 1859, by which, field batteries are required to drill twelve days in each year, of which at least six days shall be consecutive, and other volunteer corps once in each year during six consecutive days. Under this act, the commissioned officers of the different corps receive no pay, the non-commissioned officers and privates receive $1 for each day's bonâ fide drill, with the provision that no more than thirty dollars shall be paid to any one company for one such day's drill; if there are more than thirty men in a company, this sum may be divided amongst them to the number of fifty men, beyond that number no pay is allowed. The sum of $162,351.54, was expended on the militia volunteer service of the Province, in 1858, by the Canadian Government.

The following represents the strength of the Dundas Militia in 1859.

1st Battalion.—Williamsburgh. A. G. McDonald, Lieut. Col. Commanding. Service men 726; Reserve men 187. Total 913 men.

2nd " Matilda. David Robinson, Lieut. Col. Commanding. Service men 548; Reserve 150. Total 698 men.

3rd " Mountain. Edward Brouse, Lieut. Col. Commanding. Service men 434; Reserve 35. Total 469 men.

4th " Winchester. John P. Crysler, Lieut. Col. Commanding. Service men 549; Reserve 114. Total 663 men.

Total for the County: Service men 2257; Reserve 486. Together 2743, to which is to be added commissioned and non-commissioned officers, say 60 to each battalion, 240. Total effective strength, 2983.

There is but one volunteer company in the County of Dundas, styled, the first Volunteer militia rifle company of Williamsburgh, formed in 1857, James Holden, Captain, 33 non-commissioned officers and privates. The armoury at Morrisburgh contains 50 minie rifles and accoutrements, and 1000 rounds of ball-cartridges.

As in times past the militia of Canada have proved its chief defence, so in the time to come we must look to them as our surest bulwark. It is not well, even in times of profound peace, to shut our eyes to the possibility of its interruption. The lessons taught us in days gone by should not be forgotten by us thus early. The evil day might yet overtake us, and from a quarter the least expected, and what would be the consequence should it find us altogether unprepared? The example of our fellow subjects in Britain speaks to us, and tells us in accents not to be mistaken, of their faith in the doctrine, that the surest guarantee for peace is to be found in a state of preparation to resist hostile aggression; and that while trusting to Providence, and cultivating friendly relations with all, we should at the same time " *keep our powder dry.*"

Although well aware that difference of opinion exists on this subject, we have no hesitation in expressing our unqualified approval of the incipient volunteer movement in Canada. We regard it as nothing more than the exercise of the same precaution, which we manifest in our ordinary avocations. As we do not await the coming of the winter's storm to erect shelter for our flocks, so neither should we delay measures of self-defence till the ruthless invader has burned the roof over our heads. There are bounds of prudence and moderation beyond which it were suicidal for us to carry the movement; but we look forward with confidence to the time, when our young men will *cheerfully* fall into the ranks, and utterly reject the proferred *mercenary dollar*. It is desirable that they should know something of self reliance, and of military restraint, and above all that they should become familiar with the *ready and efficient use of the Minie Rifle.*

The following lines, written by an eminent Scottish clergyman, embody with exquisite pathos, all that we would say on this subject:—

Rifleman's Song.

AIR—"My lodging is on the cold ground."

Behold our stern mountains, our fields fresh and fair,
    Where no foot of invader has trod:
See our homesteads of peace, see our temples of prayer,
    Where in freedom we worship our God;
        But what if we heard from our bugles' alarms,
            That invaders had stepped on our shore?
        Then, Riflemen! Riflemen! stand to your arms!
            To the front, ev'ry man with his corps!

Behold our dear country, brightest isle of the sea—
    Brightest gem which on earth ever shone;
The refuge of patriots, the home of the free,
    Whose white cliffs are old liberty's throne.
        But what if we heard from our bugles' alarms,
            That invaders had stepp'd on its shore?
        Then, Riflemen! Riflemen! stand to your arms!
            To the front ev'ry man with his corps!

Behold our loved Monarch! the purest and best—
    The truest that Europe has seen!
O! never was Sov'reign so honored and blest
    As Victoria the mother and Queen!
        But what if we heard from our bugle's alarms,
            That invaders had stepped on her shore?
        Then Riflemen! Riflemen! stand to your arms!
            To the front ev'ry man with his corps!

Behold the bright vision, when justice shall reign,
    And the peace-march shall beat o'er the world,
When brother shall never by brother be slain,
    And the war-flag for ever is furled.
        O, then, when our bugle no longer alarms,
            Nor invaders are feared on our shore;
        Then Riflemen! Riflemen! lay down your arms,
            Then farewell ev'ry man to his corps!

REV. NORMAN M'LEOD, D. D.

Glasgow, 1860.

CHAPTER VI.

The County of Dundas—Situation, extent, population, and first settlement of—The Primeval forest—The U. E. Loyalists—The log shanty—Government grants of lands and implements—Difficulties encountered by first settlers—Hard times—Employments of first settlers—Their character—Dawn of improvement—The first schoolmaster—Brant and his Mohawks—Laws of the early settlers—Captain Duncan—Sir John Johnson—Steichmann—Reflections.

The County of Dundas is one of the United Counties of Stormont, Dundas, and Glengary. This Union of Counties was formerly known as the old Eastern District of Upper Canada. Dundas County lies between the parallels of 75° and 76° Longitude west from Greenwich; and the parallel of 45° N. Latitude, passing obliquely through the county, cuts it near the centre.

It is bounded by the River St. Lawrence on the south, by the County of Stormont on the East, on the North by the Counties of Russel and Carleton, and on the West by the County of Grenville.

It lies nearly midway between Montreal and Kingston; and a line drawn at right angles to the river St. Lawrence, from the centre of Dundas, would intersect the Ottawa River at, or very near, the city of Ottawa, the Capital of Canada. The distance between these two points, by an air line, is about 45 miles. The County of Dundas includes within its limits the four townships of Williamsburgh, Matilda, Mountain, and Winchester, embracing an area of about 250,000 acres, of which, in 1860, 237,000 were assessed at the value of $2,072,000.

The population of the county, by the recent Census (1861), is 18,824, of whom 15,190 are natives of Canada, 2097 of Ireland; 600 of the United States, 466 of Scotland, 285 of England; 152 of Germany; 23 of Nova Scotia and New Brunswick, 7 of Prussia; 3 of the East Indies; 1 not known.

EARLY HISTORY OF THE COUNTY.—The proclamation of peace between Great Britain and the United States of America, in 1783, witnessed at least a partial fulfillment of the prophesy, that " men shall beat their swords into ploughshares, and their spears into pruning-hooks." The brave and loyal subjects, who, during the fierce revolutionary struggle, had remained faithful in their allegiance to the British Crown, being no longer required to fight their country's battles, were now destined in a very different way to add to their country's greatness. It was announced that liberal grants of lands in Canada would be freely given to the now disbanded soldiers. This was simply characteristic of that principle of high honor, and justice, which, in every period of its history, has distinguished the British Government. The properties of all who had resisted the Republican Government in the States, were of course confiscated, and, peace being proclaimed, not only was the soldier's occupation gone, but his farm, and all his earthly possessions, were forfeited for ever.

A proclamation was issued, that all who wished to continue their allegiance to Britain, should peaceably rendezvous at certain points on the Frontiers. These were, Sackett's Harbor, Oswego, and Niagara, on the Upper Canada confines, and Isle aux Noix, on the borders of Lower Canada. We have seen it stated in print, that the first settlers of Dundas came in this way from Niagara; but this is a mistake, arising probably from the circumstance, that, during the last years of the war, some of them had been stationed in the garrison of Carleton Island, lying between Kingston and Sackett's Harbor. There is no doubt that the disbanded soldiers of Sir John Johnston's regiment were the first settlers on the St. Lawrence between Cornwall and the west boundary of Matilda, and that they were located in the first, second, and third concessions. Jessup's corps, belonging to the same battalion, were settled in Edwardsburgh and Augusta, while the second battalion went to the Bay of Quinté. These troops were not regular soldiers of the line, but volunteers, who had espoused the royal cause at the commencement of the Revolution. Johnston's regiment was 800 strong, and was called the Royal Regiment of New York. It was composed chiefly of Germans, with a few Scotch; the former mostly of the Lutheran, the latter of the Presbyterian faith. They were all natives of the old Johnstown settlement, on the Mohawk river, not far from Albany. At the close of the war, this regiment was stationed at the Isle aux Noix, a fortified frontier post at the northern extremity of Lake Champlain, which has already been mentioned as an important fortress during the old French war. Here they passed a whole year, and were employed in adding to the already extensive fortifications of that island. While they remained there, thus employed, two Government surveyors, named Steichmann and Tewit, were actively engaged surveying the county of Dundas, for their future occupation. Late in the autumn of 1783, the soldiers were joined by their wives and little ones, who had wandered the weary way afoot, to Whitehall, through swamp and forest, beset with difficulties, dangers, and privations innumerable. The soldiers from Isle aux Noix met them there, with boats, and conveyed them the rest of their journey by water, through Lake Champlain. Imagination fails us when we attempt to form an idea of the emotions that filled their hearts, as families, that had formerly lived happily together, surrounded with peace and plenty, and had been separated by the rude hand of war, now met each other's embrace, in circumstances of abject poverty. A boisterous passage was before them in open boats, exposed to the rigors of the season—a dreary prospect of a coming winter, to be spent in pent-up barracks, and a certainty, should they be spared, of undergoing a life-time of such hardship, toil, and privation, as are inseparable from the settlement of a new country. As soon as the journey was accomplished, the soldiers and their families, were embarked in boats, sent down the Richelieu to Sorel, thence to Montreal, and on to Cornwall, by the laborious and tedious route of the St. Lawrence. The difficulty of dragging their boats up the rapids of this river was very great; to us it is really quite inconceivable. Arrived at Cornwall, they found there, the government Land Agent, and forthwith proceeded to draw by lottery the lands that had been granted to them. The townships in which the different corps were to settle, being first arranged, the lots were numbered on small slips of paper, and placed in a hat, when each soldier in turn drew his own. As there was no opportunity for examining the comparative quality of the lands, so there was little choice in the matter, but by exercising a spirit of mutual accommodation, it frequently resulted, that old comrades who had stood side by side in the ranks, now sat down side by side, on the banks of the St. Lawrence. All these preliminaries having been arranged, on the 20th of June, 1784, the first settlers landed in the County of Dundas.

With what feelings of intense interest, mingled even with awe and melancholy, must these settlers have regarded this introduction to their new wilderness home! How impatient each to view the particular spot where his lot had been cast! Every where save in the neighborhood of the Longue Sault rapids the landscape wore an aspect of wild and gloomy solitude: its solemn stillness interrupted only by the deep murmuring of the mighty river as it rolled along its flood to the ocean. On leaving the river, the native grandeur of the woods, tenanted only by the Indian hunter and his scarce more savage prey, must have filled them with amazement. Well might they exclaim, is this our inheritance, our future home! Are these to be at once our enemies and our associates! Can it be that these giant denizens of the forest are to succumb to our prowess, and that this vast wilderness is to be converted into fruitful fields!

Even in this land of forests, few perhaps have ventured fifty miles from the abode of man, and surveyed a Canadian forest in its primeval grandeur. Indeed twice that distance from our homes, would not suffice, at the present day, to place us beyond the ring of the woodsman's axe. It was but last summer, that two adventurous æronauts were carried in a balloon, during a few hours, a distance of three hundred miles to the north of the Ottawa, and, surveying the scene around them, they concluded that they had reached the uttermost part of the earth. After days and nights of hopeless wandering through the woods, and nearly famished with hunger and cold, even in that remote region they discovered a party of lumbermen, to whom they owed the preservation of their lives.

The settlers in Dundas County, however, had preceded even the lumberman, and found in the trees of the forest a mine of wealth.

From the time of their arrival in Canada, they were known by the name of the "United Empire Loyalists," subsequently abbreviated into U. E. Every man capable of bearing arms was entitled to assume the name of a U. E. Loyalist. Some of them were indeed at a tender age. The late Colonel Crysler, then a drummer in the regiment, was in his fifteenth year, but was placed upon an equal footing with his father; and at a distant day, each of his numerous sons and daughters ranked as children of the U. E's Each soldier was entitled to draw one hundred acres on the river front, besides two hundred acres at a distance remote from the river. This was the soldier's bounty. If married and with a family, or if at any future time he should marry, he was entitled to fifty acres more for his wife, and fifty for every child; this was his family land. Besides all this, each son and daughter, on coming of age, or at marriage, was entitled to a further grant of two hundred acres. The greater part of Mountain and Winchester was thus drawn by children of the U. E. Loyalists.

The first operation of the new settler was to erect a shanty. Each, with his axe on his shoulder, turned out to help the other, and in a short time, every one in the little colony was provided with a snug log cabin. All were evidently planned by the same architect, differing only in size, which was regulated by the requirements of the family, the largest not exceeding 20 feet by 15 feet inside, and of one story in height. They were built somewhat similar to the modern back-woodsman's shanty. Round logs, roughly notched together at the corners, and piled one above another, to the height of seven or eight feet, constituted the walls. Openings for a door, and one small window designed for four lights of glass 7 × 9, were cut out—the spaces between the logs were chinked with small splinters, and carefully plastered outside and inside, with clay for mortar. Smooth straight poles were laid lengthways of the building, on the walls, to serve as supports for the roof. This was composed of strips of elm bark, four feet in length, by two or three feet in width, in layers, overlapping each other, and fastened to the poles by withs. With a sufficient slope to the back, this formed a roof which was proof against wind and weather. An ample hearth, made of flat stones, was then laid out, and a fire back of field stone or small boulders, rudely built, was carried up as high as the walls. Above this the chimney was formed of round poles notched together, and plastered with mud. The floor was of the same materials as the walls, only that the logs were split in two, and flattened so as to make a tolerably even surface. As no boards were to be had to make a door until they could be sawn out by the whip saw, a blanket suspended from the inside, for some time took its place. By and by, four little panes of glass, were stuck into a rough sash, and then the shanty was complete; strangely contrasting with the convenient appliances and comforts of later days. The total absence of furniture of any kind whatever, was not to be named as an inconvenience, by those who had lately passed through the severest of hardships. Stern necessity, the mother of invention, soon brought into play the ingenuity of the old soldier, who, in his own rough and ready way, knocked together such tables and benches as were necessary for household use.

As the sons and daughters of the U. E.'s became of age, each repaired to Cornwall, and presented a petition to the Court of Quarter Sessions, setting forth their rights; when, having properly identified themselves, and complied with the necessary forms, the Crown Agent was authorized to grant each of them a deed for two hundred acres of land, the expenses incurred, not exceeding in all, two dollars. In addition to the land spoken of, the settlers were otherwise provided by Government with everything that their situation rendered necessary—food and clothes for three years, or until they were able to provide these for themselves; besides, seed to sow on their new clearances, and such implements of husbandry as were required. Each received an axe, a hoe, and a spade; a plough, and one cow, were allotted to two families; a whip and cross cut-saw to every fourth family, and even boats were provided for their use, and placed at convenient points of the river. These were of little use to them for a time, as the first year they had no *grists* to take to mill, and the Longue Sault Rapids lying between them and Cornwall, whence they received their rations, it was found to be a very difficult matter to bring them by water.

But that nothing might seem to be awanting, on the part of Government, even portable corn mills, consisting of steel plates, turned by hand like a coffee mill, were distributed amongst the settlers. The operation of grinding in this way, was of necessity very slow; it came besides to be considered a menial and degrading employment, and, as the men were all occupied out of doors, it usually fell to the lot of the women, reminding us forcibly of the Hebrew women of old, similarly occupied, of whom we have the touching allusion in Holy Writ, " Two women shall be grinding at the mill, the one shall be taken and the other left."

In most cases, the settlers repaired to Cornwall, a distance of twenty-five miles, each spring and fall, or during the winter, and dragged up on the ice, by the edge of the river, as much as he could draw on a hand sled. Pork was then, as now, the staple article of animal food; and it was usual for the settlers, as soon as they had received their rations, to smoke their bacon, and then hang it up to dry; sometimes it was thus left incautiously suspended outside all night: the result not unfrequently was, that, while the family was asleep, the quarter's store of pork would be unceremoniously carried off by the wolves, then very numerous and troublesome, and in no wise afraid of approaching the shanty of the newly arrived settler. Frequently too during the night, would they be awakened by these marauders, or by the discordant sound of pigs and poultry clustering round the door to escape from their fangs.

For several years after the settlement, they had the choice of but two mills: literally they were situated between two extremes, Gananoque above, or the Cascades below them, equi-distant about sixty miles. To one of these two points they were compelled to resort, for the purpose of having their wheat ground. Several parties joining together would take forty or fifty bushels at a time, with five or six men to work the boat, stemming the rapids of the Longue Soult, or of the du Plat and Galouse.

Not long after their settlement here, Jacob Merckley, father of our respected townsman of that name, and his brother-in-law Shaver, being in want of some plenishings for the shanty, not to be obtained nearer home, set out upon a pilgrimage to Montreal, distant, by the tortuous path they had to travel, some 125 miles. It was in dead of winter, the snow was very deep, and they had no choice as to conveyance, but to foot it. The back was however made for the burden, and, being young and supple, they set out on their dreary journey, with light hearts, dragging behind them their hand sled with provisions and blankets for the journey. The only beaten path was on the ice, by the margin of the river. The whole stretch of shore was all but an unbroken forest, obstructed with tangled brush, and covered with snow full four feet deep. After six days steady marching, they reached Montreal, and, having procured the articles required, started on their return trip, "homeward bound." In addition to numerous other "*notions*," they had purchased an iron pot, or cooler, for boiling sugar, which weighed over one hundred pounds, and it required the united strength of the two to make headway, at even a very slow gait; however by resting frequently, they managed to make some progress. Having occasion to cross a wide bay below St. Anne's, and keeping far from shore to shorten the distance between the two points, they were much impeded by the snow drifting up their track. On they pressed, pulling away with might and main. They had scarcely reached the middle of the bay, when Shaver *gave out*, and sank exhausted on the ice. No friendly voyageur was there in sight, to bear a helping hand What was to be done? To leave the fallen brother, and go to seek assistance, might have been to let him perish in the snow; neither could he leave his precious cargo, lest it might be plundered in his absence. In his extremity, he raised him up in his arms, deposited him on the top of the load, and animated with superhuman strength, he, single handed, dragged his double load across the ice, and safely reached the nearest dwelling, where, remaining a day, the invalid was sufficiently restored to resume his place at the ropes, and they eventually reached home, safe and sound, having occupied three weeks in the excursion. Such were the difficulties met and surmounted by the early settlers; and the bare recital of them, might well put to the blush their less hardy descendants, who may utter the now frequent complaint of "hard times"

There was in former times a deal of valuable timber standing in the county of Dundas. Huge pine trees were cut for ship's masts, measuring from ninety to one hundred and twenty feet in length, and from forty to forty-eight inches in diameter, when dressed for market. One such piece of timber must have weighed from twenty to twenty-five tons. These mast trees were dragged from the woods by from twelve to sixteen pairs of horses. A single tree was sold in Quebec as a bow-sprit for $200. Of white oak, averaging when dressed from forty-five to sixty-five cubic feet, and of the best Canadian quality, there was abundance, this found a ready market at from 2s 6d to 3s. per foot; inferior quality of this timber was converted into stave blocks, and also shipped to Quebec. At a later period, large quantities of elm, and ash were sent to market from this county, while beech and maple, then considered worthless, were piled up in log heaps and burned, the ashes being carefully gathered, and sold to the merchants, to be made into potash.

There being ample employment on the father's farm, yet uncleared, for all his sons, there was little inducement for these to think of setting up for themselves; as a consequence, the lands the children had drawn, were of little value to them in the meantime. U. E. rights became a staple article of commerce, and were readily bought up by speculators, almost as fast as they came into the hands of the rising generation. A portion of what remained to the farmer or his family, was soon sold in payment of taxes, at sheriff's sale, and these lots too, usually fell into the hands of land jobbers Many of the lots had never been seen by the parties who drew them, and their comparative value was determined, either by their distance from the river, or the pressing necessity of the party holding them. It thus happened that lands in Winchester, which in a very few years brought from twenty to thirty dollars per acre, were then considered worthless; and lots even more favorably situated, in respect to locality, were sold, if not for an old song, at least for a new dress, worth perhaps from three to four dollars in cash. We have even been told credibly that two hundred acres of land, upon which now stands a flourishing village, was, in these early days, actually sold for *a gallon of rum*. The usual price of fair lots was from $25 to $30, some even as high as $50 for 200 acres. At $30 the price would be 15 cents per acre. These same lands were even then resold to settlers, as they gradually came in from Britain and the United States, at a price of from $2 to $4 *per acre*, thus yielding a clear profit to the speculator of one thousand per cent. upon his investment, a profit, in comparison with which, the exorbitant interest of these days, sinks into utter insignificance.

The summer months were occupied by the early settlers, in burning up the huge logs that had previously been piled together, and in the sooty and laborious work of re-constructing their charred and smouldering remains into fresh heaps; the surface was then raked clear of chips and other fragments, and in the autumn the wheat was hoed in by hand. During winter every man was in the woods, making timber, or felling the trees to make way for another fallow. The winters were then long, cold, and steady, and the fall wheat seldom saw the light of day till the end of April; the weather then setting in warm, the dormant breaks of wheat early assumed a healthy and luxuriant vegetation. Thistles and burdocks, the natural result of slovenly farming, were unknown, and neither fly nor rust, in these good old days, were there, to blight the hopes of the primitive farmer. The virgin soil yielded abundantly her increase; ere long there was plenty in the land for man and beast, and, with food and raiment, the settler was contented and prosperous.

There was in the character of the early settlers, that which commanded the admiration and respect of all who were brought into contact with them. Naturally of a hardy and robust constitution, they were appalled neither by danger nor difficulties, but manfully looked them fair in the face, and surmounted them all. Amiable in their manners, they were frugal, simple, and regular in their habits. They were scrupulously honest in their dealings, affectionate in all their social relations, hospitable to strangers, and faithful in the discharge of duty. As for their moral and religious character, we are proud to reflect, that, although without any clergyman, of either religious persuasion, the Lutherans and Presbyterians, from the beginning, lived together in good fellowship and peace. They united in observing the sanctity of the Sabbath, in holding lay-reading and in singing hymns on the day of sacred rest.

While we say this much of the early settler, let us not be understood as wishing to hold them up as paragons of perfection—as examples in all things to their descendants. They had their failings, as well as their virtues, but we must make allowances for the circumstances in which they were placed. They were charged by the early missionaries, and perhaps with some degree of truth, "as wofully addicted to carousing and dancing," but these were the common and allowed amusements of the times in which they lived. It may however be said with truth, that forms of licentiousness and profligacy, which are not uncommon in the present day, would have aroused the indignation of the early settlers, and met with reprobation, if not chastisement at their hands. It is true, they were not of those, who made broad their phylacteries, or were of a sad countenance, disfiguring their faces, and for a pretence made long prayers. Innured to a life of hardship and toil,—without the check of a Gospel ministry, and exposed to the blunting influence of the camp, the barrack, and the guard room, we must be content to find them but rough examples of Christian life. The scrupulous and distrustful vigilance, however, with which modern professors of every creed, eye their fellow-men, and require every pecuniary engagement, no matter how trivial, to be recorded in a solemn written obligation, stands out in striking contrast to the practice of the early settlers, among whom all such written agreements were unknown, every man's word being accounted as good as his bond. Lands were conveyed, and payments promised, by word of mouth; and verbal agreements were held as sacred as the most binding of modern instruments.

Christianne, the wife of the late Jacob Ross of Osnabruck, outlived nearly all the U. E. Loyalists of her time. Her descendants to the third generation grew up around her, and ofttimes listened to the thrilling story of her first coming to Canada, and the subsequent hardships and trials to which, at different periods in the course of her long lifetime, she had been subjected.

The following brief but touching narrative respecting her, was related to us by Mr. Samuel Ault, her grandson, and will be perused with interest, by many who were familiar with her features, and admirers of her virtues.

Mrs. Ross was a daughter of Michael Merckley, a loyalist, who lived in Schoharrie, near the Mohawk river, in the State of New York. She and her sister Eve, and her brother a little child, were taken prisoners by a scouting party of Indians, under the following circumstances:—

Her mother was dead. Her father was absent from home with a niece of his. Christianne was seventeen years of age, Eve was fifteen, and the little boy between five and six These three were left in charge of the house. The girls became somewhat alarmed at the prolonged absence of their father, and as evening drew nigh, their young hearts beat with anxiety, and all eyes were eagerly intent upon the road by which they expected his return. At last, he and his niece, both mounted on horseback, appeared in sight, riding in great haste towards the house. The little boy clapped his hands, and wiped off the tears from his swollen cheeks. The eyes too of the girls brightened up, and their hearts were filled with joy as they ran to the door to meet the embrace of their father.

Scarcely had the girls crossed the threshold, when a party of Indians in ambush, fired a volley from their rifles, before any explanation could be given or received. The father and cousin fell from their saddles to the ground, and, ere the breath had left their bodies, their scalps were taken off. The house was plundered, and with the barn and other buildings set on fire, while the poor little weeping, trembling orphans, were carried off by the blood-stained savages to their camp.

With loud cries and in tears, the three children were hurried off in charge of their cruel captors. A more touching sight one cannot imagine, and a tear bedims the eye as we try to realize it. "I want my father! I want my father!" cried the little boy "I want to go home to my father!" Yes,—he went to his father—the Indians became enraged with the pitiful cries of the little innocent, and ordered the girls to go on in advance with the squaws, keeping the lad in rear. Separated from his sisters, his cries became louder, till at last, as the only way of stopping his noise, they dispatched him with a blow of a tomahawk. His sisters saw no more of him, save his reeking scalp, which was held up before them, with the warning that unless they quickly held their peace a similar fate would be theirs. They were five weeks marching to Fort Niagara, and frequently were threatened with death when they gave vent to their feelings, and in many instances owed their lives to the interposition of the squaws.

At Niagara they remained seven weeks in possession of the Indians, when they were sold to Sir John Johnston, who commanded the Indians in the British service there.

He took the two sisters with him to Montreal, who remained in his employment as servants for nearly two years. At the close of of the war, Christianne married Ross, a discharged soldier, and came to Cornwall for the purpose of settling on a farm which he drew from Government. He exchanged that farm for one in Osnabruck, the same upon which his son and grandson now reside. They were supplied by Government with most things requisite for house keeping in the woods, but had no cow, and to remedy this want, they concluded that while Mr. Ross was busy making a small clearing, his newly married wife should return to Montreal, and do service for one year more, in order to raise means to purchase a cow, which she did. Thereafter they lived the most peaceful and happy lives imaginable till separated by death. They were strict adherents of the Lutheran Church, up to the time that their minister, Mr. Weagant, became an Episcopalian.

Christianne lived to the patriarchal age of 98, retaining to the last full possession of her mental faculties; she departed for "the better country," about three years ago, full of hope and resigned to her call. Her German bible and prayer book had been her companions through life and her comfort in old age, and even in death they were not divided, for at her own request they were buried with her in the same coffin.

Most of the first settlers have long ago passed away; a few, here and there, still remain, living exemplifications of the excellence of character which we have thus imperfectly described.

In the year 1788, the first grist-mill in the county was built by two enterprising men, Messrs. Coons and Shaver, in Matilda. It contained but one run of stones, and had a small saw mill attached to it. This mill stood upon a point of the river, about one mile below the present village of Iroquois. The saw mill never worked well, and was soon abandoned. The little grist-mill was however very successful; it would grind 100 bushels of wheat per day, and turned out better flour than one-half of the mills of the present time. Soon after this, another mill, upon what was then considered to be a magnificent scale, was built by John Monroe, on the point below Mr. Flagg's, also in Matilda. This had three or four runs of stones, besides a gang of saws, and worked admirably for ten years, when it unfortunately took fire, and was burned to the water's edge. It was immediately replaced by another, but this time with only one run of stones, cheaply constructed, and in every respect inferior to its predecessor. It stood thirty-five years, when a large field of ice striking violently on the point, carried the mill off bodily, or at all events demolished it. These several mills were all driven by the current of the St. Lawrence.

A few stores were now added. The first in this neighborhood appears to have been opened by Richard Loucks, who also kept a tavern, about a mile below the present limit of Dundas, as early as 1787. At this period the County of Dundas was not known by its present name; indeed there were as yet no counties named in Upper Canada. It formed a part of the then Lunenburgh District (of which more hereafter), which extended from Gananoque to the present Province line near Lancaster.

The settlers could now supply themselves with the necessaries of life, from the mill and the store, and the roving and dissipated life of the soldier was forgotten, in the staid and sober habits of the hard working farmer. A few of a more adventurous turn of mind, at times would man a boat, and, ascending the river to Oswego, take a circuitous route by lakes and rivers, betimes carrying their boat shoulder high, for miles at a stretch, and finally reach the green valley of the Mohawk, dear to them still in memory. Returning, they brought such articles of merchandize with them as they could transport, and, providing themselves with a passport at Carlton Island, they swiftly glided down the river.*

The duty of instructing their children seems from the very earliest time of the settlement, to have been recognized; and although of necessity a few years elapsed without a school house, yet from the very first they had their schoolmaster. A good old German, whose name we cannot recal, gratuitously spent his time in going from house to house teaching, two weeks at a time in different neighborhoods, where the children congregated, and received such instruction as the limited time and capabilities of their teacher afforded.

We learn from Major Clark, now residing in Edwardsburgh, that his father taught the first regular school in Dundas. He arrived with his family in Montreal, in the year 1786, and proceeded to the Bay of Quinté. When passing Lachine, Mr. Clark was much struck with the novel sight of a large encampment of Indians, on the precise piece of ground now occupied by that

---

* The following is a copy of such a passport:—

Inward.
John Loucks,
two men,
two women,
three children.

Permit the boat going from this to pass to Kingston with their provisions, family, clothing, beding, household furniture, and farming utensils, they having cleared out at this post, as appears by their names in the margin. Given under my hand at Fort Ontario, 21st day of May, 1795.

To whom concerned.

C. McDONELL, P. O.

beautiful grove of maple trees, which attracts the eye of almost every traveller. It is not uninteresting thus to fix the date of this well-known ornament to Lachine, should it escape the fate of maple groves in general, and ever reach a good old age. The Indians in question, were a party of the Mohawk warriors, in number about 400, who had adhered to the royalists during the American war, and had left their homes—the land of their sires for ages untold—that they and their children, might dwell under the benignant protection of their "Great Father and Friend," across the "Big Lake." They were in charge of the celebrated Indian chief, Captain Brant, and were by him conducted in a flotilla of canoes, to a tract of land on the Grand River in Upper Canada, in the centre of which now stands the flourishing town of Brantford, named in honor of their leader. It may seem very much out of our way, yet this digression is so tempting, that we cannot refrain from giving a few remarks respecting this remarkable man, condensed from an interesting sketch of his life, presented in Smith's History of Canada.

"Joseph Brant, or Thayendanegea, born on the banks of the Ohio in 1742, was the son of *Tehowaghwengarghkwin*, a full blooded Mohawk of the Wolf tribe. Brant received his education at Lebanon in Connecticut, and, having been taken notice of by Sir William Johnston, accompanied him to the wars, at an early period of his life, being only thirteen years of age when he engaged in his first battle. He became a firm ally of the British, and assisted with his tribe during the remainder of the French war. During the whole of the revolutionary war, Brant and his Mohawk warriors faithfully continued their allegiance. At the close of it, the Mohawk chief proceeded to Montreal to confer with Sir John Johnston, and from thence to Quebec, to claim from General Haldimand, the fulfilment of his pledge, that the Indians should be restored at the expense of the Government, to as favorable a condition as they were in, before the contest began. The Seneca Indians, wishing to perpetuate the friendly feeling existing between themselves and the Mohawks, offered them a tract of land in the valley of the Genesee; but the Mohawks were determined "to sink or swim, with the English." Brant visited England in 1785, where he was well received. When introduced at Court, he proudly declined the honor of kissing the King's hand, but added that he would gladly kiss that of the Queen. During his stay in London, he was invited to a grand masquerade, or fancy ball. He went richly dressed in the costume of his nation, wearing no mask, but painting one half of his face. His plumes nodded as proudly in his cap, as though the blood of a hundred Percys coursed through his veins, and his tomahawk glittered in his girdle like burnished silver. Among the guests was a Turk of rank, whose attention was particularly attracted by the grotesque appearance of the chief's singular attire. He scrutinized him very closely, and, mistaking his complexion for a painted visor, took the liberty of attempting to handle his nose. Brant, who had noticed the observation he excited, was in the humour for a little sport; no sooner therefore did the fingers of the Turk touch his nasal organ, than he raised the war-whoop, and, snatching his tomahawk from his girdle, whirled it round the head of his astonished assailant. Such a piercing and frightful cry had never before rung through the halls of fashion, and, breaking suddenly upon the ears of the merry throng with startling wildness, produced a strange sensation. The Turk himself trembled with terror, while the ladies shrieked, screamed, and scattered themselves, in every direction. The jest however was soon explained, and all was right again.

Brant was three times married, and died at Wellington Square, in 1807, aged sixty-four. He was a man of rare intelligence, a brave warrior, a steadfast ally of the British, and as humane as he was brave. His youngest son, Joseph, was appointed chief in his stead · he also received a good education; he was appointed to the rank of Captain, and also superintendent of the "Six Nations." In 1832 he was elected a member of the Provincial Parliament.

His election was contested however, and eventually set aside. That year he was carried off by cholera, and was buried in the same vault with his father."

But to return to our first *Dominie*—Mr. Clark remained two years at the Bay of Quinté employed in teaching. In 1788 he came to Matilda, at the instance of Captain Frazer, who at his own expense purchased a farm for him, at the cost of one hundred dollars. A few of the neighbors assisted in the erection of a school house, in which Mr. Clark taught for several years. He was a native of Perthshire in Scotland, and was universally respected. Before the close of 1792, the settlers in Dundas had erected two churches, and established several schools. They had also two grist-mills, and a number of stores, and taverns; and thus a new era dawned upon the happy little colony of U. E's.

LAWS AFFECTING THE EARLY SETTLERS. We may naturally enquire what kind of laws prevailed at first amongst the settlers in Dundas.

As the country was a forest, almost unbroken, from the impassable swamp, that had stopped the upward course of the French Canadians below Lancaster, to the Western Lakes—as there was yet no Legislature, and as the French laws could not well be extended over the new settlers, coming from the thirteen formerly British Provinces, where the laws had assumed a democratic aspect, it was decided by Government, that, for these and other reasons, the first settlers in Upper Canada should live under MARTIAL LAW, till such a time as it should be rescinded, and replaced by competent courts of justice. Consequently for some years, the inhabitants of Dundas County knew of no other law than that of the camp. But by martial law at that time, in the peaceable district of Lunenburgh, was meant, only, that the English laws having, by the settlement of this part of Canada, been introduced, should be its laws for the present, and that these laws, which very few knew, should be *martially executed*, by the Captain in command, having the superintendence of the particular locality. It appears there was such an officer for the district subsequently named Dundas County. Captain Duncan, an Englishman, executed these laws, *à la militaire*, and Maria-town was his head-quarters, of which indeed he was the founder, and so named it in honor of his only daughter, *Maria*. As a soldier, he was generous and humane, and, the religious sentiment largely prevailing amongst the German settlers, his office was a sinecure. It is somewhat difficult, however, with no more certain authority than the memory of *the oldest inhabitant*, to define precisely the extent of the Captain's jurisdiction. We presume that his office corresponded to that of a chief magistrate, or justice of the peace, of the present time, with the addition of a little more discretionary power.

From a manuscript before us, in the hand-writing of Richard Loucks, an innkeeper in the Lunenburg District, under date the 14th of September, 1790, we have undoubted proof that a civil court, with all the accompaniments of sheriff, judge, and jury, sat at least once in the year, at his inn, and that its jurisdiction extended over the whole Lunenburg District. Judging also from the items detailed, a jolly Judge and Jury they must have been. Numerous accounts are therein detailed of " Licker for the gentlemen of the grant gury," including sundry charges for " *decanters broken*." Port wine appears to have been the beverage used in the " Cort Room," rum, on ordinary occasions; while Judge Duncan treated his guests at "super" with brandy and " Elisapeth." In the document referred to, we find at one time, the names of twenty-six jurymen, presided over by " Juge Dunken," and " high shriff Monro." Judge Jarvis has kindly given us his opinion in respect to this court, which he says must have been under the authority of the Act of Parliament of England, 14 Geo. 3d cap. 83 (1774), usually known as the Quebec Act, by which the Governor and Council thereby constituted, must have erected the jurisdiction. There was no Court of King's Bench erected until 1794, at which time, of course, the court we have spoken of was superseded.

Those who were convicted of high offences, were punished by banishment, and were transported for a term of years, or for life, not to Botany Bay, but to the United States, a sentence next to that of death, felt to be the most severe that could be inflicted. Minor offences were atoned for in the pillory. For a long time there stood one such primitive instrument of punishment, at Richard Loucks' inn, the centre of law and justice for the then Lunenburgh District. Tradition also sayeth, that the ancestors of some of those who are now in exalted stations in the county, were there exposed to the vulgar gaze in the stocks.

CAPTAIN DUNCAN, the military commander, and "Juge Dunken," the dispenser of Law and "Elisapeth" at the Lunenburg Inn, will readily be recognized as identical.

Duncan in his day, seemed to have monopolized every office. A store keeper, and holding a captain's rank, he dealt out Martial Law, dry goods, and groceries alternately. A member of the Legislative Council, he framed Laws, and as Judge of the Lunenburgh District he dispensed them. His universal hospitality gathered around him a host of friends, while in his capacity as magistrate, he was a terror to evil doers. He was possessed of large tracts of land, acquired partly from Government, and partly by purchase, besides other property to a considerable extent, and enjoyed a full measure of the influence and outward respect, usually attendant upon wealth. He left the country somewhat abruptly for the United States, where he remained till his death.

He had, it seems, been extensively engaged in the lumber business, and it was said that some transactions in connection with this were so imprudent, that he dared never return to Canada. This circumstance detracted from that upright character, which otherwise he had acquired.

SIR JOHN JOHNSTON's name being inseparably connected with the early settlers of Dundas, a few particulars regarding his family may be interesting. His father, Sir William Johnston, was a native of Ireland, of whom it was said, in 1755, that he had long resided upon the Mohawk River, in the western part of New York, where he had acquired a considerable estate, and was universally beloved, not only by the inhabitants, but also by the neighboring Indians, whose language he had learnt, and whose affections he had gained by his humanity and affability. This led to his appointment as agent for Indian affairs, on the part of Great Britain, and he was said to be "the soul of all their transactions with the savages."

In a previous chapter we have already noticed his military exploits on Lake Champlain, and at Niagara, as well as the part which he and his Indian warriors took in the descent of the St. Lawrence with General Amherst's army. At the breaking out of the revolutionary war, Sir John, who had succeeded to his father's title, appears also to have inherited his influence with the Indians, and to have exerted that influence to the utmost, in favor of the Royalist cause. By this means he rendered himself particularly obnoxious to the continentals, as the Americans were then called. Accordingly in 1776, Colonel Dayton, with part of his regiment, was sent to arrest him, and thus put it out of his power to do further mischief. "Receiving timely notice of this, from his tory friends in Albany, he hastily assembled a large number of his tenants and others, and made preparations for a retreat, which he successfully accomplished.

Avoiding the route by Lake Champlain, from fear of falling into the hands of the continentals, who were supposed to be assembled in that direction, he struck deep into the woods, by way of the head waters of the Hudson, and descended the Raquette River to its confluence with the St. Lawrence, and thence crossed over to Canada. Their provisions failed soon after they had left their homes. Weary and foot sore, numbers of them sank by the way, and had to be left behind, but were shortly afterwards relieved by a party of Indians, who were sent from Caughnawaga, in search of them. After nineteen days of hardships, which have had few parallels in our history, they reached Montreal. So hasty was their flight, that the family papers were buried in the garden, and nothing taken with them but such articles as were of prime necessity. His extensive family estates were confiscated, and he thenceforth became a most active loyalist, and the scourge of the Mohawk settlement, during the remainder of the war."

Sir John, served with distinction throughout the war, and at the close of it was amply reimbursed by the British Government for the loss of his paternal estates. He received large grants of lands in various parts of the country, besides a considerable sum of money. He erected several mills, and was continued as superintendent of Indian affairs in Montreal, where he resided till his death, which took place in 1822. He ever manifested a lively interest in the welfare of his old soldiers who were settled on the St. Lawrence, who frequently went to see him, when occasion called them to Montreal.

The only other name that occurs to us, as particularly connected with the early history of the county, is that of Steichmann who surveyed the county of Dundas, and whose end was a melancholy one.

About the year 1801, an armed vessel "the Speedy" of ten guns, proceeding from York to Kingston, was totally lost, and as no vestige of her was ever discovered, it was supposed that she foundered in a gale, on Lake Ontario. Every soul on board perished, and, among other valuable lives, that of poor Steichmann's was lost. Judge Gray, from Cornwall, (the same from whom Gray's Creek derives its name,) several members of the Court of King's Bench, and many others, were among the number. Their unhappy end created much sensation at the time, and spread a gloom over the whole of Upper Canada.

The attempt to recall the early history of the County, has been a work of some difficulty, from the scanty materials within our reach. No records are extant, so far as we know, of the incidents connected with it. Though much of what has been advanced, may seem trivial, and uninteresting, yet, we have thought it worthy of notice, chiefly, because it has come to us from the lips of the few old settlers who remain among us. If the statements possess no other quality, they are at least reliable, and, in so far as the writer is concerned, he has done what he could to preserve them. We close this chapter with a few reflections on the first settlement of Dundas, kindly sent to us as a contribution by an old and highly respected inhabitant of the County.

" A natural enquiry is suggested, why were *Germans* located, at the first settlement of Upper Canada, in Dundas, and partly in Stormont, in close proximity to the *Highland Scotch?*

Apparently it was not by accident, but by design. We find, that close to the French Catholics of Lower Canada, were located the Scotch Catholics of Glengarry. No doubt, in consequence of the disastrous result of the Revolutionary War, it was deemed of the highest importance to promote peace and harmony amongst settlers in different parts of Canada.

Had English-speaking Protestants been made the neighbors of French Catholics, at that time, disputes of various kinds might have been apprehended to have arisen from such relationship. To prevent these as much as possible, persons of the same faith, though not of the same nationality, were placed side by side; and, to avoid civil and religious disputes, between the British-born settlers in Upper Canada, at that time, the German element of the population, was, in several instances, used by the Provincial Government. Close to the Scotch Catholics, the German Protestants were located in the eastern portion of the Province: and it was only next to the German-speaking Protestants, that the English-speaking Protestants were located in Edwardsburgh, and so upwards, towards Prescott and Brockville. Neither speaking, nor understanding each other's language, for some time after the settlements were made, much dispute was avoided among the early settlers. We consider this fact, as a part of that far-seeing system of policy which British statesmen have ever been striving to establish in Canada; and we believe the Government has not been disappointed in this respect, for perhaps in no district of Upper Canada, do, at present, the various forms of Christianity which now prevail, exist more harmoniously side by side, than in the eastern parts of Canada West.

The various types of nationality, from which the present population of Dundas has sprung, are rapidly merging into one, and the peculiarities of each, becoming yearly less observable. The dress, habits, and language of the Germans, and even the associations connected with their "Father-land," have all alike been forgotten. One brief generation serves to strip the Irishman of his "brogue." Even the canny Scot, who clings more tenaciously perhaps than any other to his vernacular, who is wont long to retain a lingering love for "Scotia's rugged strand,"—

> "Land of brown heath and shaggy wood,
> Land of the mountain and the flood."—

he, too, speedily becomes acclimated. All, denuded of their distinguishing characteristics, are assimilating in manners and in sentiments, and are thus contributing to the building up of a homogenous British Canadian family.

CHAPTER VII.

Intermediate History—The soil of Dundas—Cranberry Marshes—Standing timber and building materials—Climate—Meteorological Record—Oldest inhabitant—Eclipse—Earth-quake—Hail Storm—Irrigation—Statute labor and roads of Dundas.

From the year 1800 to the present time, the history of the County of Dundas is simply the history of Canada, and it is at least satisfactory to know, that the progress and improvement of the County have kept pace with the prosperity of the Province as a whole. The war of 1812 found its inhabitants as loyal as of yore, and at their country's call they cheerfully donned their armor and marched against the invading foe. A detachment of the Dundas Militia, as we have seen, were present at "Crysler's Farm," another remained to protect the fort and town of Prescott. In 1837, they turned out at an hour's notice, and assisted in quelling the Rebellion; at that time they were enrolled and under duty for six months. Since then the peace and prosperity of the county have been uninterrupted, not however without some hindrances to the successful practice of agriculture.

The extensive operations in lumber consequent upon the clearing up of a new and well timbered country, resulted in a state of matters unfavorable to agricultural improvement. Having spent the winter in the woods, the farmer had to spend the greater part of the summer in conveying his timber to Quebec. The farm was neglected, and, as a consequence, he rarely raised provision enough even for his own use. In this way he was compelled to apply to the storekeeper to furnish him, which he readily did, at his own exorbitant prices, taking the timber as security for payment. If at the end of the year the backwoodsman made ends to meet, he had reason to be thankful: the majority however came out on the wrong side of the ledger. The indulgent storekeeper was as accommodating as before, and was perfectly satisfied to let the old account remain at interest, and to add to it by fresh advances, upon receiving a mortgage of the farmer's land in security. The embarrassed farmer, still clinging to the hope of redeeming his farm, embarked with renewed energy in lumber-making, resolved to "make a spoon or spoil a horn." In a few cases he was successful, but in many instances the farm fell irretrievably into the hands of the merchant. The intimate and seemingly necessary connection then existing betwixt the lumberman and the merchant, induced the ruinous long-credit system, which, perhaps more than any other cause, tended to cripple the resources of the farmers, and consequently to retard improvement: happily this system is now fast disappearing. At a more recent period, and previous to the completion of the St. Lawrence Canals, the farmers of Dundas occupied much of their time in conveying goods and passengers from Cornwall to Prescott. The yearly increasing tide of emigration, all bound for the west, gave constant employment to as many teams as could be spared at $4 per day: this to a certain extent, again tended to divert the attention of the farmers from agriculture, but being a ready-pay business, it was found to be much more profitable than the lumber trade, the materials for carrying on which were besides becoming scarce in the county. Even for some time after the Cornwall Canal was finished, all upward-bound vessels had to be towed with horses from Dickinson's Landing to Prescott, and a considerable amount of money found its way into the farmer's pocket in this way. The final completion of all the canals in 1847, and the introduction of powerful steam-tugs, removed the last hindrance to the progress of agriculture, which has since then received the undivided attention of the inhabitants, and has proved more remunerative than any of the enterprises in which they had hitherto engaged. We propose in this chapter to offer a few remarks respecting the soil and climate, the irrigation, and the roads of Dundas County, together with a few additional matters of interest, suggested by the enquiry into those named.

THE SOIL.—While the soil of the county is varied, it is chiefly of a tolerably rich loam, varying in depth from six to eighteen inches, and resting upon a substratum of bluish marly clay. It may be described for the most as level, at least with little more inclination than is necessary for carrying off the surface water. In some parts, towards the centre and rear of the county, it partakes more of a rolling character, but in no place does the land rise to any considerable elevation. It is interspersed with numerous swails or lowlands, not of sufficient extent to entitle them to the name of *swamps*, and which differ from these in the important particular that they are all capable of drainage. In most cases, where any of these swails have been cleared of the timber, a single ditch through the centre, suffices to carry off all stagnant water, and, when that is once accomplished, such lands are invariably found to be of the richest and most productive nature.

These swails, as well as the other level lands, are comparatively free from stones. On the contrary, where the land partakes of a rolling nature, we usually find the surface freely covered with boulders. The labor and expense of removing them, is in some cases very great, but is in part recompensed by the stock of durable materials for fencing, draining, and building purposes thus obtained, as well as by the dry and usually fertile qualities of the lands so cleared. A few sand knolls scattered here and there through the county, barely suffice to furnish materials for brickmaking and for building purposes.

In addition to these swails, which are always heavily timbered with elm and ash, there are three cranberry marshes of considerable extent. The largest is situated in the Township of Winchester, and covers an area of about 800 acres. These marshes, situated in the heart of a thickly wooded region, are themselves destitute of a single tree, save here and there a scrubby spruce, and present a very singular and interesting appearance. They are completely covered by cranberry bushes from two to three feet in height, and are resorted to by swarms of busy berry-pickers, at the season when they ripen. The soil, which is of a black muck, not unlike the peat moss of Scotland, is annually inundated in spring, but is left quite dry again in summer. The bushes, from accidental causes or otherwise, are burnt off every few years, the fire sweeping every trace of vegetation clean before it, as in the western prairies of the United States. The succeeding crop of young bushes rise up luxuriantly from among the ashes of the old, and are generally most prolific.

As has already been mentioned, all the choice market timber, such as oak, pine, and rock elm, has long since disappeared, while the stumps, especially of the pine, remain, a convincing and lasting monument of the dimensions of the huge denizens of the forest. Here and there are found entire pine tree, of enormous size, lying prostrate in the woods, shrouded in moss and lichens, which were cut sixty years ago for masts, and for a slight flaw had been rejected. Most of these are still quite sound, and are readily converted into saw-logs and shingle blocks. In the meantime the beech and maple saplings, which, by a mysterious law of nature, seem to supplant the coniferous species, have grown up into stately trees, and another mine of wealth has been sprung, affording winter occupation to the farmer in cutting cord-wood, and hauling it to the river. The hard wood finds a ready market in Montreal, and the soft wood supplies fuel for domestic use, for railways, and steamers. There is also abundance of cedar, used for making fences, and for floats to convey the cord-wood to market. Hemlock and balsam occupy the sandy knolls; but wherever beech and maple thrive, we are sure of finding an excellent soil, and specially adapted for wheat.

The clay of the county is not esteemed very suitable for brick-making, being slightly mixed with fragments of limestone, which are calcined in process of burning the brick, and on subsequent exposure to the weather make them liable to crack. Most of the bricks used in the county, are brought from Aultsville in Stormont; or from Waddington in the U. S., immediately opposite.

There is abundance of good building stone in the county, though not very equally distributed. The quarries are chiefly near the centre and rear of the county. The stone is near the surface, is of hard gray limestone, and is sold at the quarry for $1.50 per cord of 128 cubic feet. Common field stone suitable for rough purposes, is delivered in any part of the county at $2 per cord, and well burned lime of excellent quality at 20 cents per bushel. Upon the whole, the soil of Dundas is admirably adapted for pursuing the mixed system of husbandry. Wheat, Indian corn, and potatoes are here successfully cultivated, while it is equally well adapted for the coarse grains, for grass and for roots of different kinds.

THE CLIMATE may be fairly stated to be a mean temperature between Montreal and Toronto. The extremes of heat and cold are less severe than those of the former, while a longer continuance of snow in the spring, retards agricultural operations ten days or two weeks later than in the neighborhood of Toronto.

The oldest inhabitant says, that the climate is much less severe since the county has become more generally cleared. The winters have been shortened at both ends, whilst the clearing up of marshes and wood lands has at once admitted the fresh air and the cheering rays of the sun—greatly diminished the numbers of mosquitoes, and other like pests, and rendered the whole county more healthy and salubrious. A few facts in connection with this are not without interest, and will bear us out in these remarks. We would solicit the reader's attention to the following table of observations. kindly furnished for this work by the Reverend H. W. Davies, M.A. Principal of the Senior Grammar School of the United Counties of Stormont, Dundas, and Glengarry.

156 METEOROLOGY. [CHAP.

ANNUAL SUMMARY OF METEOROLOGICAL OBSERVATIONS TAKEN AT CORNWALL.

In Lat. 45° N. Longitude 74°56 W. for the year 1859.

Height above the Sea about 210 feet.

Months.	Highest Temp. Reading	Date	Lowest Temp. Reading	Date	Monthly Range	Warmest Day Date	Warmest Day Mean Temp	Coldest Day Date	Coldest Day Mean Temp	No. of Rainy Days	Inches of Rain	No. of Snowy Days	Inches of Snow	Total Depth Rain & melted Snow	Thunder & Lightning	Aurora Borealis	Hail
January	49°	21st	−7°.1	12th	56°.1	21st	36°.60	12th	−6°.91	0	0	2	10.00	1.800		2	
February	46°.5	21st	−5°.1	5th	51°.6	18th	33°.63	11th	1°.51	1	0.305	3	10.00	1.305		2	
March	57°.7	28th	−3°.8	2nd	61°.5	29th	45°.23	1st	7°.04	6	2.708	2	6.50	3.358	2	1	1
April	53°	4th	19°.9	5th	33°.1	4th	56°.70	5th	27°.04	3	2.301			2.301			
May	85°	27th	37°.7	30th	47°.3	26th	72°.16	9th	45°.95	4	1.631			1.651	1		
June	78°.2	23rd	34°.2	13th	44°	2nd	70°.03	4th	42°.92	5	2.001			2.081			
July		No Observations Recorded this Month																
August	97°.5	16th	42°.7	30th	54°.8	15th	70°.70	29th	54°.21	4	1.823	1		1.823		1	1
September	75°	20th	30°.2	15th	44°.8	27th	65°.60	14th	41°	12	3.932			3.932		1	
October	77°.2	5th	17°.7	26th	59°.5	13th	63°.76	20th	20°.08	3	0.897	3		0.897			
November	61°	9th	14°.7	29th	46°.5	9th	52°	25th	19°.33	7	5.867	5		5.867			1
December	59°	1st	2°.7	3rd	61°.7	1st	48°.36	13th	2°.94	0	0	4	15.00	1.500			
Sums 1859	738°.1		178°.4		556°.7		616°.77		254°.91	45	21.34	20	41.5	25.69	3	7	3
" 1860	710°.6		212°.3		498°.3		609°.8		260°.08	84	25.2	39	60.00	31.25	18	18	3
Means 1859	67°.19		16°.20		50°.97		56°.07		22°.83	4	1.95	1	3.77	2.33			
" 1860	64°.60		19°.30		45°.31		55°.57		23°.71	7.6	2.29	3.5	5.45	2.84			

We may remark, that the observations being taken at stated hours, viz., at 7 a.m., at 1 p.m.; and at 9 p.m., the average temperature is pretty correctly ascertained, but the extremes of heat and cold are thus liable to escape detection. The highest observation recorded in the above table is 97°; it is more than probable, that, two hours later, the figure might have been over 100°. In the same manner, 7° below zero is the lowest notation; had the observation been taken two hours earlier it might possibly have read 27°, or even 37° below zero, for scarcely a winter passes without some part of one day, or more, verging upon 40° below zero. It may also be remarked that "rainy days," are those upon which rain fell; the duration of rain seldom exceeding a few hours.

By the Census of 1851, the population of Dundas county was 13,811, the number of deaths in one year 64, being in the ratio of one death in 216: a ratio far more favorable to this county, than any portion of Canada or the United States, with two exceptions, and singularly enough, these two, are our next door neighbors in Stormont and Russel, the ratio of the former being 1 in 240, and the latter, 1 in 220. The next below us being a third neighbor, Carleton, which was 1 in 211. Addington and Kent of similar population, were respectively, 1 in 98, and 1 in 84, while in the State of Maine U. S. the ratio is 1 death for 77 who survive.

If we are not over wise in Dundas, the same authority tells us, that few of us are really "*daft.*" During the same year there were of lunatics and idiots, in Kent 16, in Addington 13, and in Dundas but 4, and these may have been on a visit from our western neighbor Grenville, which was notorious in this way, returning 25.

We may here state, that the *oldest inhabitant* is no imaginary personage, but a most interesting and intelligent old lady, Mrs. Coons, residing in Iroquois, now in her 96th year, and in full possession of all her faculties. Peter Shaver, Esq., of Matilda, is one of the oldest male inhabitants, now in his 84th year. Both of these have a very distinct recollection of the first settlement of the county, and of the trials and difficulties which followed. We mention their names particularly, because to them we are largely indebted for information, and for substantiating certain dates herein-after mentioned, which possess an interest far beyond the limits of the county. Did space permit, we might mention a number of peculiarities in connection with the population: for example, we have at present residing under one roof, a family consisting of two females, and four males, and comprising great-grand-father, grand-father, father, and son. The great-grand father is a hale, hearty old Scotchman, who, a year ago, carried off a prize at a ploughing match, and in summer or winter has never been a day *off work*. Under another roof, and that but a small and humble one, not long since might have been seen, sitting down to their frugal meal, twenty-two children of the same parents. It is said that the Emperor Napoleon I., when asked by the celebrated Madam de Staël. "Whom do you consider the greatest woman that ever existed?" "She that had the greatest number of children," was the deliberate reply. In that light our lady of Dundas has few superiors in Canada. Were we to enter a third house, one might almost fancy himself in the abode of an "Anakim," for the united height of the seven inmates is 43 feet 5 inches. The eldest *boy* is a handsome young man of 6 feet 7 inches, and as straight as an arrow. The second is 6 feet 5 inches, and the youngest 6 feet.

The arrival of the "Great Eastern" in New York, and the visit of the Prince of Wales, are certainly remarkable events in the history of America, yet, occurrences still more remarkable, transpired during the year 1860, making it truly a year of wonders, and as such a memorable one. By Canadian farmers, it will long be remembered as a year in which the good things of this life were dispensed to them by Providence with a lavish hand. No part of Cannada shared more largely in the late abundant harvest than the county of Dundas, for we believe that nowhere was the in-gathering farther above an average. We shall not however dilate here upon this. While on the subject of meteorology, our thoughts naturally turn to the unusual phenomena which characterized the past year, to wit—the Eclipse, the Aerolite, and the Earthquake. We have neither the ability nor the inclination to treat of them scientifically, but simply wish to place them on record, as occurrences noticed by the inhabitants of Dundas, that may be spoken of many years hence.

On the morning of the 16th July, 1860, we were privileged to witness an annular eclipse of the sun, distinctly visible to the naked eye, and, with the aid of a piece of smoked or colored glass, the phenomenon became highly interesting. It occurred between 8 and 9 a. m., and the unusual appearance of the atmosphere during its continuance, took those who were ignorant of the cause, somewhat by surprise. The sunlight was perceptibly diminished, although to a lesser extent than we remember to have witnessed in Edinburgh in 1837, when many of the stars were distinctly observed. Upon the occasion of the recent eclipse here, the dim light shed upon the landscape, gave to it that peculiar dull yellow tint, which it usually assumes when the sun is similarly obscured. The greatest obscuration was said to be 0.623, hiding considerably more than one-half of the surface of the sun.

On the evening of the 20th July of the same year, a phenomenon of a different kind occurred, namely, the passage of a bright fiery meteor, or properly speaking, an "*Aerolite,*" over our heads.

Owing to the rapid flight of these mysterious bodies, they are usually witnessed by few, and, from the limited time of observation, but little can be learned of their nature. Calculation as to their size, distance, and true course, are therefore little more than conjecture. Their appearance is that of a swiftly moving fiery globe, which frequently explodes with a noise like thunder, scattering numerous fragments of their component parts to the earth. More than two hundred instances are on record, of the fall of portions of these bodies in different parts of the world, and it is a singular fact, that upon examination, they are found to contain the same chemical elements which compose the crust of the earth. On the 14th of December, 1807, an aerolite of similar appearance to the one under consideration, exploded near Weston in Connecticut, and from it, masses of stone half a ton in weight, were precipitated to the earth. The aerolite of 1860, was observed almost simultaneously over an area of more than 1000 miles; the inference is, that it must have been of vast size, and travelling at a much higher velocity than was usually supposed. Considering its alarming proximity, we may congratulate ourselves that in this case there was no explosion observed. Its appearance is described by an observer in Montreal, "as two distinct masses of brilliant flame, in appearance larger than a man's hat, one preceding the other, with a connecting link of fire, and a train of sparks some distance behind."

A writer in the "Boston Traveller," estimates its flight at 25 miles per second, and its distance from the earth 22 miles. The same writer says, "The terrific grandeur of a solitary aerolite, moving with planetary velocity in our very midst, exploding with the noise of many thunders, and hurling 'hail of iron globes,' and stony masses over our globe, is calculated to awaken in the breasts of every one, feelings of awe, and a deep and abiding interest in these bodies. The destruction which they are calculated to produce, and the four memorable instances of mortals crushed to death in their fall, tinges their interest with feelings of melancholy and terror."

At about 6 a. m. on the 17th of October, most of the inhabitants of Canada were aroused from their slumbers by a violent shock of an earthquake, the vibrations of which continued for about the space of one minute. It was accompanied by a rumbling noise resembling distant thunder, and is said to have been the severest shock experienced by any now living in the country. The writer pleads guilty to having remained fast asleep, and is consequently an incompetent witness in this case, but its reality is amply attested by numbers in this neighborhood, who were awakened by the *violent shaking of their beds*. The sensation was usually described as if a strong man had laid hold of the bed post, and shaken it with all his force. Many arose hastily and looked under the bed, and around the room, for the " loon " that did it; while others rushed to the window to see whether a hurricane was raging outside, but, although the waters of the river were in commotion, there was not a breath of air stirring. Some came to the conclusion that they had been subjected to a fit of night-mare, and thought no more of it; few attempted to account for the phenomenon at all, and an earthquake was the last explanation that any one thought of.

This earthquake was not felt further west than Belleville, and extended thence, following the route of the St. Lawrence to New Brunswick. At Montreal, the " Pilot " newspaper of the following day, says "the houses trembled, doors were opened, bells rang, and crockery was smashed." From Richmond it was reported, " that bedsteads and furniture were moved, and stoves knocked down." At Quebec it was still more perceptible, overturning chimneys, and otherwise alarming the natives. The accounts from that quarter reminded us of the great earthquake which shook Canada in 1663, a graphic account of which was written in the Jesuit's journal of the same year. " On the 5th of February," says the report as quoted by Smith, "a great rushing noise was heard throughout the whole of Canada. The earth trembled violently, and caused the stakes of the palisades and palings to dance, in a manner that would have been incredible had we not actually seen it in many places. Men and women ran out of doors, and stood horror-struck with the scene before them, unable to move, and ignorant where to fly for refuge from the tottering walls and trembling earth......the violence of the earthquake was greatest in the forest, where even the trunks of the trees are said to have been detached from their places, and dashed against each other with inconceivable violence and confusion...... The Indians declared that the forests were drunk......Some of the mountains were torn from their beds and thrown upon others, leaving immense chasms in the places whence they had issued."

In this strain the report proceeds to a great length, each sentence adding new horrors to the description, until the reader is quite prepared to hear that Quebec, with its citadel, and all its inhabitants were swallowed up alive; but no, "the most remarkable circumstance of all, is, that all this has transpired without our losing either man, woman, or child, or even having a hair of their head touched."

The earthquake of 1860 was succeeded by several minor shocks, at intervals of a few days; it was also preceded by a considerable one in May of the same year, described by those within doors, as though a railway train had passed rapidly through the cellar of the house.

We are in the habit of connecting thunder-storms with a sultry and overheated state of the atmosphere; nevertheless, we are at times subjected to sudden and unaccountable freaks of nature. Thus, about three years ago, we were visited by a thunder-storm of unparalleled severity during the very depths of winter. Upon that occasion a barn was struck by the lightning, in the township of Matilda, and with its contents was instantly consumed. By way of offset, it is by no means unusual for us in the middle of summer to be regaled by a pelting shower of hail. The most remarkable storm of this kind we ever witnessed, occurred in August, 1860; the air was at the time unusually oppressive and warm, the thermometer indicating 85° in the shade, when, without any premonitory symptoms, we were assailed by a violent shower of hail, the individual particles of which far exceeded anything previously witnessed in these parts. The storm commenced with an irregular discharge of the large missiles, gradually increasing in quantity and diminishing in size, until the ground was perfectly white. We cannot condescend to particulars of weight, or precise dimensions, for the large pieces were devoid of shape, and were speedily dissolved; several which we picked up appeared to us fully equal in size to a small hen's-egg. Fortunately the storm was of short duration, and extended over but a small area, otherwise the damage to the growing crops must have been very great.

As it was, the windows of both churches in Osnabruck exposed to it, were left without a pane of glass.

From these aerial flights we must now return to the subject, less interesting perhaps, but more immediately in hand, and describe our county in other aspects.

IRRIGATION.—The County of Dundas is well watered. In front is the noble St. Lawrence, averaging, along its whole southern boundary, a breadth of nearly one mile and a half, and of great depth. The current is swift, having an average speed of from four to six miles an hour, while the "Rapid du Plat" shoots past the centre of the county at a rate of 9 or 10 miles an hour. In rear it is watered by the Petite Nation River, which, rising within a mile or two of the St. Lawrence, has a very tortuous course, and, receiving many tributary streams, empties itself into the Ottawa River, about 30 miles below the city of Ottawa. The tributaries of this river are fed by springs and swails; during the spring time of the year and also in autumn they assume formidable dimensions, giving motive power to numerous creek mills, which, though only in operation for from three to four months in the year, are nevertheless a valuable acquisition to those living in their neighborhood.

An abundant supply of well-water is found all over the county, on reaching a depth of from 15 to 25 feet. Besides, numerous springs are met with, affording their fortunate owners an inexhaustible supply of pure water, without trouble or expense on their part. There is also in Winchester a mineral spring, similar to the celebrated one at Massena, and had in some repute for its medicinal qualities; but as no hotel has as yet been built to accommodate visitors, it is not much frequented, except by those living in its neighborhood.

Upon the whole, then, we cannot describe Dundas as otherwise than decidedly favorable, in regard to soil, climate, and irrigation, for the successful practice of agriculture; while its geographical position, and facilities for reaching market in summer or in winter are scarcely equalled, certainly not surpassed by any other county in Upper Canada.

THE ROADS.—Within the past ten years, the roads of the county have undergone a vast improvement. During the last five years the large sum of $25,000 has been apportioned to this county, from the Clergy Reserve Fund, secularized in 1854: this has all been expended upon roads; and considerable sums continue to be annually applied to the same purpose, by the several municipalities of the county. A good deal is also done by statute labor, the amount of which is regulated by law, according to the assessed value of each individual's property. Every male inhabitant of any township, over 21 years of age and under 60, is required to perform two days of statute labor, on the roads and high-ways in such township, and every party assessed for real or personal property in proportion to the value of such property, thus: under £50, two days' labor are required; under £100, 3 days; £150, four days; £200, five days; £300, six days, and so on, adding one day for each £100, until it reaches £1000, and for every £200 above that sum, one additional day.

The result is highly satisfactory.—Remote parts of the county, formerly all but inaccessible, are now easy of access. Instead of toiling through the mud, or bumping over the rough corduroy, dreading a break-down at every step, the farmer now moves along, swiftly and aristocratically in his light spring-buggy; or with his waggon-load of grain he travels with ease and comfort to himself, and his team. The value of lands in the rear has thereby increased tenfold, precious time has been saved, and wear and tear proportionably diminished. Abundant supplies of the very best quality of gravel for road-making are found in various parts of the county, and much of the statute labor is absorbed in placing it upon the roads. The highways in the centre and rear of the county, being generally nearer the supply of gravel, have improved proportionately faster than the front roads. With the exception of two, one built by a corporation, and the other by a joint-stock company, our roads are all free from the nuisance of the toll-gate.

CHAPTER VIII.

Geology and Natural History.

General Geological features—Laurentian formation—Huronian—Lower Silurian—Potsdam Sandstone—Chazy—Trenton Group—Tertiary formation—Post-Tertiary—Composition of surface soil—Forest Trees—shrubs—fruit bearing plants—wild flowers. Animals-mammalia—Birds—Fishes.

The County of Dundas has in itself no geological features of a very remarkable kind. From its position in relation to the general system of rocks of which it forms a part, it is indeed less fertile in points of interest than are several of the counties which lie around it. Here are no high hills, bold elevations, or deep gullies, in which the rocky strata may be noted or measured, or from which indications of ancient disturbances may be obtained. From the character and formation of its rocks, clays, sands, and boulders, we would infer, that the events of its remote physical history, were for the most part of a peaceful kind, and that by a slow and orderly process the County ripened into its present fair condition. We can with certainty say, that it has never been greatly disturbed with earthquakes, and, that no volcanic fires have burned within its borders. When its lower rocks were formed there can be no doubt that they were the beds and sediments of a very ancient ocean; and such the whole land continued to be through a long succession of ages, during which its several strata were deposited. Only in comparatively recent times did Dundas emerge from its watery birth-place, and take its position as part of the dry land, which now constitutes the great continent of North America.

But if Dundas be in itself wanting in special features of geological interest, it is not without interest when viewed in connection with the system of rocks of which it forms a part. Its geological position may be described as the centre of a great trough, or basin, formed, most probably, by the depression of its area, during the time of the deposition of its sediment. The circumference of this basin appears to have remained either altogether stationary, or to have been but slightly elevated, while its centre was gradually sunk to a depth of about 1000 feet. Along the line of its diameter we consequently find the same class of rocks making their appearance, as would be seen in succession, were we to sink a shaft from its surface down to its foundation. The outcrop of the strata of rocks which underlie the surface of the county, clearly appear as we travel from its centre, in any direction, north, south, east, or west. Go we north through the counties of either Carleton or Russel, and, crossing the river Ottawa, pass on a few miles to the north, we shall traverse the intermediate strata, and reach the Laurentide rocks, which though here rising into hills, yet lie at the base of the geological system. If again we travel from the same point towards the west, we shall, in the same manner, reach the same class of rocks as before, in the county of Leeds or of Lanark. If south we direct our course, and cross the mighty St. Lawrence into the State of New York, we shall, a few miles from the river, again encounter the same belts of ancient rocks. To the east, the counties of Stormont and Glengarry, are similar in their geological character to that of Dundas, but on passing to the eastern borders of Soulanges and Vaudreuil, in Canada East, we again find the outcrop of the same strata, and reach the lower rocks of the system. In every direction we thus descend in the geological scale; from the heights we reach the depths, from the hill tops we pass to the valleys. The highest elevation is near the City of Ottawa, where we meet with the Utica shale, and the lowest depressions lie all round, and may be said to describe a circle of an irregular form, of from 80 to 130 miles in diameter, and with an area of about 10,000 square miles in extent.

Let no one, however, suppose that this mountain of rocks of about 1000 feet in height, is appreciable to the natural eye. On the contrary, the whole district which it covers, is for the most part a level plain, at least it does not attain to an elevation above the sea, of more than 300 feet, or above the St. Lawrence of more than 150, and, what may seem strange to the unscientific reader, its chief apparent elevations are really its lowest geological positions. Height and depth in geology, are it should be noted, not reckoned according to apparent position, but according as it can be shown that one stratum naturally overlies another. The overlying strata are higher in the scale than those which lie beneath, and were deposited at a period more recent than they. The clays and sands of Dundas are thus greatly higher than the crystalline rocks of the Thousand Isles, or even than the limestone which is found in its own quarries. From the bottom rocks to the surface of the land, we find a series of strata, rising in regular succession, one above the other, to the height we have noted, and each presenting a different appearance from its neighbor. Such is the general character of this great basin, of which Dundas occupies about the centre. But on looking carefully at the rocks which crop out upon the surface of this area, we find that it is made up of several minor basins or troughs. First, it is divided longitudinally into two subordinate basins, by an elevation which appears at the east corner of March in Carleton, and running eastwardly, keeps a course parallel to the Ottawa, as far as Mount Calvaire in Vaudreuil. This brings up the lower rocks in Nepean, near Gloucester and East Hawkesbury. The most northern division into which the great basin is divided is the narrowest, and exhibits no further depressions of any note, but the southern division is again subdivided into three shallow subordinate troughs, which, although they do not effect the general configuration of the country, are yet important geological features. The elevations which separate these latter, run nearly parallel to the previous one, and expose the underlying rocks, the one on the north-western part of Montague, North Elmsley, and the western part of Mountain; and the other in the southern part of Oxford and South Gower. These lines of elevation carried eastward into Dundas, will probably give the line of outcrop of the limestone in which the quarries lie, and from which building stone and lime may be obtained.*

But properly to understand the geological character of the County of Dundas, it is necessary to take a general survey of the different rocks which underlie its surface.

On looking then at its surface clays and sands we find that they belong to the Tertiary and Post-Tertiary epochs of geology. They lie at the very top of the whole system of rocks which we find covering the face of the globe. the rocks proper which underlie these deposits belong, however, to the Lower Silurian formations and lie at the very base of the whole system of stratified rocks. Between these extremities Canada presents us with an almost entire blank. The great groups of strata which naturally come between the Silurian and the upper Tertiary and form so important a feature of the rocks of the United States and of Europe, have either never been deposited here, or have been washed away by ancient seas. The coal measures, for example, which are so largely developed in Pennsylvania and other States of the Union, as also in Nova Scotia and New Brunswick, have no place at all in Canada. Every coal-mining speculation in this Province has proved a delusion and a snare, and brought ridicule upon the sanguine and foolish adventurers. We have, it is true, within our borders many valuable minerals, by which in time our wealth will be greatly increased, but within the present inhabited or surveyed portion of our territory, coal will, it may confidently be asserted, be sought for in vain. Before we find coal we shall have

---

* Report Geological Survey of Canada 1851-2.

to travel as far as the Rocky Mountains or the arctic circle. Again, the Mesozoic formations which occupy the middle field of the earth's strata, and in which animals of strange and gigantic forms have been found, are not represented at all in this Province, and not till we come to the later Tertiary system, just before the introduction of the present forms of animal and vegetable life, do we find in Canada strata analogous to those of the United States and of Europe. That these missing strata never formed part of the Canadian rocks it would be hard to say. They may once have existed here as elsewhere. If so, where they have gone to we cannot tell, all that with confidence we can assert is that they are not here now; nor as far as we know have they left any vestiges of their previous existence behind them.

Having thus stated what is not found in our system of rocks, we shall now briefly describe what we do find, and what we can claim as peculiarly our own.

We have *first* the Laurentian formation which lies at the foundation of all the rocks of the Province, and is so named by Sir Wm. Logan, from the Laurentian Mountains, a range of low hills on the north shore of the St. Lawrence. These rocks are of great thickness. That part of them which is exposed to observation and measurement is computed as having a depth of 40,000 feet, or nearly 8 miles. This may appear scarcely credible, yet actual observation so determines, and the probability is that it is rather an under-statement of the reality. These rocks, it is estimated, cover an area of about 200,000 square miles of the northern and central portions of the Province; that is, to this extent they come to the surface or lie immediately under the soil. They spread over the country to the north of the river Ottawa, and from thence crossing the Province in a southerly direction, they traverse the St. Lawrence between Brockville and Kingston; they also prevail in the northern part of the State of New York, thus forming the northern, western, and southern rim of the Dundas basin. To the east they only appear in patches in the county of Vaudreuil, but a little to the north they crop out in great masses in the county of Two Mountains. They thus encircle Dundas, and doubtless also underlie it, forming the foundation upon which all its other rocks are laid.

That this system of rocks was once stratified there can be little doubt. The stratification has however been almost obliterated by the process of crystallization through which the rocks have passed. They are, for example, largely composed of a rock called by the German name of Gneiss, which may be described as a hard, tough, crystalline rock, exhibiting curved and flexured lines of stratification, and composed in the main of quartz, felspar, mica, hornblende, and garnet. Its crystals are broken, indistinct, and confusedly aggregated; but in whatever form they appear they never altogether lose their stratified appearance. The other and the most largely developed rocks of this system are however granites of various sorts which have no apparent stratification. Many of them are remarkable for their large crystals of felspar, quartz, mica, hornblende, and garnet. Those in which hornblende takes the place of mica, are called syenite from their resemblance to the granites of Syene in Egypt. The highly crystalline form of these granites indicate a maximum of alteration, during the process of which every trace of former stratification or of fossils has been entirely obliterated. But as a counterpoise we find extensive belts of crystalline limestone and marble, which give manifest evidences of stratification. These are remarkable features of the system and wherever found, afford, in the midst of surrounding barrenness, soil of the most fertile description. Another feature of the Laurentian system of rocks is the iron ore which it contains in inexhaustible quantities. From Canada alone the world could easily be supplied with the best iron for thousands of years.

These rocks are of vast age and lead us back to the remotest periods of the world's physical history. They indicate besides a state of things on the earth not dissimilar to that which existed in later periods, and in which tribes of animals and orders of plants lived and died. Although the chemical and mechanical changes to which they have been subjected, have almost if not altogether obliterated every vestige of fossil forms of life, yet one or two doubtful and much altered corallinoids have been discovered in them. The carbon of the iron, and the crystals of graphite which they afford are also evidences of an ancient vegetation. These marks though slight are yet enough for science to determine that these rocks are not in their primitive condition, but have been changed from their original stratified form into that crystalline state in which they are now found.

The *second* system of rocks which we find in the ascending order, immediately overlying the Laurentian, and within the circle of our basin, is that of the Lower Silurian. This name has been given to them from the fact of their being well developed in a district between England and Wales anciently inhabited by the Silures. This system, in its lower and upper divisions, is widely spread over the world, and in this country stretches over a large area, attaining to a probable thickness of about 5000 feet. These rocks are not however the next in direct succession above the Laurentian. The Cambrian or Huronian series comes between the two, and in the neighborhood of Lake Huron attains a thickness of 10,000 feet. But as the Huronian rocks do not appear within the region of our survey, we shall only say of them that they are the great sources of the copper which is found so abundantly in the regions of the Upper Lakes.

The Lower Silurian rocks are divided into several formations or groups of strata, each distinct from the other in the character of its fossils and in some respects also of its rocks. The lowest of these, and that which we find in our basin in immediate proximity to the Laurentian, is the Potsdam Sandstone, so called from its large exposure at the town of the same name in the United States. This is a very compact and hard stone, much resembling quartzite. Its color varies from white to reddish and brown. It affords excellent materials for building and glass-making. It is found at the base of the hills on the north shore of the Ottawa running westerly to a point opposite Pembroke, from which place it forms an interrupted belt which runs south through the counties of Renfrew, Lanark, Leeds, and Grenville. At Brockville it crosses the St. Lawrence, and, taking a course to the south-east parallel with the river some miles from its bank, it passes through the counties of Huntingdon and Beauharnois in Canada East. At the latter place it again crosses the St. Lawrence by the St. Louis rapids, and forms the whole eastern boundary of the counties of Soulanges and Vaudreuil. It is besides found on both banks of the Ottawa as far as the borders of Argenteuil and Prescott. This rock forms the second circle of the trough in the centre of which Dundas lies. It covers no great area and does not in this Province attain a greater thickness than about 300 feet. It is chiefly remarkable as a silicious sandstone containing little lime, and as being the lowest strata which contain well preserved and well marked fossils. In it we really come to the dawn of ancient life. Some of its layers are penetrated with holes which are supposed to have been formed by the roots of an ancient sea plant, or, which is more likely, to be the perforations of ancient sea worms. (*Scolithus linearis*) It also contains a pretty little bivalve shell called a *Lingula* from its having the shape of a tongue, which curiously enough is now converted into phosphate of lime, and is the only species of animal that has survived all past geological changes and now lives in the waters of the Pacific Ocean.

Besides these and other curious forms of molluscous life there have been discovered in this rock, at the Village of Beauharnois and other places, the track and footsteps of a strange animal, which, from the distinct marks left by it, appears to have had a caudal appendage or tail, and from fourteen to sixteen legs. It is conjectured that the animal imprinting these marks was some species of crustacean or crab, but of a family wholly distinct from any thing that can be suggested by the crustacean forms of later rocks or of the present day; it has received the name of *Protech-*

nites. Lately, too, other tracks still more curious have been discovered in a quarry of this same rock near the town of Perth in the County of Lanark. "These are impressed on a bed which varies in thickness, in different parts, from an eighth of an inch to three inches. They consist of a number of parallel ridges and furrows, something like ripple marks, which are arranged between two narrow continuous parallel ridges giving to the whole impression a form very like that of a ladder; and as the whole form is usually gently sinuous it looks like a rope ladder."* The breadth of the trails is about six inches and three quarters to the outer side. The tops of the ridges and the bottom of the furrows are somewhat rounded. There runs along the track a ridge intermediate between the two parallel side ridges, which although not so conspicuous as these, is yet seldom altogether wanting. Naturalists to whom specimens of those curious tracks have been exhibited consider them to have been made by some gigantic species of mollusc or shell fish. From the resemblance of the track to a ladder, the name proposed for it is *Climactechnites Wilsoni*, the specific designation being in compliment to its discoverer Dr. Wilson of Perth. These are the chief fossils which have been found in the Potsdam Sandstone; unless it be that recent discoveries by Sir Wm. Logan lead to the conclusion that this formation is the equivalent of the Quebec group of rocks, then we shall have to consider it as containing a large and important group of primitive forms of life, which will ally the Potsdam rocks with the primordial zone of the Bohemian Geologists. This will very likely be the case.

The *third* formation to which we come in our upward course, is that of the Calciferous Sandrock—a limestone so called from its containing more or less sand. In some parts of the country this rock is called by the farmers "Bastard Limestone." It follows the same course as that of the other formations above described, only that it covers a much larger area of the country than the

---
*Canadian Naturalist Vol. V. p. 279.

Potsdam. It appears extensively in the counties of Lanark, Carleton, Grenville and Leeds. It crosses the St. Lawrence at Prescott, and forms the entire southern bank of the river down to the County of Beauharnois. It margins also the north bank from the County of Stormont down to the borders of Soulanges. From this point it runs west into Glengarry, at the northern part of which it forms a sharp angle and turns to the north, passing through Hawksbury and on to Ottawa river, on the south shore of which it is seen in many localities from Carillon to the Chatts. In Canada it is supposed to attain a thickness of about 250 feet, but in this district its probable depth is about 100. It affords good building materials at Brockville and Prescott; and although very few beds of the formation yield good lime, such however does occur in some parts, as at Brockville and Merrickville. The lime there is dark-colored, but effective in giving strength to the mortar made from it. The strata are comparatively barren of fossils, and those which are found are generally in a bad state of preservation. Several convoluted and spiral shells have been discovered, along with well-marked traces of sea-weeds, or fucoids.

The *fourth* formation to which we come is that of the Chazy, so called from a place of the same name in the United States. The name has been given to it by the New York geologists, and adopted in Canada. It follows the same circle as the previous rocks, only it is more circumscribed than they are. It passes through the eastern part of Carleton, and skirts the western part of the County of Dundas. It then runs east, parallel with the river, to the Counties of Stormont and Glengarry, and pursues a course precisely similar to that of the Calciferous Sandrock, only occupying an inner belt of the great basin. The limestones found in the southern part of Dundas and to the north west belong to this group. At Packenham they afford a marble of a dark chocolate color, very compact and susceptible of a fine polish. They also contain in some places hydraulic lime, or cement, a material that does not slake when moistened with water, but forms a mortar which hardens under water. In the neighborhood of Marmora, a lithographic stone of a superior quality is also found in abundance.*

The fossils of this formation are more numerous and better preserved than those of the previous one. They are chiefly molluscs, with crustacean trilobites, and are sufficiently characteristic to entitle the strata to a specific name.

In general the Chazy is regarded as the first member of the Trenton group of rocks, so called on account of the exposure of its most characteristic strata at Trenton, in the United States. Along with the Chazy, this group comprises the Birdseye, Black River, and Trenton limestones. These rocks are almost always pure gray, blue, buff, or blackish limestones, very regularly stratified. It is upon this group that the County of Dundas reposes. The rocks which it comprises do not all come to the surface, and can only be known to exist by sections found in river channels and in quarries. They doubtless underlie the whole county to the depth of more than one hundred feet. Their whole thickness in Canada is about 500 feet. They are extensively spread over the country which lies between the Ottawa and the St. Lawrence, and in a great measure fill up the centre of the Dundas basin. They repose upon each other in regular order, and in some places seem to blend one with the other. Some fossils are peculiar to each of the four divisions, while others, and by far the greatest number, prevail throughout the whole. At the city of Ottawa the whole attains a thickness of about 500 feet, and the several members of the group are packed full of organic remains. The waters in which they were deposited must have been filled with incalculable numbers of living creatures. Radiates, articulates, and molluscs, there abounded. There are, it is upon good reason conjectured, vastly more animals buried in one cubic mile of the Trenton limestone, than there are living at any one time on the whole continent of America.† They all too belong to extinct species, nearly all to

---
*Report-Geological Survey of Canada 1851-2.
†Canadian Naturalist Vol. I. p. 39.

extinct genera, and many of them to orders which became wholly exterminated myriads of ages ago. It would be out of place for us either to name or to describe these curious and interesting fossils. Names have been given them of a technical and learned kind, which few of our readers would understand or care to make out. We shall describe them sufficiently for our purpose, when we say that they comprise multitudes of spiral and flat, single and double-shelled shell-fish, a large number of animals like crabs and lobsters, several like the common star-fish and sea urchin of our sea-coast, multitudes of a class of animals with long foot-stalks and heads like flowers, which are commonly called sea-lillies, crowds of corals of several genera and species. In fact it may be said that the rocks of this entire group are one mass of remains of such kinds of animals, broken up into minute fragments, and cemented together with a crystalline-like substance called calc-sinter, a deposit from calcareous water. If the smallest fragment of the Trenton rocks be, for example, ground very thin and transparent, on looking at it with the low power of a microscope it will be seen to contain numerous fragments of corals and shells, packed closely together.* It may be truly said that throughout a large part of Canada, and specially in Dundas, the people live upon the graves of extinct forms of life, and build their houses with the bones of the dead. Almost all the stone edifices from Kingston eastward, are built up from the fosiliferous rocks of this formation. These animals were the sources from which chiefly the lime of the rocks was derived. The waters of the Silurian seas were largely charged with lime, and the animals which lived in them, by the aid of their peculiar organs, and by a process of secretion, drew from the water the lime which it held in solution, forming it into shells or houses for themselves, and, when they died, left it behind them for the use of other animals, their successors. We thus see how useful the tiniest creatures may be, and how their labors through countless ages may all be directed by the Great Artificer for the benefit

---

*Canadian Naturalist Vol. IV. p. 161.

of mankind. Better stones for building purposes, for our climate, could not well have been provided than are found in the strata of the Trenton group. The frost does not injure them; they are not very porous; and although somewhat sombre in appearance, their neutral tints yet harmonize well with our bright sunshine and our clear blue sky.

The rocks proper of Dundas end with the Trenton limestone. Higher than this they do not rise. But above these rocks we find large sedimentary deposits of clays, sands, and boulders, the origin and character of which we shall now endeavor to describe.

These superficial deposits, although lying very much on the surface, and exposed every where to observation, are yet, perhaps, less known and understood, than are the rocks upon which they rest. They are the most recent of the strata which ancient oceans have left behind them, and are of the greatest interest, as affording an index to the conditions of the earth and its climate, at a period next before that at which man was created.

These clays and sands belong partly to the Pliocene, or latest, Tertiary, and partly to the Post-Tertiary systems of European Geologists. Some of the American Geologists, in accordance with French precedent, class them in their first system of rocks, styled Quaternary, thus immediately relating them with the underlying Tertiary. In our earlier Canadian Reports, the upper part of these deposits received the name of Lawrencian, but this we presume will now be altogether abandoned and that name be reserved exclusively for the crystalline rocks at the base of our system. Pliocence, or recent Tertiary, and Post-Tertiary are the names by which they are at present best known, and most commonly designated.

These deposits are spread over the area which lies between the Ottawa and St. Lawrence and generally conceal the older formations. They consist of clays gravels and sands with boulders of every size. Good sections of them may be seen on the River St. Lawrence all the way down from Dickinson's Landing. They occupy, too, much of the south bank of the Ottawa, and are exhibited on all the tributary streams of the country.

They may be properly divided into two distinct formations, each deposited under different circumstances from the other, and seperable by the characters of their contained fossils. The lower is commonly known as the "Boulder formation or Drift" and the upper as the "Post-Tertiary or recent." The first has no regular stratification, and presents evidences of having been formed during a period when a force of some kind, not yet satisfactorily explained, was applied to the northern portion of the earth, in such a manner as to grind down its surface, break its rocks in pieces, and transport the debris to great distances southward.

Wherever the Drift is exposed, it is seen to consist of a confused mass of rounded stones of every size, from that of a small pebble to a large block or boulder weighing several hundreds of tons. These are usually embedded in a tough clay, and sometimes so cemented together as to require the aid of blasting to break them up. The boulders are, many of them, of the same kind of rock as that which is found in the neighborhood, but a large proportion of these consists of rocks transported from distant and northern regions. These latter are more rounded than the former in consequence of the rubbing which they have received in the course of their migration. When this Drift forms the surface of the fields, the farmer who owns the land will find himself greatly annoyed by the innumerable round stones covering his fields, hindering cultivation, and impeding his plough.* To remove the boulders from such localities is almost labor in vain, for after a few years a fresh crop will work up from the deposit below and take the place of the others, better leave such fields to natural pasture, or to primitive bush. There is not much of this Drift formation exposed in Dundas. That it lies next above the rocks is certain, and in many places will be found in the digging of wells. If it be asked, how came these stones, clays, and sands to be deposited in

---

*Canadian Naturalist, vol. 1, p. 321.

such vast masses, and to be so widely distributed over the northern hemisphere of the globe? In reply, we must say, that the question is easier put than answered. We can only suppose that previous to the introduction of our present system of things, the great part of the north was under water, and, that the Arctic ocean current, which flows from the north-east to the south-west, instead of being deflected to the Atlantic Ocean, made a clean sweep over the entire northern part of America, in its course to the shores of the Rocky Mountains, and to the Pacific. At that time it is also possible, and most likely, that the accumulations of ice in the Arctic and sub-arctic circles were carried by the current with great velocity to the south. That ice would necessarily contain masses of stone broken from the rocks of the northern regions, and these passing over the rocky bottom of the sea would grind it down into sand or break it up into fragments; and, as the ice dissolved, either under the influence of a warmer temperature, or a summer's sun, the rocks contained in it would drop to the bottom of the sea, and there be imbedded in the clay and sand; they would also be further rolled and ground into round forms by subsequent migrations of similar blocks of ice. This theory is confirmed by the fact that the surface of the limestone rocks, almost wherever exposed, is either smoothly polished, or is marked by grooves and cuts, parallel to one another, and for the most part running in a south-westerly direction. These grooves are as sharp and clear as if they had been cut only recently by a mason's chisel.* The boulders also themselves are often scored longitudinally with similar marks, all as if they had been subjected to a process of continuous rasping and rubbing. It is thus that we find rounded fragments of the Laurentian rocks spread far and wide over the continent, and also that the boulder clay contains representatives from almost every strata which lie north of it. Southern rocks are never found in the north, but northern are constantly

---

*Canadian Naturalist, vol. iv, p 325.

found in the south, and the further south they have been carried, the more are they rounded and marked.

But over this unstratified Drift formation we have a Post-Tertiary system of stratified clays and sands, which covers a great part of the country, and forms the chief part of our soils. These strata appear to have been deposited in quiet, deep water. They also contain boulders, and, in some places these are very numerous. They may, however, be accounted for on the supposition that during the Drift period, the sea was gradually sinking, until, at the Post-Tertiary epoch, it had sunk so low as no longer to be reached by the ice which passed over its surface. The result would be that, while the sediment lay undisturbed, there would also drop into it from the melting ice the stones and boulders which it contained. These stones would thus be found in greater numbers along the course of some rapid current, or in those parts at which the channel was narrow. Such we may suppose is the condition of the bottom of the Atlantic Ocean at this day. If its northern divisions were exposed, there would doubtless be found a regular deposit of sediment, containing stones and rocks brought by the floating ice from the northern arctic regions. During the time that these Post-Tertiary strata were being deposited, there can be no doubt that much of Lower Canada was under water. It is also not improbable that a process of elevation had commenced and was going on, and that in its later period the sea was bounded both to the north and to the west with indented and sinuous shores. There would then be estuaries and creeks, and, most likely, rivers and streams of fresh water flowing from the land. That there was a terrestial vegetation, the fossils found at Green's creek, on the Ottawa, clearly demonstrate. Nodules of indurated clay have there been obtained, which contain, besides marine fossils, the leaves and twigs of trees, grass and other plants all indicating a vegetation not dissimilar to that which now covers the land.

The fossils of this formation are very numerous. Skeletons of whales and seals have been found in its clays. The common

Capelan (*Mallotus villosus*) so abundant at the present day in the gulf of the St. Lawrence, as also the lump-sucker (*Cyclopteris lumpus*) a fish common in the Atlantic, have been found at Green's Creek and other places.* The remains of Littoral sea-weeds and of sponges are abundant. Several spiral shells, a scallop and a number of bivalves are found over a wide area of country, and occupy such positions as to indicate that they lived and died where they now lie. The common mussel (*Mytilus edulis*) which every one knows about who has been at the sea-side, is found in abundance. The number of species which the formation contains, is very considerable, and what is remarkable, is that they have almost all, if not all, living representatives in the Gulf of the St. Lawrence or on the Atlantic coast at the present day. The sea of these ancient days was thus unlike the sea of the still more ancient Silurian period, but was similar to that which we now find upon our coasts, in its temperature and in the forms of life which it contained.

As the materials of this Post-Tertiary sedimentary deposit enter largely into the surface soils of the County of Dundas, it may be well to say a few words as to their composition. We have noted that they are the debris of the older rocks, ground into various degrees of fineness by the action of water and masses of ice. This being the case, they will contain materials of the same character as are found in those rocks, mixed up and blended together by the violent processes to which they have been subjected. As those rocks contain quartz, felspar, mica, garnet, hornblende, iron, lime, with its carbonates and phosphates, sodium, potassium, a small amount of bituminous substance, &c., it will follow that the sands and clays will be made up, in various proportions of these elements. Our soil will thus contain in it all the mineral properties of those older rocks, and these are all both suitable and necessary for the growth and nourishment of plants. We shall thus certainly never want silica, or flint

---

* Canadian Naturalist vol. v. p. 238.

which is so necessary for the stalks of our cereal plants. Of lime we shall always have an abundance. Potassium will generally be found in serviceable quantities, unless it be carried off in firewood or for the purposes of commerce. The decay of our present vegetation has, over and above, provided in most parts of the country, a considerable amount of carbonaceous substance. The things which we most lack are the nitrogenous materials such as salts of ammonia, and the phosphates, without a certain proportion of which crops will never thrive. These are in least quantities in our soils, and may easily, by a series of crops, and light tillage, be worked out, as they have been in hundreds of acres in Canada East. It is to the supply of these that our farmers must look for the future fertility of their farms. If year by year they are taking them out of the soil in the shape of cereal crops, and neglect to return them in some other form, their children will have to lament, and wonder at, the folly of their fathers.

From the sands and gravels of this Post-Tertiary system, excellent materials are found ready-made for the construction of good roads.

Some of the clays too, especially those which contain the largest amount of Potsdam and Calciferous sand, afford good materials for brick, and may be obtained in almost every part of the country. Many of the clays are no doubt too calcareous to make good brick, but there are few localities in which clay may not be found suitable for this purpose.

We have thus gone over the main features of the geological system of which Dundas forms a part. Our survey has led us back to periods of time immensely ancient, and to conditions of our planet very different from that which it now enjoys. Forms and fashions of life have been noted which are long since extinct, but which served the purposes of wisdom and goodness for which they were created. Each, however humble, had its own place to fill and its own work to do, and each contributed its share to the forming and building up of this beautiful world for the dwelling place of man. It is besides noteworthy, that however diverse in specific forms all these ancient creatures were, from the animals which now inhabit the seas, they were yet all formed upon the same types as those of our present animal kingdom. They were molluscs, articulates, and radiates as our animals are. The same mind which planned the one planned also the other. As there are no bounds to the resources of the Divine Wisdom, so there are, in every stage of the Creator's work, an infinite variety of adaptation to new circumstances and for the effecting of further ends. Till man was made there appear, from the records of the rocks, to have been a constant creation of new forms of life and an extinction of preceding species. A few only have been carried up from the earliest times to the present; but with the creation of man, acts of creation have ceased. We know of some animals and plants dying out since the human period but of none that have been brought into being. These, and other equally manifest facts in Geology, confirm the Biblical account of creation, and are one proof, among many others, that the Creator of the world was the Revealer of the Word.

From the earth and its crust let us now for a little pass on to the vegetation with which the County of Dundas is covered.

Of the forest trees which are the most conspicuous features of the county, we need not say much. Every farmer who has handled the axe and waged war with these aboriginal occupants of the soil, knows very well what they are, and what are their peculiarities and habits. In the primitive forest, which not many generations ago covered the County of Dundas, the lordly pines (*Pinus Strobus*) which lifted their heads one hundred feet and more into the sky, must have been conspicuous objects of admiration. They yielded too a handsome profit to the first settlers, who, eager for gain, waged a war of extermination against these giants of the bush. The pine is now almost a stranger in Dundas, and, unless cultivated for its useful timber, will soon cease to form a feature of the forest. Besides this white pine, the red (*P. resinosa*), yellow (*P. mitis*), and pitch (*P. rigida*) pines are also found, but these too on account of the nature and usefulness of their wood are fast thinning out. A pity it is, that no one will plant these noble denizens of the forest, and thus perpetuate a family of trees than which none have been more serviceable to the early settlers. A few straggling Norway pines may be seen on Goose-neck Island opposite Williamsburgh Church. They have probably been introduced either by design or accident; they are not, so far as we are aware, indigenous to our soil.

Nearly all the varieties of trees which are common to Upper Canada may be found in the woods of Dundas, excepting black walnut and white wood, (*Juglans nigra*, and *Siriodendron Tulipifera*). The former only begins to appear at Brockville and the Thousand Islands, the latter has its limit still further west. Many of the species of oak, elm, beech, birch, maple, ash, spruce, larch, &c., are common to the forest. The balsam fir (*Abies balsamea*), from which the celebrated Canada balsam is obtained, abounds and clothes the landscape in the winter with its sombre green. The hemlock spruce, (*A. Canadensis*), is common everywhere. When young it is one of the most graceful of trees. In spring it shoots out with great beauty its light spreading spray and bright green silvery foliage. When old it looks scrubby, its wood is, too, coarse grained and poor. It is remarked of it that its peak always droops slightly towards the east, and may be taken as an almost infallible guide by the lost traveller.

Tamarack or hackmatack (*Larix Americana*), is also found in the swamps of Dundas. This also is a slender and beautiful tree, and its wood is of some value for mechanical and building purposes. The white cedar or American arbor vitæ (*Thuja occidentalis*), is found abundantly in moist places, probably also the red cedar, (*Juniperus Virginianus*), is found in some of the dry and rocky parts of the county. Very little oak now remains, and the red or rock elm (*Ulmus fulva*) is scarce. Swamp elm (*U. Ameri-*

cana) is however abundant, and is manufactured into staves. The white ash (*Fraginus Americana*) is also plentiful in the woods, and is used to some extent for ships oars. The hickory (*Carya alba*) so peculiar to this continent, also flourishes in Dundas. It is a tall and handsome tree. It is largely manufactured into hand spikes; 20,000 of these in their rough state were shipped from Dundas in 1859.

The maple, (*Acer saccharinum*) the most beautiful and useful of American trees, is found in great perfection throughout the whole county of Dundas. It covets a good soil, and generally occupies the most elevated locations. It is valuable for its sugar-yielding properties, but the quantity manufactured is yearly decreasing, both from the destruction of the trees, and from the fact that the farmers find they can employ their time and labor to better purpose. Alex. Colquhoun of Williamsburgh, used to make yearly about 4000 lbs., but this quantity is now reduced to between 300 and 400 lbs. The finest trees are also rapidly falling a prey to the woodman's axe. Large quantities of them are annually cut up for fire-wood, much of which is exported to the east for consumption. Beautiful samples of the variety called birds-eye maple, which might be turned to profitable account by the cabinet makers, are in this way annually consumed. For manufacturing purposes it is not in large demand, although very beautiful and suitable for ornamental furniture, it yet does not possess sufficient toughness or strength to make it profitable for general use.

Next to the maple, the beech (*Fagus ferruginea*) and the birch (*Betula alba*, and *B. lenta*) are the woods of most value, both for manufacturing purposes and for firewood. These also are produced in our forests.

Of ornamental trees and shrubs, we have the flowering dogwood (*Cornus Florida*), the wild plum (*Prunus Americana*), and cherry (*P. Virginiana*), useful in their way, and favorites with the boys. The staghorn sumach (*Rhus typhina*) grows plentifully and with its bright red flowering spikes, is frequently found in the embrace of the luxuriant fruit bearing grape-vine, (*Vitis Sabrusca*). The elder (*Sambucus Canadensis*) and the mountain ash, (*Pyrus Americana*) with their red berries, and the former with its fragrant flowers, adorn the skirts of the woods and the banks of the rivers and streams. Among the useful shrubs we must not omit to mention the well known huckleberry, which is found in Dundas. It affords a pleasant berry, much used and prized for culinary purposes, and for winter preserves. They may too be exported with profit when gathered by children. It is the *Gaylussacia resinosa* of botanists, and is widely spread over the whole northern part of the continent. Allied to it is the common but useful cranberry (*Vaccinium macrocarpum*) which abounds in the marshes and might be made an article of profitable export. The raspberry also in two species, (*Rubus strigosus, R. occidentalis*) the common and the thimbleberry, grow in cleared places of the bush and by the road sides in great luxuriance. The wild strawberry (*Fragaria vesca*) is also gathered in quantities and used as an article of food.

There are, besides these plants, a large number of flowering herbs and grasses found adorning the woods and the streams of this county.

The curious pitcher plant (*Sarracenia purpurascens*) grows in the swamps. The wake-robin (*Trillium grandiflorum, T erectum, and T. erythrocarpum,*) is a beautiful and abundant spring flower, and takes the place of the white lilly of Europe. The anemone (*Anenome Virginiana and A Pennsylvanica*) blooms with great beauty in summer, and is a good substitute for the daisy. The crowfoots (*Ranunculus acris* and *R. flamula*), deck the fields with yellow flowers, familiar to old country folks. Various violas, yellow, white, and streaked with pink, spot the green sward with their pretty flowers. The tall bright pink fire weed (*Epilobium palustre*), together with the varieties of bright yellow golden rod (*Solidago*), are conspicuous every where. The pretty fringed gentian (*Gentiana crinita*) with its clusters of pale blue flowers, may be found in dry and retired places; also the cardinal flower (*Lobelia cardinalis*), with its large spike of brilliant scarlet flowers, may be seen in the meadows and swamps. The tall Canada mullein (*Verbascum thapsus*), is also a conspicuous but harmless weed; the most that can be said of it is, that it harbours numerous tribes of insects. The milk-weeds (*Asclepias*), are also found in every neglected field. The Boneset, a bitter herb, (*Eupatorium perfoliatum*), and much used as a medicine is found. It is useful as a tonic and expectorant, and is beneficial for the cure of colds. It has a head of whitish downy flowers, with large pointed leaves clasping the stalk, and may be found abundantly in autumn along the skirts of rich woods, or by the sides of streams. The Turtle-head or shell-flower (*Chelone glabra*), with its white flowers not unlike the unopened petals of a white fox-glove, and very like the head of a snake, grows also in moist places. It is a favourite Indian medicine; being extremely bitter it makes an excellent tonic. The beautiful little golden thread (*Coptis trifolia*) may also be found in the month of June, in the shady and moist parts of the woods. It has a root of long bright yellow fibres, from which it derives its name. It is known by its pretty white flowers. The root is exceedingly bitter and is used as a medicine for its astringent properties. We shall only further name the wild verbena or vervain, (*Verbena officinalis*), a tall slender plant which commonly grows by the road sides and in dry barren places. It is from one to three feet in height, and its long tapering head is covered with small purplish flowers. We mention it specially, as we have been informed by those who have practical knowledge of the fact, that it is a sovereign remedy for the poison of the poison ivy, (*Rhus toxicodendron*), which when touched is so very injurious to some people. The ox-eye daisy (*Leucanthemum vulgare*) is beginning to appear in the county. It is a native of Europe, and has become naturalized in America, greatly to the injury of the farmer. It is a most prolific weed. Its seeds are legion, and its roots are perennial. We warn the farmers of Dundas in time to be on their guard against this pernicious weed. It should be rooted up wherever found and on no account permitted to seed. Other plants might be mentioned, but these are the most prominent with which the woods are adorned. But time and space would fail us to tell of the beauties, virtues, and vices, of all the flowering plants with which the forests and river banks of Dundas abound. On both land and water there are almost countless forms of vegetable life, each differing from the other, and all displaying in wonderful perfection the wisdom and goodness of our Father in Heaven who made them all. If the few notes which we have given prove of any interest to our readers, and lead them to note and examine the plants for themselves, they will be abundantly rewarded by the study. The grasses alone which with singular beauty wave their graceful forms by every stream, and on every meadow, would prove an interesting subject of enquiry. Some of these might be found of use in agriculture. They are sufficiently ornamental, and if only they could be cultivated with the same advantage as timothy (*Phleum pratense*), they would be of service to the farmer. We close this brief account of the vegetation of Dundas, expressing a hope that some farmers will do posterity the service of planting upon a few acres of their, for the most part, too large farms, some of our finest and most valuable trees. If any one will do this, we are sure that their children will bless them, and the generations to come will call them wise.

Before concluding this chapter, we must give some brief account of the indigenous animals as well as the plants which inhabit our County of Dundas. We shall, however, only allude to some of the most curious and striking. The moose-deer and the beaver, which once had their abodes in the forest, have long since disappeared. The antlers of the former and the meadows of the latter may still be seen, to attest that once they existed here. Within the last ten years, individuals of the wolf, the bear, the fox, the deer, the racoon, and other wild animals, have been killed within two miles of the river front. In 1859 a huge American cougar, or panther, (*Felis concolor*), measuring 8 ft. 4 in. in length, was shot at Croil's Island. It was discovered perched high up in a tree by one of the farmers. Its depredations amounted to some twenty or thirty sheep. The skin was stuffed, and is now we believe in the Ottawa Museum. The wolverine, the lynx, and the wild-cat are reputed inhabitants of the forest, and are said to be sometimes seen, but of these we cannot speak with certainty. The common red fox (*Vulpes fulvus*), the silver-gray (*V. argentatus*), and the black fox (*V. decussatus*), are frequently found about the farms and in the woods. The skin of the first is worth one dollar, of the second from five to ten, and of the third forty. There are also crosses of the different breeds.

Of the smaller wild animals, the martin (*Mustela Americana*), the mink (*Putorius vison*), the muskrat (*Fiber zibethicus*), the skunk (*Mephitis chinga*), &c. &c., are frequently seen.

The seal is by no means an uncommon visitor, although we may well wonder how it surmounts the rapids of the St. Lawrence. Scarcely a winter passes without one or more of them being seen. During one winter a group of them wintered with us, and were frequently observed sporting themselves in the water, and at times lying upon the edge of the ice. One of them was shot and brought ashore, and was represented to be little else than a shapeless mass of fat. It weighed about 200 lbs.

The birds that visit us are the eagle, hawk, crow, owl, whippoor-will, bat, swallow, robin, lark, tern, gull, snipe, kingfisher, blackbird, woodpecker, cuckoo, wild pigeon, goose, duck, lune or northern diver, wood duck, snowbird, hummingbird, with many others. Many very large and beautiful specimens of the white owl are annually shot and stuffed.

The fish to be found in the river along our shore are the maskinonge, pike, pickerel, salmon, sturgeon, bass, chub, sucker, perch, eel &c.

These fall an easy prey to the angler in a great variety of ways, the old fashioned hook and line is used for the smaller kinds, maskinonge and pike are taken by trolling with a live minnow, or with a piece of brass in the form of a spoon, which receives a vibrating motion from the headway of the boat, and seems to allure the hungry fish. But by far the greater number are caught during the darkness of the night, by the expert use of the spear, aided by the light of a flaming pine-wood torch, kept burning in an iron basket in front of the canoe. Nothing can be conceived more beautiful than the aspect of the river on a calm summer's night when it is thus illuminated by these fishermen, frequently 20 canoes, each with a bright light burning in the bow, may be counted at one time. The effect is more observable when one is driving on the road on a dark night. The approach of one of these "fish lights" cast a lurid glow upon every thing around, as it stealthily passes along the shore, and the sooty countenance and eager attitude of the spearman, as he wheels suddenly from one side to another, become distinctly visible. It sometimes happens that a sturgeon weighing from seventy to eighty pounds is taken in this way, and it requires no small tact as well as strength to land him in the boat. Large numbers of sturgeon are taken at the Longue Sault Island, and are chiefly valuable for the "sounds" which are converted into isinglass. Eels are numerous from two and a half to three and a half feet in length. In winter they resort in "schools," to mud banks, in which they bury themselves in unconscious slumber; but even here their enemy finds them out, their usual resorts come to be known, a hole is cut in the ice, and with a spear twenty feet or more in length, the cruel fisherman continues to strike into the mud, until he comes upon the sleeping family. Not unfrequently three or four hundred will be taken out of one nest. The flesh is esteemed good. The skin is used for making ligatures, being remarkably tough, and sometimes also is used as a belt around the body, as an antidote to lumbago or rheumatism. Lizards and frogs (alias

Canadian nightingales) abound. The bull-frog may be heard roaring, literally like a bull, at the distance of a mile or more.

Bears are usually caught in large iron traps, and afterwards shot. The wolf in a similar manner. The fox, more wily, is not so easily trapped. Frequently he is hunted into a hollow lying tree; the open end being plugged, he is gradually pinned up at one end, where a hole is cut with an ax, and reynard, pulled out by the brush, receives his death blow by a smart stroke on his snout. The deer is hunted by hounds, and invariably makes for the nearest river. If he reaches it, he plunges in and swims for his dear life with amazing rapidity. Canoes are manned and an exciting chase ensues. When he is shot or felled with an oar if the venison cannot be transported, the carcase is suspended from the nearest tree and flayed, the hunters regale themselves with a steak of venison, dressed by the camp-fire, and the hide and horns are brought home as a trophy.

Space will not permit us farther to enlarge on the natural history of our county. We have said enough to show that it contains much that is both curious and useful. It is to be hoped that ere long, under the auspices of our Agricultural Society, accurate lists may be obtained of the plants and animals which make their home in the county, and that some of the rising generation of educated young men will undertake this labor of love.

CHAPTER IX.

Canadian agriculture—Rotation of crops—Systems of farming—Dutch, Scotch, Irish systems—Breeds of domestic animals—Of renting lands—Of the shares system—Of tile draining—Of laborers—Implements of husbandry—&c., &c.

Agriculture in Canada, is in a singularly interesting and peculiar position. Unlike the densely peopled regions of the old world where agriculture has grown up with the growth of ages, it here exists in all the stages, which, during the world's wide history it has ever assumed. We do not require to move far from home to find ourselves cut off from all traces of civilization: in our own county we may travel for miles through the woods, and save the rough road on which we travel, may see little to indicate that the foot of the white man has ever gone before us. In seeking to reach a distant back woods settlement by the shortest route, we might find ourselves in the gloomy recesses of a seemingly interminable forest, and if in the distance we should discover the blue curling smoke, ascending among the branches, curiosity would lead us, as we neared some newly erected shanty, to pause and admire the scene. Emerging from his lowly cabin, might be seen the sturdy pioneer stalking forth to begin the labors of the day, all the modern appliances of Art and Science are nothing to him, his axe upon his shoulder, he feels that he has all he needs. With an eagle eye he scans the giant denizens of the forest, and selects the first victim that is to fall beneath his blows. He pauses not to enquire of the man of science whether he is to cut his timber when the sap is in the branches, or when it is not. He enters into no scientific calculation as to the precise angle of obliquity, with which he is to guide his axe, but, with a strong arm and a good will, he plunges it to the eye at every stroke—the old king of the forest trembles on his seat, and with a crash that makes the woods ring again, he lies buried in the snow, in the very spot that the woodsman had marked out for him; another and another follow, and in a few years a large portion of the forest disappears, and a wide clearance invites the labors of the practical farmer. But the absence of any fixed system, soon sinks the virgin soil, replete with the essentials of fertility, below the level of older countries, and it requires all the energies of the modern agriculturist, to restore and maintain its fertility.

A judicious system of alternating crops is one of the fundamental principles of good farming. It is unreasonable to suppose that any soil, however fertile, should continuously produce for ever any one kind of crop. The medical man opens a vein in the human body, and withdraws a portion of that life sustaining fluid which animates the mysterious system, and, at proper intervals, he again and again, fearlessly repeats the operation. He believes, he knows not how—that nature will reproduce, and replenish the arteries with a healthier supply, but were he to omit to staunch the ebbing stream of life, who would express surprise, if his patient, gradually enfeebled, should at last sink under the treatment, and be beyond the reach of nature's restoring touch. Precisely so is it in agriculture, we may abstract a certain portion, more or less according to the richness of the soil, and nature will in process of time restore the elements of which we have deprived it, but there are bounds which we cannot transgress with impunity, and doubtless the want of a proper system of rotation of crops, is mainly the cause why vast tracts of land in Canada, formerly fertile, are now worn out and worthless.

The system of agriculture pursued in any country, is a sure index to the intelligence and prosperity of the farming community.

What, it may be asked, is the system of farming pursued in Canada, or in the County of Dundas? Without fear of contradiction, we reply, it is the system of expediency, or in other words, to take from the soil all it will yield, and return to it no more than necessity compels us. There are many obstacles to the practical working in a new country, of the established principles carried out in older countries. The want of capital and of skilled labor, and more than all, the long period of the year during which agricultural operations are entirely suspended, owing to the peculiarities of the climate, account for, and in some measure even justify, the system of expediency which is every where observable. It were absurd to look for any clearly defined system of husbandry from the backwoodsman, manfully struggling to subdue the mighty forests, at the same time contending with poverty no less difficult to be overcome. What more natural than that he should take advantage of circumstances just as they occur, and make the most of them. Yet, much of the slovenly and surperficial farming of Canada is to be attributed to the facility with which the early settler drew from his new clearance, luxuriant crops with a small amount of labor. Having made the discovery that a third, fourth, and even a fifth crop of wheat could be raised in succession from a given field, he began to think that this would last for ever, and only became convinced of his mistake, when his land became literally worn out.

While the absence of systematic farming is true regarding Dundas County as a whole, we have nevertheless a few excellent, systematic, and as a result, money making farmers, whose systems, be they good or bad, we shall endeavor to describe, leaving the reader to draw his own conclusions.

The following system is pursued by one of our most extensive and successful farmers, who may be regarded as the type of what is commonly called in Canada, a Dutch farmer. His farm embraces 500 acres, whereof 300 acres are cleared, and 200 in woods. The whole is enclosed with cedar fences, proof against all intruders, by which means his cattle have the exclusive, and unrestricted privilege of roaming through the woods, with all the benefits thereto appertaining.

Of his cleared farm, 120 acres are devoted to pasture, 100 to meadow, and 80 to tillage. His stock consists of 20 milch cows, six working horses, two brood mares, and sixty sheep. He makes from ten to twelve acres of summer fallow each year, to which he applies all the manure made upon the farm, and as much more as he can procure from the neighboring village of Morrisburgh; say from 50 to 60 two horse waggon loads of farm yard manure to the imperial acre. The proportion of different grains is regulated entirely by the adaptation of the different fields entering into his rotation. He sows each year a certain portion of fall wheat and rye, the former he does not consider a reliable crop, the latter seldom fails to yield a large return. He carefully avoids running to extremes in any particular branch, and ascribes his success mainly to the diversity of his productions, together with general economy in management. He employs cheap labor, say, three men at $8 per month for the year round, and he keeps a sharp look out upon them; being married men with families, their wages are paid chiefly in farm produce. He generally has an apprentice or two who work gratuitously, and who on coming of age, receive a *douceur* of $100, or perhaps a horse, or a couple of cows, as the case may be. In hay and harvest time, he employs six of the best men that can be had, at from 75 cents to $1 per day. At these times he conceives it to be important to be strong-handed, and always takes time by the forelock. He begins to cut his clover hay in the end of June, and when the timothy is ripe, he cuts it down in the morning, spreads it out immediately, and puts it in the barn before night. He uses a horse rake, but no reaping machine, and the greater portion of his grain he thrashes with the flail, just as it is required for his cattle. He raises annually eight calves, and sells as many head of cattle at three or four years old. Two colts at four years old, bring him yearly $100 each. He has his own wool made into cloth for his own wear, he eats his own mutton, beef, pork, and poultry, and has always some of each to sell. He has neither Ayrshire cows, nor Clydesdale horses, but has great faith in both, and will take the first opportunity to get into those breeds. He wages a war of extermination against wild mustard, thistles, and quack, and very rarely do his crops disappoint his expectations. He has in different parts of his farm eight wells. with chain pumps—keeps his troughs always full of water, and supplies his stock of all kinds with abundance of salt during summer. All his grain is freely salted as it is stowed away in the barn, and the straw is in consequence highly relished by his cattle in winter. His brood mares run all winter on the straw yard, and suckle their colts till the first of April, when the colts are weaned and cared for. His cattle are fed in winter on straw with a very little hay, but receive neither roots nor grain, and in spring, they never need to be "*tailed.*"

He carefully provides for the escape of every drop of surface water, but does not underdrain his land. Every thing is profitable with him, but hay particularly so, his average return of which is $1\frac{1}{4}$ tons per acre, his maximum $2\frac{3}{4}$, and his minimum crop $\frac{1}{2}$ ton per acre. He sells largely every year of hay at an average price of $10 per 2000 lbs. He states his belief, that the average yield of hay from the whole county in 1859 did not exceed $\frac{1}{2}$ a ton per acre. Roots are in his opinion too expensive as food for cattle, he therefore grows none, and where extra feeding is required, he prefers ground grain mixed with bran. His principle is to keep no more stock than he has abundance of food for.

His usual rotation of crops is as follows :—

On heavy rich land.	*On lighter soil.*
1. Summer fallow, manured.	1. Summer fallow, manured.
2. Wheat.	2. Corn or Potatoes.
3. Corn or Potatoes, no manure.	3. Barley, seeded to grass.
4. Barley or Peas.	4. Grass cut, three years.
5. Oats.	5. Pasture, two years.
6. Summer fallow, manured.	6. Peas, followed by fallow.
7. Wheat, seeded to grass.	

The following treatment of old meadows is found successful in his hands. Break them up in the autumn, summer fallow during the following season without manure, and seed down in August, *without* a crop. To every ten bushels of Timothy seed sown, he adds 120 lbs. of red clover, and sows half a bushel per acre of the mixture. If his cattle cannot consume the after-math, he has been in the habit of cutting a second crop of hay. But he is now of the opinion, that the better plan to secure the permanency of meadows, is neither to cut nor depasture the second crop. Luxuriant fields of clover are thus left by him, to be cut down by the frost, and to be withered and decayed by the action of the atmosphere, forming during winter a protection to the roots of the plants, and in spring taking the place of a liberal top-dressing. In this way meadows never "freeze out," they retain the clover much better, and will bear cutting much longer. He opines that grass seeds as well as grain, are generally sown too thin; that farmers are notoriously too careless in extirpating weeds; that practical farmers *work* too much, and that gentlemen farmers *oversee* too little. It is a mystery to him to hear intelligent men speak of farming as unprofitable, and the summing up of his evidence, leaves no doubt in our minds, that his system *pays*, and this he corroborates, by the following figures.

In 1830, he went on to a farm of 250 acres, with two horses, two cows, and $400 of debt. In 1840, he purchased 250 acres adjoining, for which he paid cash down $4,000. Up to 1860, he has spent at least $4,000 in cash, for buildings, fences, and other improvements. He has cleared during the last 20 years, more than $600, per annum, and has now $10,000 out at interest of 10 per cent. He values his farm at $14,000 and is quite satisfied that it now yields him not less than ten per cent. per annum, clear of all expenses.

A Scotch settler who came to Canada sixteen years ago thus relates his experience.

"I landed in Quebec with my wife and family, and with seven

sovereigns in my pocket—found my way to Glengarry where my brother-in-law resided, from whom I took a farm to work upon shares. He found me in seed, stock, and implements. I laid in a stock of provisions for the summer, and went to work with a good will, and with a cash capital of five shillings currency in my pocket. I had an excellent crop. I returned him first the seed, and then gave him one half of the remaining produce. My share gave me provisions for a year and something to spare. The following year I rented a small farm at £20 a year, where I remained three years with moderate success, at the end of that time I had provided myself with stock and implements. I next rented the farm which I now occupy, along with the adjoining one, at £33 per annum. At the end of three years it was offered for sale, I had no money to pay for it, but I judged that the land was good for the money. The boys were growing up to be men, I said to them that if they were industrious, we could pay for it; they said they would do their best. I bought it for £300, to be paid in 6 annual instalments of £50 each, with interest till paid for, and had a year to make the first payment. Forty acres had been cleared but were in a rough state. We all set to work to clear up and improve the land; we stinted ourselves to six acres every year, and now at the end of 10 years my whole farm is cleared and paid for. When first we came into the bush, the roads were all but impassable, now we have an excellent gravel road passing the door and extending all the way to the St. Lawrence. My farm is worth to day in cash £1000, and I am out of debt. The older boys have left home and are doing well for themselves, the two youngest are with me, and work the farm, we manage every thing "within ourselves" and employ no hired labor. My farm is the best 100 acre lot I know of, and every acre is available. I have never underdrained any of my land, it would be much benefited by it, but labor is too dear to attempt it. 28 acres among the stumps are devoted to pasture, the remaining 72 are fenced off in 12 fields of six acres a-piece. I adhere to a regular course of cropping and I attribute much of my success to my system of rotation. Hitherto my crops of grain have been excellent. I sow yearly 24 bushels of wheat upon 12 acres, and my average return has been 240 bushels. Of oats, I sow 12 acres, with three bushels per acre, which average me 30 bushels per acre. Of barley 12 acres, which I sow at the rate of $2\frac{1}{4}$ bushels per acre. My returns vary from 35 to 50 bushels per acre. I sow three acres of peas, three bushels seed per acre, average 20 to 25 bushels per acre. Of corn and potatoes I plant 6 acres. The remaining 24 are in grass.

The following is my rotation of crops:—

1st. 6 ac. Oats ploughed from sod.
2nd. 6 " Wheat, with a half dressing of manure ploughed fall and spring.
3rd. 6 " Barley, sowed after the wheat with one ploughing.
4th. 6 " Oats, sowed in early spring, upon the fall furrow.
5th. 6 " Peas, land ploughed in fall, harrowed in spring, and the seed *ploughed* in.
6th. 6 " Potatoes and corn, land fully manured in the fall.
7th. 6 " Wheat, sowed in spring upon fall furrow.
8th. 6 " Barley, half dunged and seeded to grass.
9th. 24 " Grass, cut three years and pastured one.

The whole of the hay and straw, oats, peas, corn, and potatoes, are consumed on the premises, which secures me a large pile of manure, my wheat straw is all used for bedding, and I am thus enabled to manure 12 acres each year. I keep ten cows, four horses and a few sheep, I sell yearly about 140 bushels wheat, 360 of barley, and $100 worth of pork. My expenses are merely nominal.

In summer time, we live upon bacon, beef, and pork hams, nicely cured and smoked, and fried with eggs, supplemented with cheese, bread, and butter, all home made, and of the best. In October, we kill a beast. The blacksmith takes a quarter, the shoemaker another, the tailor or the carpenter a third, and ourselves the remaining one. In December, we kill a second, cut it up, freeze it, and pack it away in barrels with straw, where it will keep till the first of April. The hides go to the tanner, who takes one half of each, and gives me the other when tanned; the shoemaker comes to the house once a year and makes out of it boots and shoes for young and old. The tallow is rendered and made into candles, and all the refuse scraps at " killing time " are boiled up with lye, and converted into barrels of soap. And then the women folk spin the wool and weave the stockings, sew the quilts and counterpanes, and make the featherbeds, so that come what may, we are always sure of a living. When a son or daughter is to be married, I sell a span of horses and a cow or two, give them a decent outfit and am none the poorer, as there are always young ones coming on to take their places."

Truth is ofttimes stranger than fiction. The following is no fancy sketch, but a truthful picture of life in the backwoods, exhibiting the chequered experience of many an emigrant from the Emerald Isle. An intelligent Irishman thus relates the story of his life in Canada.

"Two and twenty years ago, I emigrated from Ireland, and found my way to the township of Mountain, in the County of Dundas, where I took possession of one hundred acres of land, for which I promised to pay $200, in five annual instalments. The lot was partially cleared, the soil was good, and, being new, I raised excellent crops during the first three years. Elated with my success, I became careless and extravagant. I scarcely knew how my money came, I could not tell how it went, and to tell the truth, I did not much care. I was, in short, a prodigal, and ere long found myself over head and ears in debt. Although poor, I was honest, and gave up my farm to satisfy my creditors, but even after having done this, there remained $1200 of debt, which I had no means of paying. I was now houseless and homeless, with a large family of little children, depending upon me for food and raiment. I was fairly brought to my wit's end, and, reviewing my past life, I resolved to be prodigal no more. I sought out a lot of Crown land, and squatted upon it; it is the same lot I now occupy. The soil was naturally poor, much inferior to the one I had left, there was not a tree cut upon it. I cleared a small spot to build upon. My neighbors lived in shanties; I was ambitious, I made a "*bee*," and built me a log-house 18×24, with a chamber overhead, and cellar beneath. It was surrounded by great trees, whose branches over shadowed it, and completely excluded the rays of the sun: it was the best building in all the settlement, it is the one I still live in, and it is now the worst, but I have bricks, and boards, and timber on hand, and will build another next spring, if I am spared till then.

I set to work to clear up a portion of the land. My boys and girls turned out, and assisted me to roll up the log heaps, and prepare for a "burn." There was neither church nor school for ten miles around, and I never thought to see any in my day, but I was determined that my children should learn at least as much as I could teach them. Mornings and evenings I acted as schoolmaster, and during the day, set the older to teach the younger ones. When the boys went with me to the woods, we took a slate with us, and when wearied with work, sat down upon a log heap and worked out a few sums. I was always good at figures, my neighbors soon discovered this, they pitied my poverty, saw that I was industrious, and tried to encourage me. I was appointed assessor for the township, which helped me along. By and by the municipal councils, were established, I was found to be useful, and for my services obtained sometimes as much as £40, or £50 a year. Three of my daughters became school teachers, and brought home their earnings, which kept us comfortably while we were clearing the land. I have seen hard times in my day. Seven years ago, the partner of my joys and sorrows was suddenly taken away from me, and I was left a disconsolate widower, with nine motherless children. Poor things, they have been good children to me, and as you see, do all they can to make me comfortable: but oh! what is home without a mother? I have joined the Methodist Church; their missionaries found us out, or ever there was a road to our house, and now we have a nice church, and regular service every sabbath day, within a mile of our own door.

I have long since paid off that $1200 of debt, and besides the farm I live on, have bought and paid for seven hundred acres of land adjoining, which I purchased from the Crown, for five shillings per acre. These lots are worthless for agricultural purposes, being all swamp land, but contain a mine of wealth in the pine trees which grow upon them. I get out about 1000 standard saw logs every winter, which I sell for as many dollars, it costs me $250 for hired labor, leaving us $750 for our own time.

We grow enough grain on the farm to furnish us with all the necessaries of life. We have every thing we want, and are content. I never thought of following any system of cropping, and am too old to begin now. I never bother myself about Agricultural Societies or premiums, but the boys are "concaity" and will go into all these improvements by and by."

Dairy farming is not extensively practised in the County of Dundas. We have but one farmer who devotes exclusive attention to this branch of agriculture. His farm extends to 300 acres cleared, of which 150 acres are pasture, 50 acres meadow, and 100 acres tillage. He pays an annual rental of $450, or $1.50 per acre, keeps fifty-six cows, which he values at $35 per head, makes annually 230 cheeses, averaging 60lb. each, which he sells for ten cents per pound, raises 13 calves, and fattens six pigs, both chiefly fed upon whey, and disposes yearly of as many old cows, as he can replace with young ones. He keeps six head of horses and ten sheep. His average cut of hay is one ton per acre, and he usually grows enough of hay and straw to feed his cattle during winter. His cows are stabled at night without bedding: after harvest they are fed daily some oats in the straw, up to the 1st December, when they are all put dry. He feeds his cows in spring with bran, but neither roots nor grain. He keeps in summer two hired men, and one female "help." Certain evidence as to whether this system *pays*, or not, is awanting.

Very little attention has as yet been given to what is called the improved breeds of cattle, more or less, there has existed a prejudice against them in this county. It is difficult to give the objections to their introduction a tangible form. The prevailing idea seems to be, that they consume too much food in winter, in other words, we are disappointed to find that they cannot endure the same amount of *starvation* as the natives. Jesse W. Rose, was, many years ago, the first to introduce the Durham and Ayrshire breeds of cattle, but on leaving the county his stock became scattered, and being in most cases subjected to doubtful treatment, they were pronounced inferior to the natives. A few however fell into good hands, were well cared for, and presented in themselves the best refutation of the erroneous ideas held respecting the breed.

Mr. Elliot of Matilda has some good stock and keeps them well, we have pleasure in submitting the result of his observation and experience in this matter.

He conceives the most desirable breed of cattle for this county, to be a cross between Durham and Ayrshire, and the next best to that, Durham crossed with the native cattle. With nothing more than fair treatment, they thrive with him equally well with the native breeds, far excel them as milkers, and when fat, readily bring double the price as beef. He finds the yield of milk from a half Durham, one-fourth Ayrshire, one-fourth native cow, to be 25 quarts per day for three months after calving. A steer 18 months old, was killed in December, 1859, which at no time had been stall-fed, and had during summer only the run of the common pasture, rendered scanty by an exceedingly dry season, yet, the four quarters weighed 500 lbs, worth at the time 4 cents per lb., the hide and tallow 100 lbs. more, at 8 cents, thus realizing $28 for a yearling steer. With similar treatment, a native at the same age, would be esteemed dear at half the money. He does not believe in what is called "high feeding," but takes particular care of his calves, by giving them plenty of such good homely fare as every farmer can command, a warm stable in cold weather, and a comfortable bed to lie upon. The first year, he says, forms the character of the beast. With ordinary attention he has no trouble in raising Durham and Ayrshire cattle. He believes that as much money will be made out of one animal of this kind, as from two natives similarly fed, to say nothing of the pleasure of seeing handsome and well-favored kine about his premises. The impression upon his mind is, that the cattle of Dundas County are, as a general rule, well summered, and very badly wintered.

There is great room for improvement in the breed of horses, this class of stock is fast deteriorating in size and symmetry. There is not at the present time a good entire horse in the county. As with cattle, so with horses, a strong, unfounded prejudice has hitherto existed against heavy horses. An imported Clydesdale, a valuable, and excellent specimen of the breed, was introduced some years ago, but he was regarded as an *innovation*, and as he was not appreciated he was withdrawn; the scanty stock, however, which he left in the county, are now the very best horses we have, and can scarcely be bought for love or money.

The much talked of horse of all work is a manifest popular delusion. The fast man must still drive his fast horse, the working man his working horse. When a heavy load is to be started from an "ugly" place, the 2.40 animal will not do. The horse of all work is well adapted for a light harrow, or for "tickling the surface" with a light plough, but to plough heavy land with a good deep furrow, we want heavier metal.

Our object in raising horses is two-fold,—for our own use, and for sale. For our use we want horses that are active, moderately heavy, of quiet dispositions, easily kept in good condition, and above all, that are true to work. These qualities are rarely combined in the fast horse, but are invariably found in the half-bred Clyde. If we raise them to sell, the first question that the American buyer asks when a horse is offered for sale, is, what does he weigh? Many people ridicule the idea of selling horses by weight, nevertheless it is customary, and appears to have at least as much reason in support of the practice, as the modern mania for weighing babies of a day old, which are pronounced "likely" or otherwise according as they fall short of, or over-run ten pounds avoirdupois. It is certainly not more ridiculous to take into account the amount of weight that a draught horse can throw into the collar, than to estimate the seconds in which he can travel a mile. Besides, not one horse in a thousand, attains a speed that will ensure his sale at a fancy price, the nine hundred and ninety-nine which are bred with that view, are unfitted for working profitably on the farm, and are unsaleable except at a very low price.

Much improvement has of late years been manifested in regard to sheep. The most desirable breed for the county, is thought to be a cross between the Leicester and Cheviot, combining the properties of superior mutton, heavy fleeces of moderately fine wool, with a healthy constitution. The native breed is more easily imagined than described. They have not a good point that we can lay hold of,—crooked necks, long legs, and light fleeces;—restless and roving in their disposition, they will bound over the highest fences, from this cause the ringleaders of every flock require to be "shackled," or to have a bell strapped around their necks. Sometimes they may be seen with a "poke," three feet in length, jutting out in front of them, at other times with a heavy block of wood fastened to their ancles. This is humane treatment, however, in comparison with that of the French farmers of Kakouna, who deliberately cut off the hoofs of their sheep to the quick, and leave them to hobble in agony on their knees.

We are more happy in pigs than in sheep. The small Berkshire breed, weighing when dressed, about 300 lbs., prevails, and is the *ne plus ultra* of pork. This breed is more easily fed, comes sooner to maturity than any other, and when placed upon the table is unsurpassed.

The average annual rental of fair farms in the county, may be stated to be $1.50 per acre, including pasture, meadow, and tillage. Farms are frequently let from year to year, and seldom for a lease of more than five years. To some extent this betokens a mutual distrust between landlord and tenant, and is a barrier to the permanent improvement of lands so let. As the great majority of our farmers are their own landlords, it is unnecessary here to refer to the numerous disadvantages to the landlord, the tenant, and the soil, induced by the short sighted policy of granting short leases.

A different method of letting land, has during the last few years become somewhat prevalent, that is the *shares* system, which is carried out in three ways. Firstly. The tenant finds all his own implements, stock, and seed, performs all the work of the farm, and yields the landlord *one-third share* of the gross produce of the land, including hay and straw. Secondly The tenant finds his own implements and stock, and one-half of the seed sown each year, and yields to the landlord *one-half share* of the gross produce. In this case the landlord usually bears half the expense of threshing all the grain. Thirdly. The landlord finds all the implements, working horses, and seed, and receives *two-thirds* of the gross produce. The second method is most commonly adopted, and is not unfrequently the *dernier resort* of what Mr. Hogan describes as the " would-be gentlemen farmer." The following case is in point.

A farmer whom we shall style number five, purchased a farm of 500 acres, whereof 250 were cleared. During ten years he prosecuted his calling with energy and assiduity : he procured the best stock within his reach, the best implements to be had in the country, employed the best laborers at the *highest* wages, and erected buildings in every respect complete and convenient for conducting farm operations to advantage. At the end of ten years there was but one trifling desideratum, he could'nt exhibit a balance sheet, in other words, *it did'nt pay !* In this respect

THE SHARES SYSTEM.

alone, he resembled the immortal Mechi of Tiptree Hall, at the end of his ten years probation, with this difference, however, that he failed in securing for himself *a name*. Discouraged but not in despair, his farm was subdivided, and is now in the hands of several tenants, who work it under the *shares* system, paying as rental one half of the produce. The following rotation of crops is observed.

1st. Summer fallow or hoed crops, manured. 2nd. Wheat or barley, seeded with 1 peck timothy and 5 lbs. clover, per acre. 3rd. Meadow cut three years, plaster sown 2nd and 3rd years. 4th. Oats or peas, followed by green crop, manured.

Of 250 acres, 56 were rented for $75, or $1.35 per acre; 194 acres were rented on shares, and yielded $4.90 per acre. In 1859, hay averaged 1 ton per acre, valued at $14. Wheat 15 bushels per acre, at $1.10 per bushel. Oats 35 bushels per acre, at 35 cents. Buckwheat 29 bushels per acre, at 40 cents.

Each tenant is found with a dwelling house, barn accommodation, and a garden of one acre. The landlord retains one half of the pasture, and keeps his own stock in summer and winter, the manure being divided amongst the tenants. His farm yielded him in 1859 as follows:—

One half of produce from 194 acres let on shares,.........	$940 04
Rents from other portions of the farm, houses let, &c.,..	130 00
Live stock, wool, &c., sold,.................................	296 00
This sum credited as rental for mansion house and grounds,...	365 00
Total receipts,............................	1731 04
Less expenditure for seed and plaster,....................	130 80
Net revenue,..............................	1600 24

Cash value of his farm say $16,000. Interest received, 10 per cent. per annum, or deducting the item of $365, credited as rent, a net interest of 8 per cent. on the value of his farm. He notes, that the above figures include 20 tons of hay at $14: this is 50 per cent. above the usual price, but it was a season of unusually light crops, and he considers the aggregate return of that year as about a fair average.

Under-draining is much needed in the county and but little practised. Like many other improvements it only wants a beginning. Were a few of our enterprising farmers to test for themselves the advantages arising from thorough under-draining, despite of many difficulties in carrying it out, it might soon become general. It is but 25 years since the system became general in Britain, and already nearly all the arable land there, has been thoroughly drained, while immense tracts of moor, and other wild lands have been brought into the highest state of cultivation, which, but for the tile drain must have remained unproductive. British husbandry is based upon this system of drainage, without it, the system of "high farming," which has resulted in such a wonderful increase in the products of the field, could not have been carried on

There can be no doubt that under-draining is as needful in Canada as in Britain, and the experience of those who have tried it, goes to show that it will pay, if judiciously done. The amount of capital required, and the peculiar circumstances of a new country, may retard for a time its general introduction, but in the mean time every farmer should test the matter for himself, by operating upon a small field, and carefully noting the results. The proper depth of drains, the width between them, as well as the general plan of drainage, are important considerations, and can only be fully learned by experience and observation. Proper tools also are required for cutting the drains, and considerable dexterity in using them, which is only acquired by practice.

The following hints may be of service to a beginner.

Be sure of a good outlet, and that the mouth of the drain be at least six inches clear of the bottom of the open ditch into which it empties.

The drain should be cut not wider than is necessary for a man to work in, and should taper to a width of four inches at the bottom: this is readily done by using the proper tools, and much time and expense are saved in excavating as well as in replacing the soil thrown out.

No tile drain should be less than three feet in depth, else the frost will displace and otherwise destroy the tiles, and the whole labor will thus be lost. A good descent throughout the whole length of the drain is indispensable, as the slightest deflection is sure to be filled up with sediment. Where the land is flat, the entire length of the drain should be laid open, and the level determined by the water in the drain before a tile is laid. If there should be no water in the drain at that particular time, it will be safer to draw a barrel of water for this purpose than to trust either to the eye, or the spirit level.

In all cases a covering of wheat straw, chips, or shavings should be placed over the tiles, before filling in the earth. Four feet in depth is better than three feet, if sufficient level can be obtained.

The distance between drains depends upon the nature of the soil, and the depth of the drains. At the depth of three feet, drains may be placed in ordinary soils 20 feet apart: at four feet in depth they may be from 30 to 40 feet apart. 20 feet would give 130 rods to an acre, requiring about 2000 tiles of 13 inches each. The expense of digging, laying tiles, and filling in, at a depth of three feet, is about 12½ cents per rod, at 4 feet deep 18 to 20 cents per rod. The entire cost of tile draining one acre, varies according to circumstances, price of tiles, &c., from $25 to $40 per acre: this is a large sum in proportion to the nominal value of the land in Canada, yet, where the soil is naturally good, and the subsequent management good, it may be done profitably.

The exorbitant price of tiles has hitherto been a serious drawback to the introduction of draining; the facilities for making them are now however such that this will ere long cease to be an objection. Mr. Gibbs of Yorkville, in U. C. advertizes 1½ inch tiles, for $4½ per thousand; 2 inch, for $5.00; 3 inch for $10.00, &c., each tile 13 inches long. Such prices must command a ready sale in that neighborhood. As a machine for making drain tiles can be had for $300, there is no reason why they could not be made as cheap elswhere, if required. Tile draining is the best, and in the long run perhaps the cheapest method of under-draining, but it is not the only method. Where tiles cannot be had at a reasonable price, numerous substitutes may be used advantageously. Where small stones abound on the surface, they may take the places of tiles. Great care however is requisite in making stone drains from their tendency to "choke up:" it is necessary that they should be covered with three feet of earth, this requires a deep, wide, and consequently an expensive drain to receive the materials. Narrow strips of hemlock boards nailed together in triangular shape, answer very well, so long as they last, but the best substitute for tiles, is common cedar rails; three or four of these laid in the bottom, blinded well with cedar bark or chips, make an excellent drain, and very durable, although the expense is little less than that of tiles, it has this advantage, than every farmer can find the materials on his own farm, without paying out *the money*.

Perhaps the greatest errors in the Canadian system of husbandry consist in attempting to cultivate more land than our capital enables us to do thoroughly, and in keeping more stock than we can keep well. Were less attention manifested to increasing the extent of our farms, and more to the proper cultivation of what we already have, we should not only secure a vastly increased revenue from our farms, but we should do this a great deal more easily to ourselves, and at a much lower expenditure in proportion to the produce raised. By keeping too much stock, the straw upon the farm is nearly all eaten up, instead of being converted into manure, and there being in country parts, no facilities for purchasing manure, it becomes impossible to keep the land in a productive state. To remedy this, root crops should be more generally cultivated. An acre of land will produce 1000 bushels of mangle-wurtzel, or of carrots, at much less cost of labor, than is required to grow 50 bushels of corn. A small quantity of these roots fed daily to cattle, sheep and horses, is productive of great benefit. There is also great room for improvement in the breeds of cattle and horses in the County of Dundas and in adjoining counties. We are decidedly behind Western Canada in these particulars. As regards our breed of horses, we are at a low ebb, and the sooner we improve in this respect, the better it will be for us. $15,000 worth of the *best* horses were sold in 1859. At that rate we shall soon having nothing left but the dregs.

OF LABORERS.—The greater part of the labor of the farm in Canada, is performed by the farmer himself, his sons and his daughters: the former managing all the out of door operations, and the latter, the dairy and domestic departments. Herein lies the secret of the farmer's success. Whatever qualifications a farmer should have, mental or physical, all are agreed upon this point, that *a good wife* is indispensable. What it is the aim of the husband to accumulate, it becomes the province of the wife to manage, and wherever we hear of a managing wife, we are sure to find a money-making farmer.

The average size of Canadian farms is 100 acres each, with from 50 to 60 acres cleared, two thirds of which may be in pasture and meadow, the remainder in tillage. The demand for labor is therefore limited, and the supply is generally equal to the demand. In 1852 there were in the county, 1258 laborers, 53 male, and 74 female servants. At the same time there were 1570 farmers. One half at least of the female servants are employed by others than farmers, so that not more than 37 farmers' wives required hired "help" during that year.

The usual rate of wages for laborers is from $12 to $14 per month for the summer; $10 to $12 for the year round; $7 to $10 for the winter. Daily laborers in summer receive from 50 cents to $1, in winter 50 cents, and expert cradlers earn $1.25 per day—all boarded. Laborers are chiefly immigrants—Irish, German, and a few Scotch; they seldom continue at service longer than four years, and if during that time they are industrious and economical, they will have laid by enough to stock a small farm; remaining as tenants for a few years, they meantime look for a desirable bush lot that they may call their own. So soon as a suitable one turns up, and they can muster $100 as a first payment, the transition from tenant to landlord takes place, the log shanty is erected, and the labors of the early settler are re-enacted, with this material difference, that the modern backwoodsman is surrounded with tokens of civilization, in roads, markets, and mills, which far more than compensate for the difference betwixt paying now, $1000 for his farm, and receiving it as a gift from the crown, seventy-five years ago.

The agricultural implements of the county are keeping pace with other improvements. The first portable threshing machine was introduced twenty-five years ago: it was one of the American eight horse-power threshers, without any separator whatever: the whole power was expended in turning the cylinder, of two feet diameter, at an enormous velocity of 1500 revolutions in a minute, (the maximum speed of the drum of the best British mills, is 400.) It literally devoured the sheaves, required ten to twelve hands to attend it, and left the barn in a state of great confusion. If kept on full speed for ten hours, it would thresh 500 bushels of wheat, or twice that quantity of oats. Soon after, this was superseded by one of much humbler pretensions, driven by the revolving platform horse-power—A Yankee notion. About 1840, the first tread-mill, as it was called, was introduced, and thereby hangs a tale. It surprised the natives wonderfully, it was worked by one horse, and the first experiment was the last for a time. The difficulty of getting a horse to place himself in such a ridiculous position, as that of a tread-mill, was a formidable one, it was however accomplished, and he was firmly secured in his narrow and elevated stall. The drag was removed from the wheel; at the first revolution off came the belt, and away went the horse. The by-standers fled in consternation to the remotest corner of the barn, while the astonished horse increased his velocity with every stride. John Gilpin's speed was nothing to his. The rattling and din of the machinery revolving under his feet, terrified him to madness, and at the same time prevented the by-standers from suggesting any feasible remedy for the case, with desperate plunges the horse essayed to keep his feet, but it was evident that this could not last for ever. The straps that secured him to the infernal machine gave way, and with a *whirrl* that filled the beholders with dismay, he was violently discharged upon the floor, whence, with a couple of summersaults, and effecting a breach through the barn door, he eventually landed, *hors du combat* in the yard. The neighbors alarmed by the noise, hastened to the scene, and assisted in saving the pieces. The horse regained his equilibrium, but was never caught on a treadmill again.

In 1859 there were ten reaping machines, and 200 threshing machines in the county, the latter, chiefly of Paige's and Johnston's make, Montreal. Cash price delivered here $200. They are very compact, durable, and effective mills, with separator and fanning mill combined, and will thresh and clean, from 60 to 100 bushels of wheat, and from 150 to 250 bushels of oats per day.

Circular saws mounted on a frame ready for work, and costing $40 each, are much used; they are driven by the same horse power, at a lower elevation, and will cut 30 cords easily in a day with 4 or 5 men to assist.

Of ploughs we have an endless variety, economy in weight and price seems to be the chief aim of the makers, and in this they have succeeded tolerably well, but there is much room for improvement as to shape, none of the country-made ploughs can turn a furrow so well as the Scotch plough, and of this description there are not over a dozen in the county.

The 40 tooth diamond Scotch harrow, covering nine feet, is

fast superseding all others on cleared land. No grubbers are used in the county, and subsoil ploughs very rarely. Cultivators used between drills of corn and potatoes, are commonly used, and recently, a larger size of this implement, covering 5 feet, and working to a depth of 8 inches, has been introduced, and worked to good advantage upon summer fallow.

Turnips, carrots and mangolds, are sown by hand, we have no machines for drilling in grain, nor broadcast sowing machines, the latter would be a valuable acquisition. Wooden rollers are used to some extent, but they are very perishable, and cast iron ones too dear. Two horse lumber waggons costing $70 each, are used to transport all the commodities of the farm. Carts are not much used, they are made with wooden axle trees from $20 and upwards, the price of a good lumber sleigh with box complete is $24. Excellent fanning mills are made at Morrisburgh, by McKenzie, at the price of $24 each, and are largely exported to adjacent counties. These embrace the principal implements at present in use, they are all manufactured in Canada, and with the exception of a broad-cast sowing machine, no others are at present required.

CHAPTER X.

Social aspect—Character of inhabitants—Territorial divisions—Municipal and legal institutions—Judge Jarvis—Educational statistics—Benevolent and literary societies—Agricultural societies.

The late Sheridan Hogan, M. P. P., whose sudden disappearance, shrouded in the darkest mystery for eighteen months, has recently been accounted for by undoubted proof that he had been foully murdered, was the author of an admirable prize essay upon Canada, written in 1855 for the Canadian "Paris Exhibition Committee," in which he thus graphically alludes to the habits of the farmers of Upper Canada. "The farmer of Upper Canada has plenty and he enjoys it, and a large proportion of the people sit at the same table with their servants and laborers. As a general rule, the gentleman farmer, or rather the gentleman *who would not be a farmer*, because he would not learn the value of labor, nor how to direct it when he employed it, has lamentably failed. The gentleman, however, who is willing to strip off his coat, and as the Yankee quaintly observes, to march forward to the music of his own axe, may be certain of plenty, and of leaving his children well off." Akin to this was the remark of a somewhat purse-proud Scotchman, who had risen from being a ploughman to a position of affluence. His commiseration was asked for an individual who was represented to be of "*gentle birth*," "na, na," said he, "there's nae gentlemen in Canada," and we believe there was full as much truth as poetry in the assertion, whilst the sentiment of Burns, at once poetic and true, finds an echo in the minds of most of our farmers.

> "What tho' on hamely fare we dine,
> Wear hodden gray, and a' that,
> Gie fools their silks, and knaves their wine,
> A man's a man for a' that."

Were we to relate our own experience in the matter, we should doubtless arrive at a conclusion somewhat similar. There is found to exist in Canada a mutual dependence, or identity of interest between master and servant, which completely removes the distinctions subsisting in older countries between these relations. The result is, that the farmer who is willing to place his servants upon terms of equality with himself, is never at a loss for *help*, and his work is well and cheerfully performed; while on the other hand, those coming from the old country, and who feel disposed to stand upon their dignity, more or less experience great difficulty in meeting with suitable *servants*, and still greater difficulty in retaining their services. The annoyance to such persons from this cause is sometimes very great. Thus, a female *help* newly arrived one day, frequently disappears the next, simply because she was asked to sleep in an attic, or had not pickles, pies, and preserves, served for her tea, or perhaps was not invited to spend the evening in the drawing room. Another because she was not allowed to *sit with the family*, or a third because she was expected to milk cows, draw water from the well, or carry an armful of wood to the cooking stove. In like manner a *help* of the masculine gender, has before now bid us good morning, because he was asked to clean out a pig stye, or to dig a post hole, or a ditch. We confess, however, that "helps" of this kind are the exception. Upon the whole, we may congratulate ourselves that even in this respect we might go further and fare worse. The philosophical view of this blending of classes is, that it begets a friendly and harmonious feeling among all ranks of a community. To a certain extent it has this effect, for in Canada, honesty, industry, and intelligence, never fail to be recognized, in whatever station the man is found. Not unfrequently those who are learned in literature and law, have to chew the bitter cud of disappointment, and in aspiring to positions of elective distinction, have to succumb to the practical farmer, or the industrious mechanic, whose accomplishments are summed up in the one comprehensive term, " plain common sense."

As a class our farmers are industrious,—persevering rather than enterprizing—slow to compromise themselves by word or deed, but honest in their transactions. The faculty of accumulating property is fully developed. Seldom flush of money, they are yearly surrounding themselves with all the necessaries and most of the comforts of life. The home-spun hodden-gray, manufactured in whole or in part by the farmer's family, forms his daily dress, while the finer fabrics of Scotch Tweeds and English broadcloths, supply him with a suit for Sundays. The wives and daughters of our farmers, are neat and tidy in their persons, industrious and frugal in their habits, and not slow to lend a hand when help is needed in the barn or in the field; but when attired for *"meetin,"* even Broadway itself, does not present a more elaborate display of hoop and crinoline, with all the fashionable embellishments of the day.

If our farmer is blessed with a family of sons, seldom more than one or two of them remain at home. After receiving as good an education as the county affords, the rest branch out in different ways to push their fortunes in the world. Some spend a few years as common school teachers, and thereafter engage in any other more lucrative employment that may offer. A large number are occupied in the management of railways, steamers, and telegraphs. Some have studied medicine at Toronto, Kingston, or Montreal, and only a very few have turned their attention to law. They are rarely found behind the counter, while divinity appears to possess no attractions whatever; at least we are not aware of any such students, natives of our county. This is certainly a matter of regret, and must be regarded as an indication, either that the office of the ministry is not appreciated and supported as it ought to be amongst us, or that the principles of self-denying Christianity are still latent.

Love of home is a prominent trait in the character of the young men of Dundas; hence, very few have been tempted to the gold diggings of California or Australia, and scarcely any of them take up their abodes in the neighboring States. The general immunity from crime of the United Counties of Stormont, Dundas, and Glengarry, is best attested by the fact, that during a considerable portion of the past year, the gaol at Cornwall was reported to be without a tenant.

TERRITORIAL DIVISIONS.—Up to the year 1788, the whole of Canada, East and West, was comprised in two Districts. In that year, the Governor General, Lord Dorchester, by proclamation subdivided the same. The following extract from which, embraces all that pertained to the County of Dundas. " Whereas our Province of Quebec stands at present divided into only two districts, and by virtue of two certain acts.........provision is made for forming and organizing one or more new Districts, now, therefore, know ye, that our Governor of the said Province, doth hereby form the several new Districts, hereinafter described and named, to wit: The District of Lunenburgh, bounded on the east by a tract lately known by the name of Lancaster, protracted northerly and southerly as far as our said Province extends, and bounded westerly by a north and south line, intersecting the mouth of the river Gananoque, now called the Thames, above the rifts of the St. Lawrence, and extending southerly and northerly to the limits of our said Province, therein comprehending the several towns or tracts, called or known by the names of Lancaster, Charlottenburgh, Cornwall, Osnabruck, Williamsburgh, Matilda, Edwardsburgh, Augusta, and Elizabethtown." The other three Districts named in the proclamation were, the Mecklenburgh, the Nassau, and the Hesse Districts. These with the Lunenburgh, comprised Upper Canada.

In 1792, after the division of the Province into Upper and Lower Canada, Sir John Graves Simcoe, the Lieutenant-Governor, issued a proclamation by which Upper Canada was divided for the first time into counties, and their boundaries were defined. The first county named was Glengarry, then Stormont, and thirdly, Dundas, " which county is to be bounded on the east by the boundary line of Stormont, on the south by the river St. Lawrence, and on the west by the late township of Edwardsburgh, running north 24 degrees west, until it intersects the Ottawa or Grand River, thence descending the said river until it meets the boundary of Stormont, comprehending all the islands in the said river St. Lawrence, nearest to the said county, in the whole or greater part fronting the same." The German names of the four above mentioned districts, were replaced by English ones, their boundaries remaining the same. They were then styled the Eastern, Midland, Home, and Western Districts.

In 1798, by 38 Geo. III, in the second Parliament of Upper Canada, the Eastern District was confined to the Counties of Glengarry, Stormont, Dundas, Prescott, and Russel. This continued till 1816, when Prescott and Russel separated from these, and were formed into the Ottawa District.

In 1849, the districts were all abolished, (at this time they had increased to twenty in number,) and counties and unions of counties, for municipal and judicial purposes took their place. By this arrangement, the title "Eastern District," the first named district in Upper Canada, and around which so many old associations had circled, was abrogated for ever. Henceforth it was to be known by the more cumbrous designation, of " the United Counties of Stormont, Dundas, and Glengarry;" signifying thereby that they should be united for judicial and other purposes, excepting Representation, with a provision at the same time, for the future dissolution of such union, when by the increase of wealth and population it might appear requisite.

It was thus a prospective measure, calculated materially to affect the existing state of matters. It served to pave the way for the erection of municipal corporations, conferring self-government in all local matters, upon the inhabitants of every township and incorporated village, as well as upon the several counties, cities, and towns in Upper Canada. This comprehensive Act (12 Vict., ch. 81,) was passed in May, 1849, and the first elections were held under it, on the first Monday of January, the following year.

Having reached the requisite population, the time may not be far off, when each of the two junior counties may see fit to petition for a separation from the senior county of Stormont. The question involves serious considerations, and we do well to enquire if it would be wise for us at present to advocate the change.

It may be said on the one hand, that our county town is 35 miles distant from the centre of Dundas. That all the offices of emolument are monopolised by the people of Stormont, and particularly by those of Cornwall, and that we have as good a right as they to a share of the public expenditure. It may be said too, that we are likely ere long to be heavily taxed for repairs upon the Cornwall Court House, if not for the building of a new one, and that therefore, we should dissolve the union before that is carried into effect, and rather tax ourselves for less expensive buildings in our own county.

On the other hand it may be replied, that since the completion of the Grand Trunk R. R., time and distance have been annihilated. Ten years ago a journey to Cornwall was a serious affair, but now-a-days it is performed with such speed, comfort, and economy, as effectually to silence the first objection to the continuance of the union. Respecting the offices of emolument we may remark, that only a favored few in the county could fill them, and if the offices were to be worth the having, the aggregate amount of their salaries could not fall far short of what is now paid to the officers of the three United Counties, so that while we might have the honor of the appointment, we should have to pay at the least, three times as much for the *whistle* as we now do. With regard to the buildings, it would cost us at the lowest calculation $6000 to construct suitable county buildings for Dundas. The contemplated alterations at Cornwall will not likely exceed that amount, so that in this respect, our tax will be less than one-third of what it would be if we were separated. Apart from these considerations, we deprecate the idea of petty tribunals, there is a dignity connected with the deliberations of the various courts of the united counties, which a quarter of a century would not impart to the county courts of Dundas. It is worthy of remark too, that while ample provision is made in the law for full payment of its proportion of all debts contracted during the union, by any retiring county, there is no hope held out, that any part of the monies contributed by such county, for united county buildings or other purposes, will ever be refunded. We therefore conclude, that it were better for us to remain as we are for some time to come, and in the meantime, the best thing that we can do, is to initiate measures for the passing of a law, whereby senior counties may be compelled to refund to separating junior counties a fair proportion of the monies contributed by them, in the erection of buildings for the use of the united counties. We believe that this would have the effect, not of hastening a disruption, but of cementing the union, until such time as it might appear beneficial to make the alteration. In any case, the county of Dundas is not likely to escape taxation for the repairs at Cornwall, when we consider the length of time that must intervene before the separation can be effected. We consider the subject of sufficient importance to quote a clause or two from the municipal act, as amended and consolidated by the 22 Vict., ch. 99, 1858.

Section 39. "When the census returns taken under an Act of Parliament, or under the authority of a By-law of the Council of any United Counties, show that the junior county of the union, contains not less than fifteen thousand inhabitants, then, if a majority of the reeves and deputy reeves of such county do, in the month of February in two successive years, pass a resolution affirming the expediency of the county being separated from the union; and if in the month of February in the following or third year, a majority of the reeves transmit to the Governor in Council a petition for the separation, and if the Governor deems the circumstances of the junior county such as to call for a separate establishment of courts and other county institutions, he may, by proclamation setting forth these facts, constitute the reeves and deputy reeves for the county, a provisional council, and in the proclamation appoint a time and place for the first meeting of the council, and therein name one of its members to preside at the meeting, and also therein determine the place for, and the name of the county town.

Section 46. "After the provisional council has procured the necessary property, and erected thereon the proper buildings for a court house and gaol, the council may enter into an agreement with the senior or remaining county or counties, *for payment* to such county or counties of any part *of the debts of the union* as may be just, and for determining the amount to be so paid and the times of payment.

Section 49. "After the sum to be paid by the junior county to the senior or remaining county or counties, has been paid or ascertained by agreement or arbitration, the Governor in Council shall appoint for the junior county, a judge, a surrogate, a sheriff, one or more coroners, a clerk of the peace, a registrar, and at least twelve justices of the peace.

Section 51. "After such appointments are made, the Governor shall by proclamation separate the junior county, and shall declare such separation to take effect on the first day of January next, after the end of three calendar months from the date of the proclamation; and on that day the courts and officers of the union shall cease to have any jurisdiction in the junior county."

The municipal system of Upper Canada, is one of which any people might be proud. Though still capable of improvement, and liable to abuse, it is perhaps the most perfect municipal system in the world. Mr. Morris in his prize essay says of it, " It is adapted in a very high degree to the wants of the country, is wrought with fidelity, and is proving highly serviceable, by teaching the people the habit of self government, and by familiarizing them with the routine of business, localizing the system of legislation, and training up every where men for the various positions in private and public-life, to which industry, energy, and ability may elevate them."

Its features and workings are already familiar to all, and therefore require no lengthened dissertation at our hands. Previous to 1841, a few cities and towns in Canada, had been incorporated by special charters, but no municipal system had extended to the rural districts. In 1841 the inhabitants of each district in Upper Canada, were for the first time constituted into corporate bodies, with powers to sue and be sued, to levy and collect taxes, and to expend the monies so raised in the maintenance of schools, in making public improvements, and in the administration of justice. Each township having more than 300 inhabitants was entitled to choose two councillors, the chairman of the district council was appointed by the Governor, and one-third of the entire number of councillors retired annually in rotation. Thus matters remained until 1849, when the districts were abolished, and the present system was introduced. Amendments were made from year to year until 1858, when all previous municipal laws were repealed, and one general and comprehensive enactment substituted.

The council of every township and incorporated village, consists of five councillors, elected annually upon the first Monday in January, throughout the whole Province. The persons qualified to be elected councillors, are, residents of the county within which the municipality lies, who are rated on the last revised assessment roll as proprietors or tenants of real property, to at least the following value, viz. :—In townships, freehold property to the value of $400, or leasehold, $800. In incorporated villages, freehold to $40 per annum, or leasehold to $80 per annum. The electors, are all such freeholders and householders as have been residents in the municipality for one month before the election. British subjects of the full age of 21 years, who were rated as proprietors or tenants on the last revised assessment rolls for real property. In incorporated villages, the annual value of such property must be at least $12, in towns $20, and in cities $30. The councillors elect, meet on the third Monday in January following their election, and then choose from among their number a chairman, who is styled the

"*Reeve*," and when the population of any township or incorporated village, numbers 500 resident freeholders or householders, such council may also elect a "*Deputy Reeve.*" The Reeves and Deputy Reeves of the several municipalities in any county or union of counties, constitute the council of such county, which is presided over by one of their number, elected by the council, and who is named the "*Warden*" of such county or union of counties.

Each of the four townships of Dundas county, have thus their several councils to manage their local affairs, and each sends a Reeve and a Deputy Reeve to the United Counties council.

The villages of Iroquois and Morrisburgh are also incorporated, the former by Act of Parliament in 1857, the latter by a by-law of the counties council, passed on the 17th of October, 1860.

The amount expended by the township's council of Williamsburgh, during the year 1860, was $3403.43, of this, $1373 was spent on roads, $819 for county rates, $630 for schools, $153.75 for salaries to councillors and clerks, and the balance for incidental expenses.

The receipts for the same year were $3691.82, of which $746.90 from Clergy Reserve fund, $2494.40 from taxation, $405 from tavern and shop licenses, the remainder from fines, &c.

The municipal assessed taxes in the county of Dundas, including township rates, amount to two cents in four dollars; the yearly assessment by school trustees, amounts to nearly one cent and one half in four dollars, and the self-imposed tax for the support of religious ordinances, about one cent and one half more, so that the total direct taxes for schools, church, and state, amount to five cents for every four dollars worth of property held :—e. g. A farmer who owns one hundred acres of land, which with his personal property is valued at $2000, should pay $10 for public taxes, $7.50 for the support of schools, and $7.50 for the support of religion, (*if he paid his share,*) in all $25 per annum.

$9000 are annually expended by the several municipalities upon the roads of the county, including the Clergy Reserve grants of $3000.

The counties' council for the united counties of Stormont, Dundas, and Glengarry, consisted in 1860, of fourteen Reeves, and eleven Deputy Reeves, in all 25, of whom 9 were from Dundas. The amount of monies expended by the county council for that year was $10,946.

Cornwall, the county town of the united counties, is distant by G. T. R. 25 miles from Morrisburgh, and 32 from Iroquois. The court house, gaol, and public offices are there situated. There also are held the Court of Queen's Bench, of Quarter Sessions, and the sittings of the counties' council.

The county of Dundas was named in 1792, in honour of Mr. Dundas, at that time colonial secretary in England.* When this part of Canada was originally surveyed in 1783, the townships were numbered, and it was not until some time after that they were named, and even for many years after being named, they continued to be designated as the 1st, 2nd, 3rd townships, and so on. To this day, the township of Osnabruck is more frequently styled the "*third town*," than by its own euphonious German name. The

---

* Henry Dundas, Esq., born the 28th April, 1742, was the youngest son of Robert Dundas of Arniston, (in Scotland), Lord President of the Court of Session. He was appointed Lord Advocate of Scotland in 1775: having subsequently filled some high official situations in the Government of England, during the administration of Mr. Pitt, he was elevated to the Peerage in 1802, as Baron Duneira and Viscount Melville.

Lord Melville was impeached by the House of Commons in 1805, for alleged malversation in his office as Treasurer of the Navy, and after a trial by his peers, in Westminster Hall, adjudged not guilty

Obiit, 1811   Seat, Melville Castle, Edinburgh.
Motto. "Quod potui, perfeci."   (*Burke's Peerage.*)

At some future, perchance far distant, day, having separated from its sister counties, a motto may be sought for the official seal of Dundas. If so, we hope that the one above given will be selected, in memory of the statesman whose name the county bears, as well as for the sentiment it conveys, "I have done what I could."

numbers commenced with Charlottenburgh, and continued in consecutive order to the Bay of Quinté. Lancaster, though naturally the first in order, was not then numbered amongst the townships. It was considered utterly worthless, and was more commonly known as the "*sunken*" township.

Williamsburgh was doubtless named in honor of Prince William Henry, Duke of Clarence, who in 1831 ascended the throne of England as William IV. Prince William visited Canada and Nova Scotia in 1787. He was then in the navy, and commanded the "Pegasus" of 84 guns. After visiting Quebec and Montreal, he passed some time at Sorel, and sanctioned the change of the name of that place to his own, "William Henry," which it still bears. Matilda probably owes its name to the Princess Charlotte Augusta Matilda, late queen of Wirtemburgh, eldest daughter of King George III, by Queen Charlotte.† Winchester derives its name from the Earl of that ilk, who preceded Dundas as Colonial Secretary. Mountain was so called in honor of Dr. Mountain, the first Protestant Bishop in Canada. This township was partially settled at a very early period in the history of the county; a few families having come in by the way of Kemptville, long before the swamps lying between it and the St. Lawrence became passable.

LEGAL INSTITUTIONS.—By an ordinance of the Governor in Coun-

---

† King Geo. III. died in 1820, at the advanced age of 82, having reigned sixty years. He had by his Queen Charlotte, nine sons and six daughters, whose names afford a key to many of the townships in the eastern part of C. W. They were as follows:—

(1) Geo. IV. (2) Frederick, Duke of York. (3) William Henry, Duke of Clarence, (William IV.) (4) Charlotte Augusta Matilda, ob. 1828. (5) Edward, Duke of Kent, ob. 1820, (father of Queen Victoria.) (6) Augusta Sophia. (7) Elizabeth. (8) Ernest Augustus. (9) Augustus Frederick, Duke of Sussex. (10) Adolphus Frederick, Duke of Cambridge. (11) Mary, Duchess of Gloucester. (12) Sophia. (13) Octavius. (14) Alfred. (15) Amelia.

cil of the Province of Quebec, in 1784, there were certain regulations made for the trial of causes, under and over £10 sterling, in the Court of Common Pleas, and regulating the time of the defendant's appearance *in Montreal*, in case that he resided above the Longue Soult, on the Ottawa River, or beyond Oswegotchie, in the upper parts of the Province.

The first act in the statute book of Upper Canada, regarding the jurisdiction of courts was in 1792, Geo. III, chap. 4, which prohibited the summary proceedings of the common pleas, and required the intervention of a jury in causes above forty shillings, Quebec currency. Chap. 6 of the same year, established a court of requests, to be held by two or more justices of the peace, in divisions to be established by the county quarter sessions. This jurisdiction was afterwards extended to £5 currency, where the debt was ascertained by the defendant's signature. In 1794, the Court of King's Bench was erected in Upper Canada, and the same year district courts were established, having jurisdiction in matters of debt from forty shillings to £15.

In 1841, by the 4th and 5th Vict. chap. 3, the Courts of Request were abolished, and the name, "District Court," was changed to "County Court." This act has since been amended by several other statutes, and now finally settled by the consolidated act of 1859. Under which, the jurisdiction of the County Courts extends to $400, and that of the Division Courts to $100.

The Court of Queen's Bench holds semi-annual Courts of Assize, and Nisi Prius as in England. It is held at Cornwall, usually in the months of April and October. The County Court and Quarter Sessions sit four times in the year, at the same place, and are presided over by Judge Jarvis. He also presides over the Division Courts, which are held six times in the year in the front townships of Dundas, and four times in the rear townships. The amount of litigation in the county, may be gathered from the fact that it is not uncommon for the Judge to dispose of 100 cases in a day. In the course of the year 1859, the number of cases passing before him in the Division Courts of the County of Dundas, reached 2920. The sums sued for amounted to $45,525 for Dundas, and $118,836 for the three counties.

The Division Court is, in Upper Canada, the court of lowest jurisdiction, and, its sessions being held in various localities within each county, a great variety of trifling suits are disposed of speedily, cheaply, and, in most cases, satisfactorily. The decisions are usually given upon the judge's own responsibility, but he may call in the assistance of a jury in any case, or, either of the parties interested may demand a jury. This privilege, however, is rarely exercised. So much so is this the case, that the practical working of this court seems opposed to the generally received opinion as to the beneficial results usually attributed to the system of "trial by jury." In nineteen cases out of twenty, the common-sense farmer considers his cause safer in the hands of one disinterested individual, than of a dozen of his brother farmers.

Judge Anderson was the first District Judge for the Eastern District. Like Duncan the former Judge for the Lunenburgh District, he had been a Captain in Sir John Johnston's regiment. He however retired in 1818, and was succeeded by Judge Sheek. This gentleman, was the proprietor of the mills at Mille-roches, and from him Sheek's Island takes its name. In 1822, Judge Sherwood, an eminent lawyer of Brockville, father of the present Receiver General, the Hon. George Sherwood, was appointed, and held the office until 1825, when he was promoted to the King's Bench. The vacancy was filled by the appointment of David Jones, Esquire, of Brockville. Mr. Jones was a lawyer in good practice residing in Brockville: when the act of 1842 was passed, requiring the Judge to reside in the county, he did not consider the appointment sufficiently important to warrant his removing to Cornwall, and Judge Jarvis was appointed in his place, in January of that year. Judge Jarvis had previously been Judge of the Ottawa District from 21st December 1825 and of the Johnston District from June 1837, consequently he has now been presiding on the Bench for a period of over thirty-five years; longer than any other Judge in Upper Canada. Our worthy Chief Justice, Sir John B. Robinson, was not promoted to the Bench till August 1829.

Judge Jarvis was sworn in as an attorney, in November 1820, on the same day with the late Sir James B. McCaulay, Chief Justice in the Common Pleas, and was called to the Bar, in Hilary term 1823. He commenced practice in 1820 in Cornwall, where he has since resided. At the time he was called to the Bar, he stood No. 68 on the Barrister's Roll, there are now only 14 above him, and he stands No. 8 on the Benchers Roll as a director of the Law Society. At the time of his appointment to the Bench of these counties in 1842, the Division Courts were established, consequently he had the onerous task of organizing them.

Mr. Jarvis was born at Fredericton, in the Province of New Brunswick, on the 21st April 1797, he is consequently in his 64th year. He came to this Province with his father's family in 1809, and resided at Toronto till 15 years of age. He entered the army in 1812, at the commencement of the last American war, during the whole of which he served. He was present at the battle of Queenston Heights, in the light company of the 49th, when the brave and lamented General Brock with sword in hand placed himself at their head, and led them up the mountain at double quick time, in the teeth of a sharp fire from the enemy's riflemen. He stood within a few feet of the General where he fell, and in the retreat that followed, was made a prisoner. He was with the Grenadiers of the 8th regiment at the battle of York, on the 27th April 1813, where his regiment was almost annihilated by the overwhelming numbers of the enemy. He was present at the battles of Stoney Creek, Beaver Dams and Black Rock, as well as at Chippewa, with the 8th, where they were severely handled. He commanded a company of that regiment in the hard fought action of Lundy's Lane, where that extraordinary conflict was sustained till midnight. Present at the unsuccessful assault of Fort Erie, he also took part in repulsing the memorable sortie of that Fort in September. From the 29th of July till the 21st September, he never had his clothes off, every other day he was on piquet, and during the whole time, under constant fire from the enemy's guns. Nearly every day it rained, and huts constructed with the branches of trees, formed their only covering.

During the rebellion, Judge Jarvis raised three troops of lancers, most of whom were the young braves of the County of Dundas, Lt. Martin Carman, Cornet George M. Crysler, Major and Pay-Master. J. W. Loux, now M. P. P. for the County of Russel, and others were among the number.

Judge Jarvis' life has thus been devoted to his country since childhood, and while we doubt not his services were duly appreciated in every station which he has occupied, in none could they have been more so, than in his capacity as County Judge, a station for which his natural qualifications are eminently suitable. Gentlemanly and affable in his manners, prompt and impartial in his decisions, he has won for himself the esteem and respect of the inhabitants of these United Counties.

EDUCATIONAL.—Before speaking of the schools of Dundas, it may be interesting to glance at the history of our school system still in its infancy, and to measure its already marvellous proportions, by a few figures from the Superintendent's Report for 1858.

As already mentioned schools have existed in the County from its very first settlement. The first Legislative enactment however for the support of schools, was in 1807, when the sum of £800 was appropriated for the establishment of public schools in Upper Canada. It was then enacted, that there should be *one public school* in each of the eight Districts in Upper Canada, and that £100 should be paid annually to the teacher of each school. Five trustees were appointed for the management of each school, by the Governor, and all their proceedings were rendered subject to his approval.

No further provision was made until 1816 when the sum of

£6000 was annually appropriated for the establishment of *common schools*, to be divided amongst, the then, ten Districts of Upper Canada, according to population. The Eastern District ranking among the highest, received £800 yearly, as large an amount as had previously been allotted to the whole Province. At this time the inhabitants were first empowered to elect, as at present, three trustees for each school, with nearly similar powers. A board of education was also established in each District, to whom the trustees were to report once in three months, the Board itself reporting to the Governor, once a year. No allowance to any single school was permitted to exceed £25 annually.

This act was partially repealed in 1820, when it was enacted that only £2500 should be paid annually from the public chest in aid of common schools. Each of the Districts receiving £250, and no single school to draw more than £12 10s. per annum. In 1824, the continuance of the last act referred to was extended, and a sum of £150 per annum in addition, granted, for the encouragement of common, and *sunday* schools, to be expended on such books and tracts, as were designed to afford moral and religious instruction. In 1836, the public grant was increased to £5650.

The next act to provide for the advancement of education in Upper Canada was the 2nd Vict. chap. 10 in 1839. This act provided that, when the old District schools should be declared to be Grammar schools, and trustees for them were elected by the Governor, the sum of £100 per annum should be granted to each such grammar school, and £200 to each District, for the purpose of building a school-house, on the condition that the inhabitants of that District should raise a like sum.

After the union of the Provinces, by the 4th and 5th Vict. ch. 18, in 1841, a permanent fund was established for the support of common schools; £50,000 was granted annually, which, by the 7th Vic. in 1843, was to be equally divided between Canada East and Canada West. In 1846 the school system was revised, and a Normal and Model School established at Toronto, by an appropriation of £1500 for providing suitable buildings, and an annual grant of £1500 for the support of the Normal School. In 1849, in addition to the existing grant, *one million* acres of land, were set apart to form a fund for school purposes.

All former School Acts were swept away by the comprehensive act of 13 and 14 Vict. c. 48, in 1850, which was entitled "An Act for the better establishment and maintenance of common schools in Upper Canada," which, with a few supplementary and explanatory clauses, including the erection of separate schools, with equal privileges for Roman Catholics and Protestants, inaugurated the present school system of Canada—a system which, upon examination, will be found to exhibit a wonderful combination, and no less wonderful simplicity of mechanism Hitherto it has worked harmoniously, and been of incalculable benefit to the Province, insinuating its influence into the remotest settlements, and diffusing civilization, intelligence, and enterprise over the length and breadth of the land. Much of the success of the school system, is unquestionably due to the chief superintendent, Dr. Ryerson, who may be said to have originated it, and under whose management it has attained its present efficiency.

In 1858 there were in operation in Upper Canada 3866 common schools, with 4202 teachers, and 293,693 scholars; 94 separate schools, chiefly Roman Catholic, with 118 teachers and 9991 scholars; 75 grammar schools, with 4459 scholars, besides the Normal and Model Schools, with about 400 scholars. The Legislative grant for all the schools of Upper Canada in 1858 was $177,913; to colleges $20,000, and to Literary and Scientific institutions $17,000. At the same time there were in operation, 11 colleges, 46 private academies, 255 private schools, with an aggregate of 7467 pupils. The number of youth receiving instruction during the year at school and college was thus 316,000, and the large sum of $1,727,498 was expended in their education, from all sources, public and private, showing an average of $5.46½ per annum for each scholar.

During the year, 170 superannuated or *worn-out* (so called in the report) teachers, received pensions varying from $5 to $70 each per annum, according to the number of years they had been in the service.

The whole system is controlled by a council of public instruction and a chief superintendent of education, who is *ex officio* a member of the council, and who, as well as the council, is appointed by the crown. The council meet from time to time in Toronto, where a handsome departmental building was erected for its occupancy in 1852, at a cost of $100,000. The grounds surrounding it extend to eight acres, and are tastefully laid out with a view of being at once useful and ornamental. They comprise a gymnasium, as well as afford practical illustrations in horticulture and agriculture. There is also a museum attached, containing numerous interesting collections of sculpture, painting, geological specimens, models and engravings. The public are admitted to the museum upon leaving their names in the visitors' book, at the Education Office,"*and their sticks and umbrellas in the ante-room.*" The department includes a depository for public school libraries, for prize books, and for school maps and apparatus, during the last five years 182,267 volumes have been distributed to schools and institutions. The expenditure for books, maps and apparatus in 1858 was $32,664. Then there is the departmental library, the Chief Superintendent's office and apartments for his clerks and staff of assistants; the Normal and Model Schools occupy a space in rear of the main-building, and are connected with it by a spacious corridor.

The Chief Superintendent receives a salary of $4000 per annum. His deputy and numerous staff of clerks and assistants receive together, $10,143. The amount returned as contingencies under the head of education, in the public accounts for 1858 was $50,000 more. Two Grammar School Inspectors are paid $1000 each, and each local superintendent of common schools at the rate of $4 per school, say $15,464. It thus costs us the formidable sum of $81,607 annually, to oil the wheels of this gigantic engine. The total public expenditure, under the head of education, for Upper and Lower Canada in 1858 was, $529,365 21.

We have in Dundas County, one grammar School, 72 common schools, and a few private schools.

THE GRAMMAR SCHOOL is situated in the village of Iroquois. It is a substantial stone edifice, erected in 1843, by John A. Carman, Esq , and was by him generously made a present to the county; one acre of eligible land is attached to it, which was also a gift, from Mr. Coons. The land and building are valued at $3000. It is styled the "Matilda County Grammar School," which of course is an anomaly, and ought to be rendered "The Dundas County Grammar School." This school receives government aid in the same ratio as other junior county grammar schools, the appropriation being made to counties, and unions of counties in proportion to population, and to individual grammar schools according to the average attendance at each. It is conducted by two teachers, male and female, the former teaches the higher branches of English, mathematics, and the classics. Music, drawing, &c , are taught by the latter. The number of pupils in 1858 was 55, and the tuition fees as follows—English, mathematics, and classics $3 to $4 per quarter, Music, &c., $7 per quarter. The teachers' salaries are $600 and $300 respectively, and the government grant $394 per annum. The grammar school is governed by a board of eight trustees, holding office for three years. Two are appointed annually by the counties' council, two of their number retiring yearly by rotation.

The grammar-school trustees have at present no powers for levying assessments for the support of the school, in this respect their position is inferior to that of the common school trustees. It is true they may apply to the county council for aid, but it is also true that the county council may refuse, and very often have refused to have anything to do with them. There is unquestionably room for amendment in this feature of the grammar school law.

THE COMMON SCHOOLS. In 1859 there were in Dundas county 72 common schools in operation, 73 teachers and 10 vacant schools. The number of children in the county of school age that is from 5 to 16 years, was............ ....5009.

The number attending school was............... ...4244.
The number who did not attend any school .... 661.
Number not reported, including private schools... 62.

The average time during which all the schools were kept open was 10 months and 6 days. Of the 72 schools, 49 were free schools, that is, supported by a direct tax on the real property within the school section, and the school thrown open to all, free of tuition fees; the remainder were supported by a charge of one shilling and three pence per month for each scholar, and the deficiency made up by assessment.

The receipts of common schools were,

From Legislative grants......... ....$2196.00
Municipal grants 2191.00
Local assessment by trustees 6144.20
Rate bills at 1s 3d. per month 652.09
Balances, and other sources 552.82

Total receipts for schools in Dundas Co. in 1859.$11,736.11

The average annual salary of teachers in the county was, male teachers, boarded, $174, without board $248. Females, boarded, $97, without board $141. The highest salary paid was $460. The lowest to male teacher $120. One half of the teachers board, week about, with the inhabitants of the School section; it is to be hoped this antediluvian custom will soon be abolished. Of the teachers, 43 were males, and 30 females; only 10 held a first class certificate, 52 a second class, and 11 a third class certificate.

The sum of $33,360 was expended in 1858 from the public chest in aid of literary and scientific institutions. Of this sum, $6580.00 was paid to observatories in Toronto and Quebec, the remainder was appropriated chiefly to Mechanics' Institutes. Of these there are in all Canada about 140, each receiving from government an annual sum, varying from $100 to $200.

Of benevolent and literary societies in Dundas we have to present but a very meagre catalogue. There are two temperance societies, neither of them in a very flourishing condition; two lecture associations, under whose auspices courses of lectures are delivered during the winter months, and *seventeen* " Orange Lodges." Of these last, 13 have been organized within the last five or six years Their present strength is said to be about 500. There are no efficient public libraries, reading rooms, scientific or literary institutions in the county, beyond what has been mentioned, excepting it be our agricultural societies, which now fall to be noticed.

The first agricultural society in the county was established in the year 1830. One Bartholomew Tench, a merchant in Matilda, seems to have been the first to move in the matter; he drafted a constitution for it, and used his influence to induce the farmers to join it. Its first president was Peter Shaver, Esq., and John Flagg, Esq., was Secretary-Treasurer. During the first few years of its existence, being a novelty, it attracted some attention, and numbered about forty members It was not long, however, before envy, jealousy, and discord, found their way into the agricultural wigwam, and the efforts of the directors to please every body resulted, as a matter of course, in their pleasing nobody. From the first, this society received from government two dollars for every one subscribed, and as the members gradually decreased, so in proportion did the share of the spoil increase to those who remained. A township society was soon afterwards formed in Matilda, the one in Williamsburg still retaining the name of the county of Dundas Agricultural Society.

In 1847 both societies had dwindled down to ludicrous proportions, when a few disinterested parties came to the rescue, and year by year, very slowly indeed, the county society began to emerge out of the state of confusion and misrule which had obstructed its usefulness. In January, 1852, it was deemed desirable to abolish township societies altogether, and to unite in one, the whole eastern district. A district society was then organized of which the Hon. Philip Vankoughnet was chosen president, and in October of that year, an agricultural exhibition was held in Cornwall, which passed off remarkably well.

The Act of 1852, establishing a bureau and board of agriculture accompanied by a new code of laws for the management of agricultural societies, opened up a new era in their existence. Under this act $1000 were granted annually to counties or unions of counties, or $600 annually to any single county in such union. This act was amended in 1857, when it was provided that each county returning a member of parliament should receive a sum not exceeding $800 annually towards the support of agricultural societies therein, with the proviso that they should have in each such society at least fifty members, paying not less than five shillings each annually. By this arrangement the government agreed to pay *three* dollars for every one raised by the local society, up to the specified amount; it was also provided that three-fifths of this governmental grant should be divided amongst the several township or branch societies, organized under this act.

In February, 1853, the present county society was reorganized, Jacob Brouse, Esq., being chosen president. Branch societies were established in Mountain and Winchester in 1857, and are still upheld with considerable spirit in these townships.

The various agricultural societies throughout the Province are exerting an influence for good, by stimulating a generous rivalry, and by bringing articles of real merit prominently into public notice. It is questionable, however, whether they are doing *all* the good that they might, considering that the large sum of $111,032 is annually expended by government in their support. Hitherto the farmers of the Province have not manifested their appreciation of this liberal policy, as they ought to have done, and much of the money expended by agricultural societies, has been little better than a squandering of the public funds. The important ends of seeking, by this means to introduce a better system of agriculture, and better breeds of live stock, have, in many cases been entirely overlooked in pandering to the selfish propensities of the many, who seem to regard an equal distribution of the dollars and cents as more desirable. Were liberal premiums awarded for the best cultivated farms, and to the men who should in the most intelligible language, tell their brother farmers by what process they have been enabled to grow the best crops, much more good might be done, than by expending large sums of money in small premiums, for a bushel, or a bag of the best grain, and roots of different kinds, and in a variety of ways even more objectionable.

CHAPTER XI.

Population of Dundas and adjacent Counties—Exports and Imports of the County—Manufactures—Progress.

Having a tender regard for those of our readers who have an antipathy to wading through columns of figures, we shall condense as much as possible what we have collected for this chapter. Dry and uninteresting though the figures may be to some, none but those who have made the attempt, can form any idea of the time and labor necessary to procure the information which they represent. Indeed, but for the assistance of Mr. Johnston, the census commissioner for the county, added to the kind aid of Mr Hutton, the Secretary of the Board of Statistics at Quebec, we could not have attempted to give accurate details of the population, the various religious denominations, or the agricultural productions of the county.

The following figures exhibit the population and relative increase of the counties bordering upon Dundas, and which from their position are commonly known as "Central Canada."

County.	Population, 1852.	1861.
Leeds	30,280	35,827
Lanark	27,313	31,658
Carleton	23,637	29,503

Grenville	20,707 24,293
Prescott	10,487 15,412
Renfrew	9,415 29,503
Russel	2,870 6,818
Stormont	14,643 18,150
Dundas	13,811 18,824
Glengarry	17,596 21,154

The following is the population of the towns and villages within the above counties, in so far as they have been published.

Ottawa City	14,754	Kemptville	1059
Brockville	4,091	Merrickville	908
Prescott	2,568	Morrisburgh	857
Perth	2,500	Renfrew	695
Cornwall	1,899	Iroquois	617
Smith's Falls, about,	1,200		

The population of Dundas County is distributed as follows:—Williamsburgh, 5529. Matilda, 5473. Winchester, 4149. Mountain, 3683.

The number of farmers in Williamsburgh, 545. Matilda, 597. Winchester, 553. Mountain, 511. Total, 2206.

AGRICULTURAL PRODUCTS OF DUNDAS, 1860.

		Bus. Fall Wheat.	Bus. Spring Wheat.	Bus. Barley.	Bus. Rye.	Bus. Peas.	Bus. Oats.	Bus. Buck Wheat.
1	Williamsburgh	508	51,964	17,789	530	10,448	112,177	9,464
2	Matilda	320	58,881	27,556	77	14,002	122,269	6,177
3	Mountain	940	61,190	4,961	1,753	10,598	76,287	3,859
4	Winchester	1,284	62,002	7,057	310	11,181	77,838	3,122
	Totals	3,052	234,037	57,363	2,670	46,229	388,571	22,622

	Bus. Corn.	Bus. Potatoes.	Bus. Turnips	Bus. M'ngolds	Bus. Carrots.	Bus. Beans.	Lbs. Hops.	Tons Hay.	Bus. Timoth.
1	7,069	46,454	481	2,145	3,956	116	87	4,002	262
2	10,912	69,934	150	1,000	2,084	46	88	6,420	19
3	7,023	42,362	991	180	3,223	43	3,346	3,642	48
4	6,222	38,108	2,299	818	4,179	316	139	3,571	357
	31,226	196,858	3,921	4,143	13,442	521	3,660	17,635	686

	Lbs. Flax.	Lbs. Wool.	Lbs. M.Sugr.	Galls. Cider.	Yds. Cloth.	Yds. Linen.	Yds. Flann'l.	Barrels Beef.	Barrels Pork.
1	3,248	14,447	32,489	174	4,068	1,015	9,338	381	1,325
2	150	16,895	10,295	2,818	3,436	231	9,352	975	1,465
3	50	9,776	16,396	—	2,643	47	8,755	295	1,245
4	377	10,222	18,575	—	2,341	140	6,419	210	1,417
	3,825	51,340	77,755	2,992	12,488	1,433	33,864	1,861	5,452

	Heads Cattle.	Heads Horses.	Heads Sheep.	Heads Pigs.	Total value of live stock	Lbs. Butter.	Lbs. Cheese.
1	4,064	1,865	4,566	1,662	$188,644	163,758	21,955
2	4,582	3,787	4,722	1,813	156,147	197,655	13,969
3	3,337	1,299	3,073	1,389	106,933	122,930	2,310
4	1,658	1,464	3,166	1,385	111,117	134,195	2,288
	13,641	8,415	15,527	6,249	562,841	618,538	40,522

We have only given the totals of 32 out of the 64 columns which occupy the agricultural sheets of the census for the single county of Dundas. In order to arrive at the figures given, it has been necessary to add more than two thousand lines of figures in each column. This may afford some idea of the amount of labor to be accomplished before the personal and agricultural census of the 78 counties of Canada, besides cities, towns, and villages, can be presented to the public.

Thirty-four enumerators were employed upon an average eight days in taking the census of Dundas, and recording about 550 names: their remuneration was two cents for each name. The labors of the enumerators were superintended by one commissioner in each county; by him the sheets were all revised, in many cases corrected, in not a few instances entirely re-written, and each column added up, before they were forwarded to the Head Office in Quebec. The commissioners received a salary of 12s. 6d. per day while so employed.

The total cost to the Province of taking the census will be about $200,000.

The number of shops and stores in the county of Dundas, for the sale of merchandize, was in 1859, seventy-two; of these, 30 were in the township of Williamsburgh, 24 in Matilda, 11 in Winchester, and 7 in Mountain. The invoice value of the goods sold in the county was as follows:—

In the township of Williamsburgh............ $112,500
"   "   Matilda.................... 57,600
"   "   Winchester................ 56,250
"   "   Mountain 13,875

Total value of goods sold in 1859.........$240,225

Traders sell at an average advance of 25 per cent. for cash, upon invoice prices, so that the farmers of the county paid the sum of $320,300 for store goods. The number of families in the county was about 3000, shewing an average annual expenditure by each family for merchandize of $106.76.

Nine shopkeepers in Williamsburgh sell for $7,500 each. Five sell for $4,500, six for $2,250, five for $1,050, and five for $750 each. In Matilda, four sell for $4,875 each, seven for $3,000, six for $1,800, and seven for $900 each. In Mountain, one sells for $6,000, four for $1,500, and two for $937½ each.

The disparity betwixt Williamsburgh and Matilda, is caused by Morrisburgh being near the boundary of Matilda, while Iroquois, the trading point of the latter, is six miles from the boundary line, consequently a large portion of the people of Matilda trade in Williamsburgh.

With respect to the annexed table of exports from the county, it may be remarked, that the figures represent only such quantities exported by the river and railway, as could be traced with certainty. A large additional amount of produce found its way to Ottawa, Kemptville, and Prescott, by private conveyance, of which no account is taken. The table is therefore but an approximation, and is valuable as shewing the diversity, rather than the precise quantity of exports.

EXPORTS AND IMPORTS.

PRODUCE EXPORTED FROM DUNDAS COUNTY—1859.

			$	cts.
5,677	Barrels	Flour at $6..................................	34,062	00
37,000	Bushels	Wheat at $1.10.............................	40,700	00
18,474	"	Oats at 35 cents	6,465	90
32,238	"	Barley at 60 cents.........................	19,342	80
2,000	"	Peas at 60 cents...........................	1,200	00
535	Barrels	Potash at $30..............................	16,050	00
180,000	lbs.	Butter at 15 cents........................	27,000	00
4,327	"	Poultry at 5 "	216	35
2,700	"	Lard at 8 "	216	00
65,000	dozen	Eggs at 10 "	6,500	00
13,500	lbs.	Wool (washed) at 30 cents	4,050	00
25,650	"	Hides (dry and green) at 8 cents........	2,052	00
22,000	"	Pork, Beef, Ham, Bacon, at 7 cents......	1,540	00
10	tons	Bran and Shorts at $13	130	00
578	head	Cattle at $20..............................	11,560	00
150	"	Horses at $100............................	15,100	00
2,583	"	Sheep and Pigs at $3.....................	7,749	00
9,000	cords	Fire wood at $1 50 to $1.75.............	14,500	00
1,633,000	pieces	Cut Staves at $5¼ per 100...............	8,573	00
250,000	"	Sawed Staves at $5½ per 100.............	1,375	00
750,000	"	Racked Hoops at $3.50 per 100..........	2,625	00
100,000	"	Shaved Hoops at $9 per 100	900	00
580,000	feet	Sawed Pine Lumber at $8................	4,640	00
128,000	"	Squared timber at $35...................	4,480	00
20,000	pieces	Hickory Hand-spikes at 6 cents..........	1,200	00
30,000	feet	Oak Steamboat Buckets at $19...........	570	00
200	pieces	" " Paddle arms at $1.........	200	00
100	"	" " Fenders at $1 50.........	150	00
		Shingles and Lath	45	00
200		Fanning Mills at $24.....................	4,800	00
8		Buggies at $90............................	720	00
80		Ploughs at $8.............................	640	00
4		Sleighs at $32............................	128	00

Total exports from the county............ $239,480 05

The value of produce exported to the United States entered at the Custom House, was $40,189.

The value of free goods imported from U. S. was......... $24,901
The value of duty paying goods   "   "   6,399

Total imports from U. S., 1859..................... $31,300

Free goods are those imported under the Reciprocity Treaty, two-thirds of which are composed of travellers' horses and carriages, settlers' household stuff, &c.

244 MANUFACTURES. [CHAP.

The amount of freight forwarded by the Grand
Trunk R. R. in 1859, was, from Williamsburgh, 1177 tons.
Do.   do.   do   Matilda.......... 1025 "
                                              ─────
       Total,.................................. 2202 "

MANUFACTURES.—The following table shows the number of mills and manufactories in the county of Dundas, in 1859.

Flour Mills.	Number runs of Stones.	Saw Mills.	Number of Saws.	Carding Mills.	Tanneries.	Carriage Factories.	Foundries.	Chair Factories.	Stave Factories.	Lock-gate Factories.	Fanning Mill Factories.	Total worked by power.	By Water-power.	By Steam-power.
8	19	26	43	4	8	4	1	3	2	1	1	42	31	11

The above mills and factories work chiefly for the home market, and their exports are included in the general exports of the county. Grist mills grind upon an average six bushels of wheat per hour, each run of stones. Saw mills cut 2,500 feet per day, each saw, while working. The carriage factories turn out annually 38 buggies at $90 each, 70 cutters at $32 each, 30 waggons at $70 each, and 30 sleighs at 24 each.

The steam stave-cutting machine in Matilda cuts 10,000 staves per day, or from 60 to 70 per minute, while working. It is driven by a steam engine of 25 horse power, which is worked by consuming the refuse shavings alone for fuel, and gives employment to ten hands. Ash and elm are the materials from which the staves are manufactured. These are brought to the mill in blocks split out of large trees, and sawed in stave length, worth about $3 per cord. The blocks are soaked in boiling water until softened, sliced off ⅝ of an inch in thickness, by a ponderous knife, at the rate already mentioned, and are then shaped and and finished by machinery, and sent to Montreal to be made into flour, salt, and plaster barrels.

Staves cut by circular saw are a trifle more valuable than those cut by the steam soaking process, and are made at the rate of from seven to eight per minute.

The fanning mill factory in Williamsburgh, has an engine of eight horse power which runs by consuming shavings and saw dust, employs six hands at $1 per day, and turns out 250 mills per annum, at $24 each. 200 of these are sent to Montreal, Ottawa and Glengarry. In the foundry are cast 65 tons of metal annually, 400 ploughs are turned out at $8 each when finished, 75 stoves at $20, besides other castings.

The lock-gate factory is the property of Mr. Chaffey, and is situated in Morrisburgh. It comprizes a saw mill, with upright, and large circular saws, planing machines, drilling and boring machines, with other conveniences for the building of the huge lock-gates that are used in the St. Lawrence canals. In 1859 seven pairs of gates were made at $3000 a pair, which might very properly be added to the exports of the county.

A first class grist mill, of stone or brick with flume complete, costs from $3500 to $4000 per run of stones. A first class saw mill complete, except the dam, costs $1000 to $1500 per saw. A first class steam engine (high pressure) costs $100 per horse power delivered in the county.

A well finished farm-house of brick or stone 36 × 26 with kitchen, &c., 24 × 18, one story and a half in height, with cellar underneath, costs $1600. A large number of the farm-houses in the county are of this class. A few however are to be found of higher pretensions, that have cost from $6000 to $10,000. In the new settlements are to be found every variety of dwellings, from the humble shanty, with its stoop, valued at five pounds worth of labor, to the snug frame building with its shady verandah, worth $1000 in cash.

A barn 16 feet high and 36 feet wide costs $4 per foot in length. A board fence with cedar posts sunk four feet in the ground, or a well-built straight cedar fence costs $1 per rod of $16\frac{1}{2}$ feet. Bricks cost $4 per thousand at the kiln: stone $1.50 per cord at the quarry; and lime 15 cents per bushel at the kiln.

It augurs well for the future progress of Dundas, that, whatever measure of prosperity it enjoys, has arisen from the perseverance and energy of its inhabitants, rather than from fortuitous circumstances connected with the locality. It has shared less than most counties, in the yearly influx of emigrants that has peopled rapidly other portions of the province. Possessing no extensive water power, it has not attracted the attention of capitalists, and as a consequence, we have no manufacturing villages to boast of. Neither the soil nor climate are superior to other districts of Canada, but we do not look upon any of these as indispensably necessary to the attainment of success in agriculture.

East Lothian possesses no water power, and boasts of no manufactories. It is situated on the bleakest and most exposed coast of Scotland, with a soil naturally cold and tenacious, and a climate any thing but favorable to agriculture, yet it stands unrivalled for the intelligence and enterprise of its farmers. By a steady adherence to a fixed system of good husbandry and thorough underdraining, they have rendered that tract of country, much of which was but a few years ago barren moors, one of the most productive, as it certainly is one of the best cultivated portions of Britain.

There is no reason why the farmers of " the old Eastern District" may not, by adhering to similar principles, occupy as distinguished a position in reference to agriculture in Canada, as do those who have imparted such a world-wide celebrity to the district of East Lothian in Scotland.

CHAPTER XII.

Religious aspects—First Protestant Church in Canada—The Lutheran Church, the Rev H Hayunga—Church of England, Rev. Mr Lindsay—Presbyterian Church, Rev Mr Broeffle—The Free Church—Methodist Church, Rev Mr. Pope—Roman Catholic Church—Religious Statistics—Clergy Reserves.

We have already spoken in no measured terms of commendation of the social condition of our farmers, and in fulfilling our self-imposed task, we feel that, having put our hand to the plough, we must not turn back—we must not shrink from the consideration, how they may be truthfully described in their religious aspects. An all-wise Providence has peopled this land with Christians of every name and denomination, and it is our especial blessing that each of us may worship our Heavenly Father according to the dictates of our conscience, "none daring to make us afraid." However much we may deplore the divisions and dissensions that exist among Christian people, we should never forget that these dissensions may be the very means, in the hands of the Almighty, of hastening the time, when all shall know Him from the least even to the greatest. So far from being discouraged by these divisions, it becomes the particular duty of every Christian, by every means in his power, to advance the Redeemer's kingdom; to assist in the erection of churches in the land, in providing adequate remuneration for faithful ministers of the gospel, and in training up the rising generation in the fear of the Lord. If the bright predicted future of Canada is ever to be realized, we must rely upon something more than the equipment of our fleets, and the discipline of our armies, we must look to something more than the indomitable perseverance of our hardy sons of toil—we must rest our hopes of future greatness upon our religious, and educational institutions. Do we already consider ourselves *a great people?* Let us rear a monument to our greatness, as great, and more durable than the Pyramids of Egypt, by establishing these institutions upon a firm foundation. While the world standeth let our land be known as a land filled with faithful ministers, and with a church-going and God-fearing people.

Our farmers, as a class, may themselves be exemplary in the outward observance of religious duties, but, we fear, that while solicitous for the worldly advancement of their sons, in too many cases they fail to impress upon their minds the important truth, that the great aim of life should be to prepare for eternity. A natural, but very mistaken desire on the part of parents, to remove every restraint, and gratify every wish of their children, frequently results in entirely overlooking their higher interests. Receiving a more liberal education than his father, the son soon discovers, that in worldly matters, he is the wiser man of the two, and at a very early age he begins to think and act for himself; and the time of life when the youthful mind is most susceptible of good impressions, finds him his own master, free to respect or discard religion from his thoughts, as he thinks fit. The result of this is a manifest carelessness in the rising generation, with regard to religion; and while parents are members of churches, their children are too often roving about from one church to another, criticizing all, and joining themselves to none. We fear that were we to ask the youth of Canada, to tell us what they considered to be *the one thing needful,* we should have to doubt their sincerity, if they did not express themselves in *dollars and cents.*

In 1852 there were 1673, or one-eighth part of the population of the county of Dundas, between the ages of 15 and 20. " This is undoubtedly the period of life when the character is formed—

the season when the passions budding and hastening to ripeness, acquire new vigor, become impatient of restraint, and eager for gratification. Then the young man looks around for companions and friends—then the calling in life is chosen—the principles of action adopted, habits acquired, and those connections in business and society formed which usually decide the character and fix the condition, both for this, and the future worlds." It would be well, alike for parents and children, and a great blessing to our country, if greater care was manifested to instil sound religious principles into the minds of our youth, to inspire them with a love and reverence for true religion, and the ordinances of the church to which they profess to belong, and to establish them in their faith. We might then hope that they would not forsake the old paths, or be carried about with every wind of doctrine.

With these general reflections, we shall now look more particularly at the different denominations of religious profession that exist in the county of Dundas, and endeavor to give a succinct and reliable history of the introduction and progress of each.

According to the census of 1861, there are eighteen different denominations of Christians residing in Dundas county, represented by the following numbers respectively:—

	Williamsburgh	Matilda	Winchester	Mountain	Total
Wesleyan Methodists	931	1787	646	1103	4467
Roman Catholics	597	843	1001	504	2845
Episcopal Methodists	420	930	1034	453	2837
Church of England	916	996	139	515	2566
Church of Scotland	718	623	284	519	2144
Lutherans	1353	155	181	21	1711
Free Church	423	100	626	389	1538
Baptists	98	16	217	128	459
Universalists	5	11	....	20	36
United Presbyterians	7	4	....	12	23
New Connection Methodists	15	....	....	....	15
Millerites	14	....	....	....	14
Church of God	9	....	....	....	9
Second Adventists	....	9	....	....	9

	Williamsburgh.	Matilda.	Winchester.	Mountain	Total
Congregationalists	6	....	2	....	8
Unitarians	....	3	....	....	3
Mormons	....	....	....	1	1
Quakers	....	1	....	....	1
No Church	22	81	9	18	130
Protestants	....	7	....	....	7
Infidels	1	1	....	....	2
Totals	5529	5473	4139	3683	18824

THE LUTHERAN CHURCH.—In connection with this Church, we shall first state what we believe to be a historical fact, one which cannot fail to be interesting to every Protestant in Canada, and which is not generally known. It is this—that the first Protestant Church that was built in all the Canadas, from the Atlantic to the Pacific, was built in Williamsburgh, in the County of Dundas.

The Lutherans of Williamsburgh, in the year 1789, five years after their settlement here, commenced to build a frame church 60 feet by 40 feet in size, on the centre commons; in fact upon the very site of the edifice occupied at present by the Church of England. The new church may be said to have risen out of the ashes of the old one, for nearly all the timber of the first, being white oak, and sound, was used again in constructing the second, and even the arched window-frames of the old church, indicative of the Dutch style of architecture, are the same that characterize the present building. The winter setting in earlier than usual, the frame was not raised that season, but in March, 1790, it was commenced anew, and the work went on rapidly.

About the same time they sent an invitation to the Rev. Samuel Schwerdfeger, who resided near Albany, to be their pastor. This he accepted the more willingly, as even his sacred office had not shielded him from the consequences of the revolutionary war. While his exhortations tended, perhaps, to confirm the inhabitants of the old Johnston district in their allegiance to their king, he and his family were thrown into a dungeon by the Republicans, and suffered a variety of hardships. He arrived at Williamsburgh in

June, 1790. By him the first Protestant church in Canada was that same year consecrated to the service of Almighty God. Its name was "Zion's Church." In the church books it was called the German Protestant Church. The English called it the Dutch church.

We might here also correct, what appears to be a mis-statement, lately given by Montreal newspapers, to the effect that 21st of December, 1789, was the date when the Jesuits' church in Montreal, was for the first time allowed to be used for Protestant worship in Canada. Mrs. Jacob Coons, now living here, informs us that she was married in that church (now known by the name of the Recollet Church) in the fall of 1783, by the Chaplain to the Forces, six years anterior to the time referred to. She was then 17 years of age, and still retains a very distinct recollection of occurrences about that time. Mrs. Coons states that at the time she was married there was no Protestant church in Canada that she knew of, nor any until the one in Williamsburgh was built, the date of which she has good reason to remember, as her husband was a carpenter, and assisted in building it. It is certain there was none in Montreal, and that the present St. Gabriel Street Presbyterian church, the first Protestant church there, was not commenced until the year 1792. Christ's Church Cathedral in Montreal was commenced in 1805, and was only completed in 1814, so that the church in Williamsburgh was completed two years before any other Protestant church began to be erected.

In the year 1793, the Lutherans petitioned Government for one half of the centre commons, in Williamsburgh, for a glebe for their congregation. They received a "Licence of occupation," from the Surveyor General, which implied the granting of a deed at some future time, but as yet no deeds for such lands had been issued. An attested copy of this licence of occupation, is in the archives of the Lutheran Church in Williamsburgh. They took possession of the land, cleared a part of it, planted an orchard, and built a parsonage house, which was replaced only ten years ago by the present handsome brick parsonage.

A second church was built by the Lutherans in Matilda, in 1792. Mr. Schwerdfeger officiated in both these churches, exclusively in the German language; he died in 1803, having officiated for nearly fourteen years, very acceptably to the people. In 1804 the Rev. Mr. Myers became pastor of these Lutheran churches. He was shortly afterwards sent to Philadelphia for ordination, which he received, and returned to Dundas: but, being inadequately supported, he resigned the charges in 1807 and removed to Lancaster in Pennsylvania.

The next year the Rev. J. G. Weagant received a call from these churches, which he accepted, and for some time preached for them acceptably, residing in the parsonage. He too appears to have been inadequately supported by the people, and yielding to inducements, too tempting for most men to resist, he, in 1811 secretly joined the Church of England, and was re-ordained by Bishop Mountain, in Quebec. Upon his return from Quebec, he pretended still to be a Lutheran Minister, and preached as usual, up to that time, officiating as his predecessors had done, in German exclusively. Suspicions soon however arose that all was not right, for he began to use the English book of common prayer, and occasionally to wear the surplice, or Church of England vestment, practices which gave such offence to some of his former friends, that they declared, they would no longer go to hear a man, who preached to them in *his shirt sleeves*. It was in vain he tried to convince them, that there was really no difference, that it was only substituting English for German. A few however, were persuaded by him to join the Church of England, and he obtained their signatures to a petition, to enable him to receive a salary from Government. The majority still remained faithful to the church of their fathers, but were thrown into a sadly confused state by the defection of their minister.

In 1814, the Lutherans again rallied, and invited the Rev. Mr. Myers, to return to them once more; upon his consenting to do so, they sent two sleighs, in the winter of that year, to Pennsylvania, and brought him and his family to Dundas. When the Lutherans demanded the parsonage and glebe, and the church which their own hands had built, from Mr. Weagant, he bade them defiance, and putting a padlock on the church door, he posted an advertisement, forbidding any of them, even to enter the church, unless they would first acknowledge the thirty nine articles of the Church of England. At length, however, a compromise was effected, by which it was agreed, that the Lutherans, might as a favor occupy the church once in two weeks, but Mr. Weagant, despite all the efforts of the Lutherans to dispossess him, retained possession of the house and glebe. During the next three years, while he was quietly enjoying the benefits attached to his new creed, his former fellow churchman, Myers, had to depend upon the measure of faith of the faithful, and now felt even more keenly than before, disappointment and discouragement arising from the straitened circumstances in which he found himself placed. His situation under these circumstances, calls for our sympathy, and when we recal to mind, that even a Peter, when severely tried, was tempted to deny his Lord and master, we regard it as less the fault, than the misfortune of Myers, that in 1817, only three years after his return, he too conformed to the Church of England. With all our charity, we dare not affirm, that either he or his predecessor, in abandoning their creed, were uninfluenced by a view to the loaves and fishes.

Mr. Myers was thenceforth settled in Matilda, and continued to officiate there as an Episcopalian Minister, till his death, which was hastened in consequence of a severe fall, by which his leg was fractured.

In 1825, the Lutherans were visited for a short time by the Rev. I. L. Senderling, but he did not accept a call, as they were now unable to raise a salary sufficient for his support. In 1826, the Rev. Herman Hayunga was sent to them, and became their pastor. He found but a remnant left of the once united and faithful Lutheran Church, and that in a deplorable condition.

Without a church, disunited among themselves, and distrusting him, lest he too might forsake them, as his two predecessors had done, his situation was far from being an enviable one. Few men indeed under circumstances like these, but would have soon sought out a more inviting field of labor; but, firm to his purpose, of at least establishing in their early faith, those who still retained a lingering love for the church of their fathers, Mr. Hayunga, suffered none of these things to move him. By his unwearied zeal in visiting from house to house, and by his earnest and faithful public ministrations, he soon gained their confidence, so that in a short time, he had the satisfaction of seeing the work of the Lord so prosper in his hands, that a respectable congregation of Lutherans was again gathered together, to worship according to their ancient faith. In one year from the time of his arrival among them, he formed a second congregation, and a Union Church, so called, was built by the Lutherans and Presbyterians conjointly, in the centre of Williamsburgh. This church was consecrated by Mr. Hayunga, in June 1827. To it he contributed largely of his private means; it was called St. Peter's Church, and it remains there a Union Church still.

In 1833, the Church of England obtained a deed from Government, for the land they already held in possession, whereby the Lutherans were for ever excluded from the church, and the church property.

Mr. Conrad Frymire, having generously presented the congregation, with three acres of land, a short distance above the old church, a Lutheran Church was there erected the same year, to which Mr. Hayunga, again largely contributed. He continued his labors in these two congregations till 1837, when impaired in health, he was obliged to resign. To him, under God, the Lutheran Church in Dundas County, owes its continuance, and whatever measure of prosperity it enjoys.

Seldom since the days of the apostles, has the office of the ministry been prosecuted with such generous self denial as by him.

During the eleven years of his unwearied labors, he never was *promised* more than $250 per annum, and seldom received $150, in the mean time ministering to his own necessities from his private means. During the first years of his ministry, he officiated in German and English alternately, and having quietly brought them through the difficult transition state, from one language to another, he latterly restricted himself to the English. He was succeeded by the Rev. Diedrick Sharts, who officiated in both of the Lutheran churches for some time: he demitted his charge a few years ago, and since his time the congregation in Front, have had no stated minister, although Mr. Hayunga has in the interim, given them frequent gratuitous services. St. Peter's is now one of the largest Lutheran congregations in this section of Canada, and fully occupies the time of its present incumbent the Rev. Mr. Bridgeman.

In 1846, the Government in part atoned for the loss of their church and glebe, by granting the Lutherans of Williamsburgh, a sum of $2000, together with $37\frac{1}{2}$ acres of land. They have at present two ministers, two churches, 300 communicants, one parsonage, and about 40 acres of land. Their number in the County in 1851 was 1527 souls, and in 1861, it was 1711. The doctrines, principles, and sentiments of the Lutheran Churches of Dundas, are the same as those of Germany, but the language, and some of their usages and ceremonies, are conformed more to those of the Lutheran Church in the United States.

If we may seem to have dwelt unduly upon the history of this church, it is because we believe it to have been the first Protestant Church in Canada, and moreover, because the history of both the Presbyterian and Episcopalian Churches, is so interwoven with it, as to be inseparable from it. In what we have written, we have but reproduced incontrovertible facts. Having undertaken the task of narrating the history of the County, we had no choice left, but to state the simple truth.

THE CHURCH OF ENGLAND.—The doctrines and practices of the Church of England were introduced into the county, in the manner we have already indicated, in the year 1811, and were promulgated by Mr. Weagant till 1835, when he resigned. His death took place soon after, for his tomb stone in the grave yard reads thus,—"In memory, of the Rev. John G. Weagant, who died Nov. 20, 1835, Æt. 73 years." He was immediately succeeded by the Rev. Gerbrand Beek Lindsay, "an Israelite indeed in whom was no guile." A faithful and earnest ambassador of Christ. Never was minister more beloved by his people than he. Even those who had unwillingly come into the pale of the Church of England, now ceased to regret the change. By his piety, and brotherly love, he adorned the doctrines which he preached, and by an unblameable life and conversation, he exemplified the beauty of holiness. Under his ministrations, the quondam Lutherans became zealous members of the Church of England.

The old church of 1790, associated with so many bygone events, was not ruthlessly demolished, but carefully taken down, and rebuilt under Mr. Lindsay's superintendence; guided by his excellent taste, a very neat and comfortable edifice replaced the original. This, the present church, was consecrated by Bishop Stewart, in 1836. Mr. Lindsay was the first to preach in this Church, exclusively in English. He officiated in Williamsburgh, in Matilda and Edwardsburgh, during eleven years, and may be truly said to have laid the foundation of episcopacy in the hearts of the people. While their original connection with the Church of England, through Mr. Weagant, was rather a matter of expediency, than of deliberate choice, it was only now, under the eloquent and earnest teaching of Mr. Lindsay that they came to love and admire it. To the inexpressible grief of his Congregation, he removed in July 1844, to Cornwall, where he died in October 1845, at the early age of 37, leaving the whole country side to mourn his loss. His name, and his Christian worth will survive, long after those who knew him, themselves have disappeared.

The Rev. Edward Boswell, D. C. L., the present incumbent, was Mr. Lindsay's successor in Dundas County, and that same year (1844) Williamsburgh was created a Rectory, and the support of the incumbent was thereby secured, for his life time at least. In consequence of the recent secularization of the clergy reserves, the salaries attached to the Rectories, will cease with the present Rectors, and in course of time their congregations will be placed, in so far as external aid is concerned, upon a par with others around them; so that upon the removal of the present incumbent, the Episcopalians of Williamsburgh, who have hitherto been members of a state endowed church, will, in common with other Protestants, virtually become members of a voluntary church.

In 1857, Dr. Boswell was instrumental in erecting a church in Morrisburgh, upon a conspicuous site, presented for this purpose, by James Hodges, Esquire, superintendent of the Victoria Bridge at Montreal. This church is built of stone, in the early English style, and was planned by Mr. Rubridge. Externally it presents an antiquated appearance, but internally, its correct proportions, stained glass lancet windows, high open roof, and receding chancel, are very pleasing and appropriate. It is seated for about 250, and cost $5,000. It was opened for worship in 1857; by the Venerable Archdeacon Bethune of Cobourg, and is called "St. James' Church."

The Episcopalians of Dundas have at present, three ministers, four churches, one parsonage, and about one hundred acres of land. The census of 1851, gave this church in Dundas 2743 adherents, the same authority places the number in 1861 at 2566.

THE PRESBYTERIAN CHURCH.—In 1795, the Presbyterians being less numerous than the Lutherans, had as yet built no church, but simultaneously with these, they had received the west half of the centre commons in Williamsburgh, in the first, second, and third concessions, amounting to about 70 acres of land. That year, they secured the services of the Rev. John Ludewig Broeffle, to be their minister, and living on terms of good fellowship with the Lutherans, were permitted by them, to occupy their pulpits alternately. The first Presbyterians in Dundas, were all U. E. Loyalists, chiefly Germans, and Mr. Broeffle officiated to them in the German language exclusively. Preaching in Matilda, Williamsburgh and Osnabruck, he resided in Williamsburgh, and for his stipend, he had to depend upon the liberality of his people, who seemed to entertain very primitive ideas indeed, in regard to the support of their minister, and we suspect have bequeathed them, as a legacy to their descendants. He was esteemed a kind and faithful minister of the Gospel, and was universally beloved, yet, strange to say, his actual stipend never exceeded $100 per annum, and he was destitute of private means. We are at a loss to reconcile the expressed sentiments of his attached flock, with the extreme niggardliness of their contributions for his support. The following original document, beautifully penned, was recently discovered, amongst other old papers in possession of one of his elders.

To all to whom these presents may come—

"We hereby certify, that the Rev. John Ludewig Broeffle, minister of the Presbyterian Congregation, has ministered unto us for these ten years past, and that he has conducted himself, in that charge, and every other trust, as a good and faithful pastor, in testimony whereof, we the elders of the Congregations of Williamsburgh, and Osnabruck in the Province of Upper Canada, have subscribed our names, the 22nd January 1805."

At the advanced age of 76, he walked from Mariatown to Osnabruck, (a distance of 15 miles) to preach there, but from the effects of this over exertion, he never recovered. He died in Williamsburgh, in 1815, having labored unremittingly, and endured all manner of privations and hardships, during 20 years. In 1823, the Rev. Mr. Johnston, who resided in Osnabruck, preached in private houses in Mariatown, and elsewhere in Dundas, for three or four years. He was followed in the year 1828, by the

Rev. Robert Lyle, who, also residing in Osnabruck, officiated besides, in Williamsburgh, where he succeeded in building a Presbyterian Church, not however without incurring a considerable debt in its construction, and which the Presbyterians of that time, made no successful effort to liquidate.

After using this Church in an unfinished state for ten years, it was sold for the benefit of creditors, and fell into the hands of Mr. Mattice of Cornwall. It was occupied by him as a store for the sale of merchandize during some years, and when the works commenced upon the canals, in 1844, he sold it to the Roman Catholics, by whom it has ever since been used as a chapel.

In September 1840, Mr. Lyle, who was a Minister of the Irish Synod of Ulster, was received into the Presbyterian Church in Canada, in connection with the established Church of Scotland. Having however unfortunately incurred the censure of the Church Courts the following year, he was deposed from the ministry. He was followed in 1841, by the Rev. John Dickey, who was also connected with the Church of Scotland, and who received yearly from the Clergy Reserves fund, a considerable salary in addition to the contributions of his flock. He was truly an apostolic man, much and deservedly esteemed. He labored in the Union Church in Williamsburgh, and also in Winchester, and built up a large congregation.

He died in 1851, and was succeeded by the Rev. Thomas Scott, during whose incumbency, a grant of $600 was given by the Clergy Reserve Commissioners, for the purpose of building a manse. The congregation accordingly purchased thirteen acres of eligible land, and erected a comfortable brick manse. Mr. Scott resigned this charge in 1858, removing to the centre of Matilda, where he succeeded in assembling a respectable congregation, and where a comfortable frame church was speedily erected. He was succeeded in Williamsburgh by the Rev. John Davidson, the first Scotchman who had statedly officiated in the county.

St. Peter's Church, which the Lutherans and Presbyterians,

have for thirty-three years, jointly and harmoniously occupied as a Union Church, having by the lapse of time, fallen into disrepair, and in the mean time, both of these bodies having steadily increased in numbers, it has been resolved, amicably to dissolve the connection, and each has in contemplation the erection of a separate church.

There is another branch of Presbyterians in the County of Dundas styled " the Presbyterian Church of Canada," this church, commonly known as the " FREE CHURCH," being intimately connected with these last, may be here noticed, although not in strict chronological order.

About the year 1847, the Rev. Charles Quin, a Free Church minister residing in Cornwall, first visited Winchester, and other parts of the county, and succeeded in organizing several congregations in connection with that body, in localities, otherwise unprovided with Gospel Ordinances. Through his instrumentality, two churches were erected, one in the township of Winchester, and another in the Colquhoun settlement, in Williamsburgh. In 1856 he was formally inducted to the pastoral charge of Winchester, at this time having a charge in Osnabruck, but after a few months, he resigned both, and became Free Church Minister of Kemptville. He was followed, in Winchester, by several missionaries and licentiates, under the care of the Presbytery of Montreal, but up to this time no permanent minister has been settled among them.

In 1859, the Rev. Mr. Thom, a graduate of Knox's College, Toronto, was inducted to the pastoral charge of Williamsburgh, preaching in Morrisburgh, in the Colquhoun settlement, and in the sixth concession each sabbath. He resides in Williamsburgh, " in his own hired house."

As an earnest of our desire to see these two bodies of Presbyterians reunited, we herein unite their statistics.

The Kirk, and the Free Presbyterians of Dundas, have together, three ministers, four churches, six stations without churches, one manse and glebe, and about three hundred communicants. In 1851, the Kirk of Scotland Presbyterians in Dundas numbered 2926. The Free Church, 46, together 2962. In 1861 their numbers respectively were, 2144, and 1538, in all 3682. Next to Methodism, the Presbyterian element seems to predominate, the increase in the last ten years has been 25 per cent., shewing a steady growth.

The Free Church in Upper and Lower Canada, had in 1859, 183 churches, and 143 ministers. The Kirk of Scotland, at the same time, 135 churches, and 107 ministers. The United Presbyterians, 119 churches, and 66 ministers.

The United Presbyterian, and Free Churches, have agreed upon a basis of union, and are expected to consummate the union at the next annual meeting of their respective Synods, to be held in Montreal on the 6th of June next, when these churches, united, will assume the name of the "Canada Presbyterian Church." *Esto perpetua.*

THE METHODIST CHURCH.—1790, is generally believed to be the year in which the Methodist missionary, William Losee, first visited the County of Dundas. He was sent here by the conference of New York, to visit this hitherto unexplored northern region During the two next succeeding years, his must indeed have been like angels visits, few and far between, for we learn that his circuit extended from Niagara to Cornwall, embracing both sides of the river, and receding from it, just as far as he could "*win.*" Losee, is represented to have possessed the spirit of a Boanerges, in an eminent degree. "He was one who would not confer long with flesh and blood, or wait for human authorization and approval in any enterprize to which he believed God had called him. "Plain and familiar, though very often abrupt in his style, he pourtrayed the consequences of an ungodly life, and so vehemently urged the necessity of repentance, that many were awakened to a sense of their sinfulness, and induced to seek protection in the mercy of God."

In 1792, we find him associated with the Rev. Darius Dunham, "a man of good talents as a preacher, plain of speech, honest and very blunt, a "character" no doubt, he was familiarly known by the soubriquet of *scolding Dunham.*" Between him and Losee, the field of labor was divided into the Cataraqui, and Oswegotchie circuits; Losee taking the latter, which embraced Dundas County, and Dunham the former. It does not appear that Losee was ever ordained, and consequently he could neither administer baptism, nor the Lord's Supper; for these purposes, Dunham is said to have left his own circuit, and visited this county occasionally. After the year 1792, we find no mention of Losee at all, which we regret, as we would gladly have followed up his career to his life's end. The presumption is, that he never attained to the status of a minister. Considering that he was held in estimation by his brethren, and that his name is still familiar as a household word with Methodists, we are surprized, that no sketch of his life has been preserved. It may be said of him, " that no man knoweth of his sepulchre unto this day," at least we have not been able to trace out his carreer. We incline to the opinions expressed regarding his status, from what appears of his life in the History of Methodism by A. G. Meacham. V.D.M.

In the year 1797, the first Methodist Church in Dundas was built upon Point Iroquois in Matilda. A more beautiful site could not have been chosen. The point upon which it stood was the highest and most picturesque headland upon the St. Lawrence, between Brockville and Montreal, and is said to have been a favorite spot with the Indians, when holding their councils of war in days of yore. It commanded a view of the river, above and below for many miles. Towards the north, the landscape then extended, in an unbroken plain of dense and gloomy forest to the horizon. The southern shore of the St. Lawrence was clothed with foliage of even a darker hue, to the water's edge, and melting away in the distance, was bounded by the Green Mountains of Vermont, dimly aising their lofty heads to the skies. On either side, the sparkling river, rolled its deep flood, circling around its numerous islands, clothed with stately trees, reflecting their dark shadows on its bosom. The church stood amid an umbrageous grove, at a place where the spacious highway, described its curve around the point. The first edifice was a frame building of very humble pretension, but in 1830, this was replaced by a large and substantial stone church. This might have been handed down to many generations, but the completion of the canals in 1847, and the facilities for milling and manufactures, thereby created, clearly indicated the lower entrance of the canal, as the site of the future capital of Matilda. A considerable village had already sprung up there, and it was deemed expedient to erect a church, at that place. The one upon Point Iroquois, besides being distant a mile from the village, became difficult of access, the site upon which it stood, together with some 400 acres of land adjoining, being isolated by the canal. This church was taken down, and the handsome stone church which, with its glittering spire, now adorns the village of Iroquois was built instead. The materials of the old building were sold for a price " and thus " remarked a worthy methodist, who seemed to regard the transaction as little less than sacrilege, " were Zion's stones, converted into a house of merchandize."

After the building of their first church, the Methodists of Dundas were successively visited by Dunham, Samuel Coate, Thomas Madden, William Case, and Joseph Sawyer. The last named, arrived in the county about the year 1805, and was the first resident minister. He lived many years in Matilda, and was much respected.

During the American war of 1812–14, most of the American Methodist Missionaries were withdrawn from Canada, and for some years after, the Methodists were regarded by the provincial authorities with a jealous eye. They were wholly supplied with itinerant, and ever-changing American missionaries, and it was not unnatural to suppose, that a tendency to democratic institutions, might through their agency, be instilled into the minds of the people, totally subversive of that loyalty which was due by British subjects to the British Crown. During this reign of terror in the history of Methodism, their ministers were not even recognized by law; nor was it until the year 1830, that the laws of Canada empowered them to celebrate matrimony, while all marriages contracted before any magistrate previous to 1793, and for some years after that, were declared to be valid. Shortly after the war, the Rev. Joseph Sawyer, then residing in Matilda, was put upon his trial for marrying a couple; he was found guilty of a high misdemeanor, and was sentenced to fourteen years banishment. He and his family were accordingly placed in a canoe and ferried across *to the United States*. Many of his neighbors with tears in their eyes, escorted him to the water's edge, to bid him farewell. This literal fulfilling of the law, was generally considered as needlessly severe, and as amounting to little short of persecution. The Government itself relented. After three months' absence, he was pardoned, when he again came to Matilda, and remained there some years. Subsequently he returned to the States, where he died not long since.

In 1818, a deputation from the British conference, consisting of the Rev. William Pope, his brother, and some others, visited Canada. The Popes took up their head quarters in Matilda, where they remained nearly two years. Their ostensible purpose was to give the Methodists of Canada, an organization, similar, and to some extent affiliated to the British Conference. When the object of their mission became apparent, the discord and excitement which followed were indescribable. The cause of Methodism in Canada, seemed to be on the eve of annihilation. The American missionaries considered their legitimate rights infringed upon, and sternly refused subjection to the new missionaries, or those who had sent them. The minority remained in connection with the New York Conference until 1828, when they formally separated from them, assuming the designation of the

"Methodist Episcopal Church in Canada," and are now known as Episcopal Methodists. "So complete" says their historian, "was the separation, that the Bishop of the United States who presided in the conference previous to the passing of that resolution, arose and declared that they must elect another president before they could proceed to further business." The number of those who separated, was fifty ministers.

In the meantime, the British ministers and missionaries firmly held their ground. So far as we have learned, they were esteemed good, pious, prudent men, whilst their *loyalty* was unquestionable, and inclined the government to regard them more favorably. Deeply imbued with a knowledge of human nature, they proved themselves equal to the task they had undertaken. They succeeded in gaining the confidence of a large portion of the Methodists in Canada, who very soon after formed themselves into a distinct conference, styled "the Wesleyan Methodist Church in Canada." Previous to this organization which took place about the year 1820, the Methodists of Canada numbered 6,000 communicants, with 36 ministers. Since that time their numbers have increased rapidly in Upper Canada, and perhaps nowhere more rapidly than in the county of Dundas. According to the census of 1851, there were in Upper Canada, of Wesleyan Methodists, 96,640, of Episcopal Methodists 43,884, and of other Methodists, 67,132, in all 207,656, within a fraction of one-fourth part of the entire population. In 1851, there were in Dundas County, of Wesleyans 3056, and of Episcopals 1007, in all 4063. By the census of 1861, their numbers are respectively, Wesleyans, 4467, Episcopal, 2837; New Connection, 15; together, 7319, shewing an increase in ten years of nearly 80 per cent. The Methodists of Dundas have nine ministers, ten churches, thirty preaching stations without churches, and one parsonage.

THE ROMAN CATHOLIC CHURCH.—The history of this church in Dundas, commences at a very recent period. Previous to 1844, there were very few Catholics in the county. In that year, the commencement of the Provincial canals, induced a large influx of Irish and German laborers, professing the Roman Catholic faith, and it was deemed desirable to provide for these the means of religious instruction. Unable to build a church of their own, they made an offer to Mr. Mattice, for the abandoned Presbyterian Church, near Mariatown, built as already said in the year 1831, but at that time used as a store. Having agreed to liquidate the debt incurred by the Presbyterians in its erection, it was handed over to them, and being temporarily fitted up as a chapel, it served the purpose of the time very well. Very few of those for whose use it was obtained remained in Williamsburgh or Matilda after the completion of the canals. The greater number of them, from the fruits of their savings on these works, were enabled to purchase farms in Winchester and Mountain, where their numbers have been greatly increased by emigrants from Ireland, and elsewhere. Since that time they have built a commodious and comfortable stone church in Winchester. They have also repaired the old church for future occupation. Their first settled clergyman was the Rev. Mr. Coyle, who left in 1856, and was succeeded by the present incumbent, the Rev. Mr. Mead. The Catholics of Dundas have one clergyman, and four churches; in 1851 they numbered 2055, and in 1861, they had increased to 2845.

RELIGIOUS STATISTICS.—There are nine Methodist; three Episcopal; three Presbyterian; two Lutheran, and one Roman Catholic, ministers in the County of Dundas,—in all eighteen, or, one minister to 1046 inhabitants. In the City of London, there is, of all denominations, but one minister to 10,000 inhabitants. In proportion to population, we have nearly ten times as many in Dundas. There are twenty-four churches, or, one for every 784 inhabitants, young and old.

The sum of $7200 is annually subscribed for the support of ministers. One is paid altogether from the Clergy Reserves commutation fund. One officiates gratuitously; the average salary of the remaining sixteen is thus $450 per annum; paid by the people. The stipend of two of the Church of England, and two of the Church of Scotland ministers, (included in the 16) is supplemented by sums varying from $200, to $450 each.

The amount of voluntary contributions for religious purposes, in the County, for 1859, was as follows:

Salaries of sixteen ministers at $450 each	$7200
For missionary purposes by Methodists	400
" " " " Presbyterians	400
" " " " Episcopalians	87
" " " " Lutherans	100
Total contributed for religious purposes	$8187

The number of families was 3000, the average annual amount paid by each, $2.73. During the same year each family paid on an average $106.76 for *store goods*, consisting of tea, sugar, dress, tobacco, and WHISKEY. This is a large amount compared with what is spent for religious purposes; were each family to give $3.50 per annum for these;—each minister would receive $600 per annum, and there would be $900 a year to spare for missions.

We do injustice to ourselves, inflict a cruel wrong upon our ministers, and bring discredit upon our Christian profession, by recognising the sum of $450 as adequate remuneration to a minister of the Gospel.

In too many cases that pittance, comes not to the minister until long over-due, and then, in dribblets, and in " plunder."* It admits of a doubt, whether the actual *cash value paid* to each of these sixteen ministers, by their people, exceeds $400 per annum. To say nothing of the expense of keeping a horse, the year round, which every country minister must do, we know of no kind of calculation by which it can be made to appear, that a man can support a family —occupy a respectable position in society—furnish his mind with sound doctrines and scholarly attainments—clothe his body with

---

* A Canadian-ism signifying barter, or, as here, *in kind*.

becoming raiment—and devote all his time and energies to the work of the ministry—upon $400! a year. Let any Canadian farmer calculate correctly what is spent and consumed in his own family, and he will be puzzled to know how his minister manages to keep soul and body together.

It is quite certain that even should we condescend to $100 salaries, we shall always be able to get lots of $100 ministers. But, we have little faith in cheap servants, still less in cheap schoolmasters, and upon the same principle we devoutly pray.—From cheap ministers, *Good Lord deliver us*.

CLERGY RESERVES.—When Canada became a British Province, it was expressly stipulated that its inhabitants, who were then chiefly French, and of the Roman Catholic faith, should be secured in the free exercise of their religion, and in undisturbed possession of all their church property and endowments. At the same time, it was deemed to be only a simple act of justice to those who might be expected subsequently to people the Province, that similar provision should be made "for the maintenance of a Protestant clergy." Accordingly, the Imperial act of 1791, conferring a British constitution upon Canada, also provided, that one seventh part of all crown-lands in Canada should be set apart, as a source from which this might be done. It was some time before the revenue arising from the sale of these lands amounted to any considerable sum, and for many years it was monopolized by the Church of England. But as the country gradually became settled, the sums realized from the sale of Clergy Reserve lands, as they were called, swelled to a large amount. The Scotch Church, having in the meantime greatly increased in numbers, made application for a share of the "Reserves Fund." After years of remonstrance, and harassing delays, their right was recognized, and they too became participators in that fund. Other bodies sprung up in rapid succession, and each claimed an equal right, as *Protestants* to a share of the spoil. It soon became apparent that no system of distribution could be devised which would satisfy all parties. The ill-fated Reserves became a bone of contention, by which the most unhappy and unchristian dissensions were stirred up in the minds of the population, of British origin, all over the Province. The manner of their distribution came to be used as a hobby-horse, on which political aspirants might ride into Parliament, and when there, was used as political poker, to stir up strife and animosity. The public mind, becoming exasperated, demanded their secularization. The Government of Canada, seeing no alternative but a rebellion, yielded to the popular clamor. In 1853 they applied to the British Government for power to "deal" with the Reserves; this was granted, and in 1854, they were transferred from the church, to the state, and the proceeds arising from their sale, handed over to the various municipalities in Upper and Lower Canada. It was however stipulated in the Imperial Act of 1853, that the rights of existing ministers, should in no wise be infringed upon, and the first act of the Canadian Legislature was to make provision for those ministers to whom the faith of the crown had been pledged, by securing to them for life, the salaries which they were then receiving from that source. An Act was passed authorizing the Government to commute with these parties, by paying to each minister such a sum, as would, at 6 per cent, secure him for life in the enjoyment of his salary. By so doing, every semblance of connection between church and state was, forever, abolished in Canada. The ministers of the Church of England and of Scotland, agreed to yield up to their respective churches the whole amount of monies severally received by them, with the understanding, that individually, they should receive their salaries as before. In the case of the Scotch Church, the ministers agreed to be content with even a smaller sum than they might have claimed, in order that new ministers entering their church might also share this allowance with them. By this act of the clergy, the whole of the commutation money received from Government, was funded for the permanent benefit of these churches.

DISTRIBUTION.

The Church of England received in Upper and Lower Canada...	£275,851	5	2
The Church of Scotland.............................	127,448	5	0
The late United Synod of the Presbyterian Church.....	2,240	11	0
The Roman Catholic Clergy of Upper Canada.........	20,932	15	0
The Wesleyan Methodists in Upper Canada...........	9,768	11	0
Total paid to Protestant Churches. U. and L. Canada, Cy.	£436,241	7	2*

The payments were made in Provinicial Debentures, bearing interest at 6 per cent. These were sold, and the proceeds invested in other securities, yielding from 8 to 10 per cent. interest, which, virtually, increased very considerably the capital amounts at the disposal of the several churches.

At the time that the Reserves were secularized, to so large an amount had the fund accumulated, that after paying the sums above-mentioned, there still remained in the hands of Government a large overplus. The amount distributed amongst the municipalities of Upper Canada in 1858 was $341,120$\frac{44}{100}$. Since 1854, the amount thus distributed cannot be much short of one million and a half of Dollars! On the 1st of January 1860, there still remained of Clergy Reserve Lands unsold in Upper Canada 261,497 acres; in Lower Canada 463,315 acres: in all 724,812 acres.

---

* Parliamentary Returns.

CHAPTER XIII.

Constitutional changes—First Canadian Parliament—Dundas returns two members—Changes at the Union—Franchise extended—Voter's Qualification, Oath, Registration—Member's qualification and remuneration—Council rendered elective—Representatives of Dundas—Political aspect—Biographical sketches—Lying Campbell,&c.—Col. Crysler—Peter Shaver—George Crawford—Reflections.

In endeavoring to sketch the history of Canada, and of Dundas, the writer has, for obvious reasons, refrained from advancing strictures upon governments, nor has he regarded any of the changes which have taken place in our institutions and laws, in the light of political partizanship. He approaches this part of the subject in the same spirit, desiring to deal with it, in a strictly impartial manner. The history of the county would manifestly be incomplete, without some reference to its political antecedents, and as all are more or less affected by the enactments of our legislature, the very brief remarks that follow concerning the past representatives of "Dundas," will, he trusts, not be altogether without interest.

During the first three years of its existence as a British Province, the government of Canada was purely military. Subsequent to that period, the French laws continued to be acknowledged in matters of civil controversy, and the laws of England were applied to all criminal cases, until the year 1774, when, by the Imperial Act, known as the "Quebec Act," his Majesty was authorized to appoint a Council, to consist of not more than twenty-three, nor less than seventeen persons, which council, with the consent of the Governor, were to have power to make laws for the good government of the Province. This form of government continued until 1791, when the province of Quebec was divided into Upper and Lower Canada, with separate governors for each. By the Imperial Act of that year commonly called the "Constitutional Act," the power was conferred upon the Governor of Lower Canada, and the Lieutenant-Governor of Upper Canada, to call together respectively a Legislative Council and a Legislative Assembly, to make laws for the peace, welfare, and good government thereof. The Legislative Council was to consist of a sufficient number of discreet and proper persons, to be named by the governor, being not fewer than seven for the Province of Upper Canada, and not fewer than fifteen for the Province of Lower Canada. Each party so appointed was to become a member of the Legislative Council, and to hold his seat therein for the term of his life. It was also provided by the said Act, that the Legislative Assembly of Upper Canada should consist of not less than sixteen members, and that of Lower Canada of not less than fifty members, to be elected respectively by the votes of the inhabitants. It thus became necessary to divide the Provinces into counties, and to specify by whom the members were to be elected. As already mentioned, Governor Simcoe, in 1792, issued a proclamation, dividing Upper Canada into counties. The representatives of the said counties were to be elected "by the majority of votes of such persons as were British subjects of the full age of twenty-one years, and possessed of lands or tenements within the county, in freehold of the yearly value of *forty shillings* sterling, or upwards.

The first session of the first parliament of Upper Canada met at Niagara, on the 17th of Sept. 1792; the second session also met there; the third, fourth, and fifth sessions met at Newark, the Governor taking up his abode in a small farm-house half a mile from the village. The second Parliament met at York (*Toronto*) on the 1st of June, 1796, and with the exception of a short session of seventeen days, held at Newark in 1798, York continued to be the seat of government, and the capital of Upper Canada, until the union of the provinces in 1840.

The first act of the Legislature of Upper Canada appointed that the common law of England should be acknowledged as the rule in all matters of controversy. The second act established trial by jury. The seventh regulated the tolls to be taken in mills. The seventh of the second session in 1793 was entituled "An Act to prevent the *further introduction of slaves*, and to limit the term of contract for servitude, within this Province." The eleventh of the same session was "An Act to encourage the destroying of wolves and bears, in different parts of the Province."

Dundas county continued to be represented by one member in the Assembly, until the year 1828, when, having largely increased in population, the principle of representation according to population, now so much a matter of controversy between Upper and Lower Canada, was applied to Dundas, which thereafter returned two members until the union, since then, in virtue of the Imperial Act which stipulated that Upper and Lower Canada should be equally represented in the Legislature of the united provinces, but one member has been returned from Dundas.

From the time of the Union until 1853, Canada East and Canada West continued to be represented by 84 members of Assembly, viz., 42 from each, and the voter's qualification remained at the old *sterling* forty shilling freehold. In 1853 the representation was enlarged to meet the requirements of the rapidly increasing population of the province. 46 new representatives were added, making the number as now 65 from each section of the province. This involved numerous alterations in the limits of counties. Some were divided into two or three Ridings, each to return a Representative. Portions of others were detached for the same purpose, and, in a few cases, new counties were created. Dundas remained unchanged, and the only alteration in the united counties was, that the town and township of Cornwall were separated from Stormont into a separate constituency, thus giving the three counties four members instead of three as formerly. In that year also, the elective franchise was extended, so as to include owners, and *tenants or occupiers* of real property. That act has since been amended by 22 Vic. ch. 82, the following extracts from which define the franchise, and the system of registration now in force.

"Every male person entered on the then last revised assessment roll in any city or town, as the owner, tenant, or occupier of real property therein, of the assessed value of $300 or upwards, or of the assessed yearly value of $30 or upwards—or, who is assessed in any township as the owner of any real property within such city or town of the assessed value of $200, or of the yearly value of $20 or upwards shall be entitled to vote at any election of a member to represent such city or town in the Legislative Council or the Legislative Assembly.

For counties, townships or villages, not being within the limits of any city every male person entered on the then last revised assessment roll, as the owner, tenant or occupier, of real property of the assessed value of $200 or upwards, or of the yearly assessed value of $20 or upwards, shall in like manner be entitled to vote for members of the Legislative Council or Assembly.

The clerk of each municipality in Upper Canada shall, after the final revision of the assessment rolls, forthwith make a correct alphabetical list of all persons entitled to vote at an election of a member of either House, within such municipality, together with the number of the lot, or other description of the real property, in respect of which each of them is so qualified, and the clerk shall certify by oath or affirmation, before the Judge of the County Court, or before any two justices of the peace, to the correctness of the list, so by him made out, and shall deliver over, on or before the first day of October in each year, a certified copy of the same, to the clerk of the peace of the county or union of counties, within which such municipality shall lie; and no person shall be admitted to vote at any such election, unless his name shall appear upon the list then last made out and certified; and no question of qualification shall be received at any such election, except to ascertain whether the party tendering his vote is the same party intended to be designated in the alphabetical list aforesaid.

The following oath and no other, may be administered by the deputy returning officer, to any person offering to vote, if required by the candidate or his agent, or by the deputy returning officer himself.

You swear (or solemnly affirm) that you are......(*naming the voter*) whose name is entered on the list now shown to you. That you are of the full age of twenty years—that you have not before voted at this election, either at this or any other polling place, and that you have not received any thing, nor has anything been promised to you, either directly or indirectly, in order to induce you to vote at this election. So help you God."

By this arrangement of registration, no one whose name does not appear upon the list can attempt to vote, without personating, and assuming to vote in the name of some other person whose name is therein recorded, and the penalty for so doing is a fine of $200, imprisonment for six months, or both, at the discretion of the court before whom he shall be convicted.

Before any person can be elected a member of the Legislative Assembly, it is requisite that he be possessed of real estate within the Province to the value of £500 currency, free of all incumbrances. The term of a session of Parliament is limited to four years, at the expiration of which the members must be re-elected, or be replaced by others. It most frequently happens, however, that the Parliament is dissolved before the period of limitation arrives. The remuneration to members of both houses, is at the rate of six dollars per day, if the session does not extend over thirty days; if it extends beyond that time, they receive severally a sessional allowance of $600, and no more: they are also allowed travelling expenses, at the rate of ten cents per mile, for the distance from their residence to the seat of government, to be computed going and returning.

By the Act of Victoria 19, ch. 140, in 1856, the Legislative Council was rendered elective, and to this end the Province was divided into forty-eight electoral divisions,—twenty-four in Upper Canada, and twenty-four in Lower Canada, each to send a member to the Upper House. Not more than twelve members were to be elected under this act in any given year, and the elections to recur periodically every second year until the whole number were elected, the order in which the several electoral divisions were to return a member being determined by lot. The qualification for a member being £2000 freehold real estate within the division, and the term of office eight years.

The County of Dundas lies in the St. Lawrence electoral division, which comprises the town of Brockville, and the township of Elizabethtown, the South Riding of Grenville, the North Riding of Leeds and Grenville, and the County of Dundas. George Crawford, Esq., of Brockville, was the first Honorable member elected in the St. Lawrence electoral division. He was returned in 1858, by a majority of 58 votes of the whole division. His majority in Dundas was 151. Mountain gave him 158 majority, Winchester 83, Williamsburgh 75. Matilda showed a majority in favor of his opponent, Dr. Brouse, of 115.

It may be interesting to preserve the names of those who have from the first, and at different times, received the honor of election to the Legislature, at the hands of the electors of Dundas. If not now, at some future time perhaps, the information might be sought for and less readily found. It will show that when no great National questions agitate the minds of a community, personal feelings and predilections have more to do with their choice of representatives, than either political convictions or allegiance to party. Sometimes local considerations may exercise an influence in this matter greater than their real importance merit; still it is better that constituencies should send to Parliament men acquainted with their local wants, and in whose uprightness and good sense they can confide, than men who are mere politicians, however brilliant their talents may be. The following list of our representatives we believe to be correct, and in order:—

REPRESENTATIVES OF DUNDAS.

PARLIAMENT.	NAMES.	WHEN RETURNED	SERVED IN ALL.	RESIDENCE.
First	Alexander Campbell	1792	5yrs	Montreal.
Second	Colonel Fraser	1797	3 "	Matilda.
Third	Captain Weager	1800	4 "	Williamsburgh
Fourth	Major Henry Merkley	1804	4 "	"
Fifth	Colonel John Crysler	1808	16 "	"
Sixth	" " "	"	"	"
Seventh	" " "	"	"	"
Eighth	" " "	"	"	"
Ninth	Peter Shaver	1824	17 "	Matilda.
Tenth	Peter Shaver and George Brouse	1828	2 "	" "
Eleventh	Peter Shaver and John Cook	1830	11 "	" Williamsburgh
Twelfth	Peter Shaver and John Cook	1834	....	Matilda. Williamsburgh
Thirteenth	Peter Shaver and John Cook	1836	....	Matilda. Williamsburgh
Fourteenth	John Cook	1841	15 "	"
Fifteenth	George McDonell	1845	3 "	Cornwall.
Sixteenth	John Pliny Crysler, Con.	1848	7 "	Williamsburgh
Seventeenth	Jesse W. Rose, Lib.	1852	2 "	"
Eighteenth	John Pliny Crysler, Con.	1854	"	"
Nineteenth	James William Cook, Lib.	1857	4 "	"

The springs, whence flow the devious streams of political popularity are unknown to us; judging from past results, however, we might almost infer, that like ocean tides, political affairs were controlled by some mysterious lunar influence; for with amazing regularity, the last five elections have each reversed the preceding one in Dundas. Crysler *ousted* Rose by a respectable majority, while Cook left Crysler minus 350 ! The liberal party exultingly claimed that they had " redeemed " the county; the conservatives contended no less stoutly that they were "sold." On the occurrence of elections alone, do politics interfere with the harmony and friendly feeling of the inhabitants. At these times, however, there is a visible line of demarkation in society; the dormant energies of both parties are then aroused, and the contest is usually carried on with much enthusiasm, and neither time nor money are spared. Old men and young, rich and poor, voters of every hue, qualified and unqualified, have been in times past indiscriminately dragged to the polls; many of the latter by their affrontery eluding the vigilance of the scrutineers, and it has not been until after the storm had subsided that illegal votes were dragged to light, and then it was of no avail, unless the defeated canditate assumed the expense of contesting the election, and if he had done so, the probability in most cases was, that an equal, or perhaps a greater number of bad votes would have been fished out of his own catalogue of names. If the existing Voter's Registration Act be faithfully carried out, much fraudulent voting, and its demoralizing false swearing will in future be obviated.

Time was when the County was young, and its inhabitants were knit together by the recollection of the days when they had stood shoulder to shoulder in the ranks, in defence of their King and Country; or, when leaving house and home they had together sought an asylum from the tumults of civil war in the wild woods of Canada. If in these days they were not all of one mind, at least they agreed to differ. Then, the recurrence of a parliamentary election was a pleasing episode in the life of the early settler, and was hailed as the occasion, when old friends long separated should meet again. Then, the proceedings were characteristic of the simplicity of character of the inhabitants: then, was no false swearing, and rarely any voting at all. The rival candidates in turn addressed the people at the hustings, and the contest was decided by a show of hands, or by one party moving to the right, and the other to the left hand; the returning officer counting heads, and declaring accordingly, amid the acclamations of both. At a later period *a barrel of rum* came to be considered as a *sine qua non* to the success of a candidate. This again was succeeded by a time when *money* freely spent yielded a mighty influence in the result of elections. In many constituencies at the present day, it is still a conspicuous element. This kind of bribery which ministers to the baser passions and propensities of our nature, is the more to be deplored, because from the infinite variety of ways in which it may be practised without detection, it is most difficult of cure. Let us hope that this *golden age* will disappear before the dawn of that brighter era, when good *common sense* shall prevail. When free and independent electors shall exercise their right of discrimination, unbiassed by "fear, favor, or affection," and according to the dictates of conscience. One thing is certain that if electors concede to any aspirant, the privilege to *buy* their votes, they may make up their minds that he will assume the right to *sell* their interests, when it suits his convenience. As none of the representatives of Dundas have so far as we know distinguished themselves above their fellow members in the arena of politics, little can be said of the political history of any of them. The first on the list of our members may have been a whig or a tory, a lawyer or a merchant, of such matters there is no record, and the little that is preserved of his history, presents few inducements to prosecute the enquiry. His character is summed up in this, that he was familiarly known at the time by the unenviable *soubriquet* of LYING CAMPBELL.

FRAZER, was one of Sir John Johnston's veterans, of good family, and extensively connected. A whole-souled warm-hearted man, the personification of what the world calls a "good-fellow."

MERKLEY, was a U.E. Loyalist—a German of the Lutheran creed, and a blunt honest farmer; possessed of limited education, and speaking very broken English. His homespun suit of Canadian gray, and his ofttimes ludicrous pronunciation of the English language, added to the energetic, and at times vehement style of his delivery, frequently elicited bursts of mingled laughter and applause from the House. He was one, however, neither to be laughed down, nor easily intimidated. He knew nothing of the art of "*chiselling*," but in his own honest and independent way, he spoke just as he thought. His sentiments were always plainly expressed, and to the point. Respected by all parties as a man of sterling integrity, he was also of jovial as well as humorous disposition, and was a frequent guest at the Governor's table.

JOHN COOK, was also of the U.E. stock, and in his day enjoyed a fair share of popularity, having served 15 years in Parliament. He is still living in Williamsburgh.

McDONELL, was a lawyer of Cornwall; he possessed considerable talents, and rather more than an average share of legal elocution. It was through his instrumentality that the Lutherans of Dundas received a pecuniary remuneration for the loss of their church and glebe. He died some years since in the prime of life.

JOHN CRYSLER, is a gentlemanly, unassuming man, of few words, but has the reputation of being a shrewd calculator, and no doubt is patiently awaiting the turn of the tide which may possibly reseat him in the Legislative Halls.

ROSE, was in turn, a merchant, a speculator, a farmer, and a newspaper editor. For many years he took the lead in the county as an enterprizing and exemplary farmer, was always a staunch supporter of the agricultural society, and was the first to introduce improved breeds of stock in Dundas, and for this deserves to be had in remembrance. In his experience, however, farming was rather honorable than lucrative: he sold out, became the editor of a western paper, which he has since abandoned, and has recommenced a mercantile business. Of limited education, he nevertheless possessed fair abilities, and expressed himself upon all occasions with great fluency.

J. W. COOK, the present member, is a nephew of the aforesaid John Cook. He is extensively engaged in the lumber trade, and is reputed to be a good man of business.

Two of our past representatives demand more than a passing notice at our hand; we have reference to Colonel Crysler, and Peter Shaver, Esq. Both of these gentlemen were U.E. Loyalists, who came to the county at its first settlement, and spent their whole lives in it. They thus came to be inseparably connected with its history, and to be universally known by its inhabitants.

Few men in any country have had a more remarkable career

than Colonel John Crysler. He came to the county in 1784, being then fifteen years of age, a drummer boy, or as he himself used to say, " a sheep-skin fiddler." He early engaged in merchandize and soon amassed a large property. When at the zenith of his prosperity, he had, as it were, the whole county under his thumb, and patent deeds for sixty thousand acres of land in his chest. As a farmer, merchant, magistrate, a colonel of militia, and for sixteen consecutive years the representative of the county in Parliament, he was a man of note, and of extensive influence. He erected several grist-mills and saw-mills in the county, and for many years was extensively engaged in the lumber business. Careless of money, his hospitality knew no bounds, his house was open to all, and his means were lavished with more liberality than discretion. Before the close of his life, however, disappointments and losses, occasioned by his indulgence to private friends, as well as by failures in his commercial speculations, supervened, and he had to confess with the wise man of old that "all is vanity." Rapidly as he had accumulated a handsome fortune, even more swiftly did his riches " take to themselves wings and flee away." He died at Finch in 1850, at the advanced age of 81 years.

Peter Shaver, Esquire, was born near Johnstown on the banks of the Mohawk River, in the State of New York, in October 1777. His father was a well-to-do farmer, had a numerous family, and was surrounded with all the comforts that rural life affords. A frugal, industrious man was he, and a hot-headed old tory to boot. At the commencement of the war he was one of the first to volunteer the services of himself and of his three eldest sons, in support of the royal cause. Leaving his wife and family on the farm, he joined the standard of Sir John Johnston, served under him during the whole of the revolutionary war, and came with his regiment to Canada, in the year 1780. During his absence his house and farm were plundered, his family rendered houseless and homeless, and his property seized upon, by bands of ruffians, who recognized no authority but that of " mob law." In this destitute condition his wife and children were permitted, under a flag of truce, to make their way, as best they might, through the woods to Canada. After enduring incredible hardships, they reached Ticonderoga, whence they hoped to be conveyed in a boat through Lake Champlain; the boats, however, were frozen fast in the ice, and nothing remained for them but to set out afoot on their weary pilgrimage along the margin of the lake. The mother carried her infant in her arms, while the elder boys drew the younger ones upon a hand sleigh, a distance of over one hundred miles upon the ice, to Isle aux Noix. Here they were for a time sheltered from the cold, in an Indian wigwam, and were afterwards transferred to the barracks. The whole family came to the county of Dundas with the other settlers in 1784, and Mr. Shaver has continued to reside there, with very little intermission ever since.

In youth, he served his apprentice-ship as a mill-wright, but did not long follow that calling. In 1799 he married, and shortly afterwards entered into the lumber and mercantile business, which he prosecuted with varied success until the year 1848, when he retired. A few years ago, Mr. Shaver was afflicted with total blindness; at his advanced age, few would have had the fortitude to submit to the pain of an ophthalmic operation, or had faith to believe in the possibility of a remedy; he however had both, and a skilful operation completely restored his sight. He is now in his 84th year, active in mind and in body, remarkable for his genial flow of spirits, his rare intelligence, and intimate acquaintance with all that is going on in the world around him. That he was respected by his fellow-men is sufficiently attested by the circumstance of his having, for seventeen consecutive years, represented his county in Parliament. He received a commission as ensign in the Dundas Militia more than fifty years ago, and was appointed Lieutenant Colonel in 1847.

In this connection we shall mention but one more name, and although the individual is neither a native of the County of Dundas, nor a resident in it, yet the position which he holds in relation to it, justifies us in noticing him.

More than forty years ago, a stout young lad with fair hair and ruddy cheeks, landed on the wharf at Quebec, a friendless emigrant from the Emerald Isle. He had left his native land, to carve out for himself, a new home in the New World. There was nothing in his outward appearance to distinguish him from other emigrants, nor was his address remarkable otherwise, than for his rich "*brogue.*" He had received a tolerably good education, and his countenance bespoke intelligence, rather than any extraordinary mental endowments. His heart was light, and so was his pocket, while his thick-set frame and brawny arms, seemed to indicate, that if ever he should distinguish himself in Canada, it would be in the backwoods, among those, " who lift up the axe against the trees."

The same individual now resides in a princely mansion, on the banks of the St. Lawrence, surrounded by numerous friends, enjoying the well-earned fruits of his own industry. He is regarded as a man of influence in high places, and the inhabitants of a District, containing one thousand five hundred square miles of territory, and polling seven thousand voters, have recently testified their respect for his integrity, by conferring upon him, the highest honor in the people's gift—a seat in the Legislative Council of his adopted country. The quondam Irish emigrant, is the HON. GEORGE CRAWFORD of Brockville, whose career we notice thus, as an example of what has been done by hundreds of others, in this rapidly rising colony, and more particularly, that his example may stimulate our youth to habits of industry and perseverance.

Immediately upon his arrival in the Country, he went "into the bush," and set to work in earnest, to cut down the trees, to pile up the log-heaps, to eradicate the blackened stumps, in fine, " to make him a clearance." At the end of seven years, of hard labor, he found that he had cleared one hundred acres of land, without having added anything to the weight of his pocket; it was even lighter than when he had begun. In 1827, he took a contract on the Rideau Canal; here he had to contend with difficulties, chiefly arising from the lack of capital; however, by dint of perseverance and energy, joined to judicious management, he came out of that contract a gainer to a considerable amount. In 1832, he tendered for a large contract on the Cornwall Canal. Upon the day of opening the tenders, he was told by one of the commissioners, that as there were other good tenders for the work lower than his, he could expect no contract, and that he might as well return home. Next morning he rose before daylight, in hopes that he might get away from Cornwall, before the friend with whom he was staying should witness his disappointment. But his host was wide awake, and heard the stealthy footsteps pass his bed-room door. He arrested the fugitive, and persuaded him to remain until the decisions were announced. How it came,—let the commissioners tell, but, before night, he was secured in a large and profitable contract. In 1842 he contracted for a large portion of the Beauharnois canal: upon this work alone he cleared a handsome fortune, which placed the cap sheaf upon his previous successes. The ball was now at his foot, his name was up, and he could have commanded as much public work as he chose to undertake. It was at this period, that he proved an exception to the general rule of humanity. He said to himself, to use his own words, " I have enough —I am quite satisfied that the world owes me nothing. It has done better for me, than I ever expected or deserved, and for this I thank a divine providence, who, I can sincerely say, has blessed me more than I could ask for, or am worthy to receive."

After his retirement from Public works, he was twice elected to Parliament, as representative of the town of Brockville, and withdrew from that position, with a view of offering himself as a candidate for the Upper House, in the newly formed St. Lawrence electoral division. In this contest he was successful.

Mr. Crawford commanded a company of volunteers during the Rebellion, and was appointed a commissioner for settling the Rebellion losses, to the inhabitants of the Province. It was mainly at his instigation, that the present location of the Grand Trunk Railway, along the front of the St. Lawrence was determined upon. Of this road he is now a director, and has been since its commencement. He is also a director of the Brockville and Ottawa Railway Company.

The political history of Canada reads us a salutary lesson, which we do well to ponder. From it we may learn the folly of attempting to redress grievances, whether real or imaginary, by any other than constitutional measures. "Vox populi vox Dei" was never more truly said of any people than of Canadians, and has been fully verified in many of the changes that have transpired. As for instance, in the secularization of the Clergy Reserves, and in the substitution of an elective Legislative Council for that formerly nominated by the Crown, and which to have advocated a few years ago had seemed little short of treason. Even the citizens of the United States, who were wont to boast that there was no freedom like unto theirs, now, freely concede, that the position of Canada as a dependency of the British Crown, is decidedly preferable to the relation that any single State of the Union, bears to the Federal Government. "It is a curious fact" says the Washington *Constitutional* of 1st Jan., 1861, "that practically the Provinces of Britain at this moment, enjoy a freedom which the black Republican would deny the sovereign States. States, they insist, may not secede—shall not secede—and shall be punished summarily if they attempt to secede. Contrast this view with that which the modern Colonial rule of Britain spreads before her Provinces. For years past Canada has been told authoritatively, that its people are masters of their own future, that they are at liberty to assume the attributes of nationality, whenever they feel equal to its responsibilities: and the imperial government will place no obstacles in their path. The Canadians have but to avow themselves secessionists and they may become the citizens of a sovereign state without the dread of being "whipped," "subjugated," or coerced after the manner in which our chivalrous coercionists would frighten South Carolina, and sister commonwealths, into the worship of some fanciful impersonation of Federal authority."

Never before did such a concession emanate from the core of Republicanism, yet it is surpassed by the following petition to the Senate and Representatives of the State of Maine, in Legislature assembled, dated the 10th Dec. 1860, and signed by over nineteen thousand republicans.

"We, the undersigned, respectfully request that your Honorable body will appoint commissioners to confer with the British Government in regard to an immediate annexation of the State of Maine to the Canadas· also to make arrangements for an immediate secession of the said State from the General Government."

We may live to see important changes in the constitution of Canada—we may possibly see all the British North American Colonies united into a great confederation, but we trust that in our day at least, the connecting link which binds us to Great Britain will not be broken—and that the banner of Old England will long continue to float over our citadels, and be regarded as the emblem and guardian of our rights, civil and sacred.

CHAPTER XIV.

The St. Lawrence Canals.—The Elliots —Steam Navigation, History of, on River, Lake, and Ocean.—Cunard, Collins, Canadian and other Steamers.—The Great Eastern.—Grand Trunk Railroad.—Victoria Bridge.—Benjamin Chaffey.

The Canals situate in the County of Dundas are worthy of notice, forming, as they do, links in the chain of the " St. Lawrence Canals," the most stupendous works of the kind to be found in the world. They were constructed with a view to overcome the natural obstructions to the navigation of the St. Lawrence, caused by the various rapids existing between Montreal and Prescott. These Canals, with the exception of the "Junction," were completed in 1849, and are of various lengths, of from one mile to twelve; in all, they are 43 miles in extent. The total expenditure of the Province on their construction up to the first of January, 1860, was $5,418,770.

"The Galouse," "the point Iroquois," and "the Junction Canals," now form one continuous canal of 7½ miles in length, terminating at Iroquois in Matilda. This Canal, the " Rapid du Plat," 3 miles in length, lying in Williamsburgh, and the " Farrans Point," of one mile in length, in Osnabruck, are all called the 'Williamsburgh Canals," and are under the superintendence of Mr. Isaac N. Rose of Morrisburgh. The Williamsburgh Canals have cost up to the present time for construction, $1,320,475, of which the "Junction" completed in 1859, cost $230,736: they are 10 feet deep, 100 to 150 feet wide, with locks 200 feet in length, and 45 in width. The locks are all of cut stone, built in the most substantial manner, and finished in the best style. The lock gates are now constructed of solid pieces of timber from 15 to 18 inches in thickness, dowelled and bolted together, and are considered to be an improvement upon the old style of framed gates; each set of gates consisting of four leaves costs from $5,000, to $6,000. A swing bridge when placed over one of these locks costs $3,000; and the cost of one of the St. Lawrence locks complete is from 50, to $60,000.

It is in contemplation to deepen all these Canals to $11\frac{1}{2}$ feet, and to lengthen the locks to 350 or 400 feet. The sum estimated for the deepening alone amounts to *one million of dollars*. The expediency however of first ascertaining the effect of Canadian Railways upon our water communications will, in all probability, prevent the immediate expenditure of any large sum for this purpose.

While the St. Lawrence Canals have conferred an incalculable benefit upon the commerce, and have added largely to the general prosperity of the Province, the hitherto limited trade of the country has fallen immeasurably short of creating the amount of traffic, which their ample dimensions were designed to accommodate, and which the large expense of their construction demanded. Unfortunately, from some cause or another, they have hitherto been unsuccessful in diverting the trade of the great lakes into the channel of the St. Lawrence; and while the works from their massive structure will remain for ages, a monument of the public spirit of a young colony, whose population when they commenced the undertaking, scarcely exceeded a million of souls, it is discouraging to record, that during the year 1859, after paying for repairs and management, the net revenue of the whole chain of the St. Lawrence Canals was but $728.86! The falling off, as compared with former years was doubtless caused by the competition of the Grand Trunk Railroad, whose facilities for carrying through freight from the sea-board to Detroit, are only now being fully brought into play: while the rapidity of their movements has enabled the Railway Company to monopolize the passenger traffic.

In May 1860 by an order in Council, the St. Lawrence Canals amongst others were thrown open, absolutely free of toll, to all vessels whatsoever, whether such vessels be American or Canadian. The decrease in the revenue from all the public works by this act, will probably be about $110,000 per annum. We must confess, that although this act of the Government bears upon the face of it the stamp of a liberal and enlightened policy, it puzzles us to ascertain the particular mode in which the Province is to be remunerated. Whether it will benefit most the western producer, the forwarder, or the shipper in Montreal, or whether as doubtless contemplated it will exercise a reflex benefit upon the whole community, remains to be seen. One thing is certain, the Province cannot afford to lose $110,000 per annum, and if it does revert to the exchequer in some indirect manner it must eventually come *directly* from the pockets of the inhabitants generally.

The Williamsburgh Canals were constructed in various sections by different contractors. The only one who has continued to reside in the County is Mr. William Elliot. He, in company with his brother Andrew Elliot had extensive contracts on these works.

The Iroquois Canal was more difficult of construction than any of the others, the greater part of it required to be blasted out of the solid rock, and much difficulty was experienced in excluding the water while finishing the bottom. The original contractors succumbed under the difficulties, stopped payment, and left the country; for a time the work was suspended and eventually it was completed by the Messrs. Elliot, who, with their well known perseverance and energy surmounted every obstacle. The "Junction" Canal was also attended with difficulty in construction, though of a different kind; here too the original contractors not only failed, but their sureties after a hard struggle to carry on the work were forced to abandon it, after having incurred heavy losses. Mr. Andrew Elliot again came to the rescue, and despite of all obstacles pushed it through to a successful termination. Both brothers have since then been engaged in extensive contracts for railways and other public works, in all of which they have been characterized by unflinching honor and integrity in the fulfilment of their agreements, and by an amount of energy rarely equalled by any contractor.

Andrew retired to Cornwall, where he erected extensive mills. William settled in Matilda, and in 1850 also erected an excellent stone grist mill there at the same time that Mr. Chaffey built the large mill upon the canal in Williamsburgh. The Matilda mill was unfortunately burned down a few years after, but was rebuilt immediately, with an additional run of stones, and every modern improvement. It has since then proved, as indeed all these mills along the line of the St. Lawrence Canals, of great benefit to the surrounding country.

Mr. William Elliot came from the Scottish side of the borders, in the year 1828. He resided two years at Lansingburg in the state of New York. In 1831 he purchased a farm near Ormstown, Lower Canada, then situated in the midst of a wilderness; his father came out in 1834 and settled upon the farm, and his brother Andrew came the following year. In 1840 Mr. Elliot commenced business as a brewer at Moullinette, where after $3\frac{1}{2}$ years his establishment was burned down which occasioned him a heavy loss. At various times he has been elected to municipal honors,—as reeve of Iroquois, and an influential member of the Counties Council, he was appointed warden of the United Counties in 1858.

In connection with the canals we may mention a few facts regarding the navigation of the St. Lawrence by steam, and of steamboats generally.

The ingenuity of our American cousins, is more conspicuous, in their aptness to discover at a glance, the practical utility of new inventions, than in their original conception, and is only equalled by the unblushing assurance with which they appropriate to themselves the credit. As an instance of this we might mention the reaping machine, claimed to be an American invention, though a Scottish implement, that had been many years in use, supplied the model of the American, so called, invention. This propensity is even more transparent in the introduction of steamboats. By Americans *Fulton* is said to have been the first to have applied the newly invented steam engine to the propulsion of boats; in other words, that he was the inventor of steamboats. And one-half of the world believe that he really was; the other half, however, happen to know that the American invention was merely the practical application of another Scotchman's successful experiment, and the credit claimed, the surreptitious appropriation of the Scotchman's fame. "Chamber's Encyclopedia," no mean authority, tells us that Symington, a Scotchman, built a steamboat, which was placed on the Forth and Clyde Canal in 1802, and which was first tested as a tug boat. On this occasion two loaded vessels of 70 tons burden each, were towed a distance of $19\frac{1}{2}$ miles in six hours against a head-wind so strong that no other vessel in the canal could move to windward on that day. This boat had a single paddle wheel in the stern, and was impelled by a horizontal cylinder of 22 inches diameter, and four feet stroke, working by means of a connecting rod and a crank on the axle of the wheel; the rudder was double, on account of the peculiar position of the wheel, and the steering apparatus placed in the front part of the vessel. The speed of the vessel going alone was six miles an hour. Symington's vessel excited great interest, and while he busied himself working it and devising further improvements, another "*chiel*" specially busied himself in "*takin notes*." Fulton, not only closely examined this novel and successful *steamboat*, but closely interrogated the builder as to the construction of every part of it. Symington showed him every attention, performed a satisfactory voyage solely on his account, and gave him all the information he wanted besides; and, to say the least of it, it was ungenerous in Fulton, that he took no subsequent notice of him. Under a feigned name, Fulton ordered an engine from Boulton and Watts, in England, took his departure for New York and immediately commenced to build a boat. The engine was sent after him, and English engineers with it, to fit it up in his vessel. In 1807 he successfully performed the trip to Albany from New York in the "Clermont," at the rate of five miles per hour running time. Thus were steamboats first introduced in America. The second was the "Car of Neptune" also built on the Hudson in 1809, and the third steamboat we read of in the New World, was the "Accommodation," which was built by the late Hon. George Molson of Montreal, and commenced to ply regularly between Montreal and Quebec on the 6th of November, 1809. This vessel was 87 feet in length, had berths for 20 passengers, and made her maiden trip in 36 hours running time, equal to a speed of 5 miles an hour. She was quite as much an object of interest to the Quebecers then, as is now the Great Eastern to all the world. The Quebec *Mercury*, announcing her arrival, remarked. "She is incessantly crowded with visitors. This steamboat receives her impulse from an open spoked perpendicular wheel on each side, without any circular band or rim; to the end of each double spoke is fixed a square board which enters the water, and, by the rotatory motion of the wheels acts like a paddle. No wind or tide can stop her." The general use of steamboats for passenger traffic in Britain commenced with the "Comet," built by Henry Bell on the Clyde in 1812.

The first steamer on the Upper St. Lawrence and the lakes, was the "Ontario," a staunch sea boat of 270 tons, which began to ply in 1817, and performed the trip between Ogdensburgh and Lewiston in *ten days*. The "Iroquois," built upon Symington's plan, with one large wheel across the stern, was built expressly for stemming the swift currents between Prescott and Dickinson's Landing. She had so much difficulty in ascending the river, that, at the Rapid du Plat and other points posts were sunk at short distances along the shore, to each of which, in succession, she made fast until steam enough was raised to carry her on to the next.

She ran only two seasons and then abandoned the route. The "Black Hawk," built at French Creek, was used by the Americans for several seasons, afterwards sold to the Canadians and succeeded the "Iroquois," under the name of the "Dolphin." This was a powerful and fast boat, and had no difficulty in ascending the river. Since that time a vast number of splendid steamers have continued regularly to navigate our waters.

In November, 1838, the "Dolphin," having on board a number of rebel prisoners, descended the Long Sault and Cascade Rapids and wintered at Lachine, the following spring she was towed up the rapids at great expense. Much difficulty was found at the Longue Sault, a particular part of which seemed to defy all their efforts to get the vessel up. The current shot down with such rapidity that the "Dolphin" was at times in danger of being towed under water, and anon was dashed with violence on the river bank. After four weeks, however, of incessant toil, and, with the aid of twenty yoke of oxen, besides horses, capstans and men, added to the working of her engine, she was got up, the first and most likely the last steamer that will ever accomplish the feat.

The "Jack Downing," a small steamer of 35 feet in length, is often mentioned among the early boats on these waters. This boat was built at Carthage, in Jefferson County in 1834, and was drawn upon wheels to Sackett's Harbour, a distance of 30 miles. It was used for a short time as a ferry-boat at Waddington, making occasional trips up and down the river, aided at the currents by the poles of her crew (3 in number). Shortly after, the "Rapid," built upon a novel principle, and consisting of two hollow cylinders, the shape of two cigars, 10 feet apart, with a large wheel in the middle, appeared, fitted up with the engines of the "Jack Downing." Her first trip down the river was also her last. After many fruitless attempts to return, she was wrecked upon a small island, and was for a time abandoned. Eventually, it was taken by way of the Ottawa and the Rideau Canal to Ogdensburgh, where it plied as a ferry-boat.

The winter of 1837 was somewhat remarkable for the long continuance of open navigation. On the 17th of January in that year, the steamer "Kingston," ran up as far as Prescott loaded *with red coats.*

It was about this time (1837) that the great problem of successfully crossing the Atlantic Ocean by steam, engaged the public mind, and was practically solved. This circumstance may be regarded as the most important era in the history of America since its discovery, and it therefore becomes interesting to trace the progress of Ocean steam navigation from its commencement.

As early as 1819, a steamer named the "Savannah" of 380 tons, sailed from New York to Savannah, and thence direct to Liverpool, arriving there on the 21st of September after a voyage of 18 days, " as she drew near the city with sails furled, and American banners flying, the docks were lined by thousands of people, who greeted her with vociferous cheers."* This proved the possibility of a steamer performing an ocean voyage of 3000 miles at a stretch. Shortly after this, a prize of £10,000, was offered by the British Government, to the party who should first perform a successful steam voyage to India. The prize was won by Captain Johnston, who sailed from England on the 16th of August 1825, in the steamer "Enterprize," of 120 horse power, and reached Calcutta on the 7th of December. The entire distance run was 13.700 miles, and the time occupied, 113 days, during 10 of which, she was at anchor. She ran under steam 64 days, and consumed 580 chaldrons of coals, the rest of the voyage being under sail. There was but one coaling station on the route, namely, at the Cape of Good Hope. The greatest days run under steam was 225 miles; the least, 80, and the speed of the vessel in smooth water was eight miles an hour.†

The enormous expense of fitting out, and working ocean steamers, added to their limited capacity for carrying freight, retarded their

---
* Scientific American.   † M. Martin's His. India.

general introduction for some years after their capabilities had been tested. In 1835, the steamer "Royal William," made a voyage from Halifax to Liverpool, but it was reserved for the "Great Western" to test the matter, as a remunerative commercial speculation. This powerful steamship of 1340 tons, built expressly for the route, departed from Bristol on the 7th April 1838, and reached New York on the 23rd, the running time occupied on the passage was under 14 days. In every sense of the word, she proved a success, and for many years this pioneer of ocean steamers, continued to cross, and re-cross the Atlantic with marvellous regularity. The "Sirius," a Clyde-built steamer made a voyage during the same year, and arrived at New York on the same day as the Great Western, having been 18 days at sea.

No sooner were these results known, than Messrs. Cunard & Co., of Halifax and London, entered into a contract for a term of years, with the British Government, to convey the mails by steam between Liverpool and Boston, calling at Halifax, and connecting there, with steamers to Quebec, Newfoundland and Bermuda. A magnificent fleet of steamships was constructed for the service. The *Britannia, Columbia, Caledonia,* and *Acadia* were the first of the line, that under the name of the "Cunard Steamers," have continued ever since, to bridge as it were, the Atlantic, with a precision, speed, and comfort, that have been the admiration of the whole world. The *Brittania,* made the first voyage to Boston in 14 days 8 hours, ariving on the 18th of July, 1840. For many years the service has been performed weekly, from each side of the Atlantic, and from the commencement they have been liberally subsidized by Government. The Imperial subsidy at present, amounts to over £3000 stg. per trip, out and home. With this assistance it may be said, that little thanks are due to the company for maintaining an efficient line of steamers, but their almost total exemption from marine disasters, especially when placed in contrast with other rival lines, and the consequent confidence placed in them by the travelling community, indicate a perfection of management, order and punctuality, that have never yet been equalled, and that are deserving of Governmental encouragement. One solitary mishap, and that, unattended by the loss of a single life, is all that stands recorded against them, during a career of twenty years. *The Columbia* went ashore in a fog, near Cape Sable, on the iron-bound coast of Nova Scotia; but though the vessel perished, yet, through the presence of mind, and discipline of the officers and crew, under providence, every soul was safely brought to shore.

The success of the Cunard line, induced the Americans to enter the lists of competition. A nobler fleet of steamers than the "Collins" line, could not well be conceived; built and fitted regardless of expense, for the very purpose of excelling, and if possible, of driving the "Cunarders" from the ocean:—subsidized too by their Government, and commanded by experienced captains, they nevertheless met with a series of disasters, through which they forfeited public confidence, and utterly failed as a commercial speculation. The *Arctic* in 1854 came in collision with a steamer at sea, off Newfoundland, and sank to the bottom, occasioning the loss of 322 lives. In 1856, the *Pacific* foundered in the deep, and no vestige of the ship nor of her living cargo was ever discovered. The line dwindled down in numbers and in repute year by year—the subsidy was at length withdrawn, and the "Collins Line" that had owned the *Atlantic*, the *Pacific*, the *Baltic*, the *Arctic*, and the *Adriatic*, ceased to exist.

In 1853, a Liverpool firm contracted to run a line of *Screw Steamers* from Liverpool to Canada—twice a month to Quebec in summer, and once a month to Portland during the winter. The Province engaged to pay them a subsidy of £1238 currency per trip, under certain conditions, one of which was, that they should not average over 14 days on the outward, nor 13 days on the homeward voyage. The ships of the first year were, the *Genova, Lady Eglinton*, and *Sarah Sands*.—Their average passages were, —*Genova*, 20 days out and 15 home: *L. Eglinton* 14 out, 12 home: *Sarah Sands* 22 out and 18 home. Next year, the

Cleopatra, Ottawa, and *Charity,* were added to the line. The *Cleopatra* made her first trip to Quebec in *forty three days;* the Ottawa never reached Quebec at all, but after dodging about some time, among the ice at the mouth of the St Lawrence, made for Portland: the *Charity* having sailed from Liverpool a month after the *Cleopatra,* reached Quebec in 27 days, and found the latter still in port. As a matter of course the contract was cancelled. An agreement was next entered into with the Messrs. Allan, who represent the present very efficient line of screw steamers, known as belonging to the "Montreal Ocean Steamship Company," originated and sustained by Canadian enterprize and capital. In terms of this contract, the sum to be paid to the Company was £25,000 a year, for fortnightly trips in summer and monthly ones in winter. In May 1859, the Company represented that owing to the depression in trade they were unable any longer to sustain the line, without further assistance. The Canadian Government, nobly stood by this Canadian enterprize, and largely increased the subsidy, requiring as an equivalent, the performance of a weekly service summer and winter. This Company now receives $416,000 per annum, and already returns yearly to the exchequer a postal revenue of $200,000. The line consists of a fleet of eight Screw Steamships, each 300 feet in length, and are from 1800 to 2500 tons burden. They are all Clyde-built ships. As a line they have brought no discredit on the name, and individually, they are noted, for their splendid accommodation, their sea worthiness, and their fast sailing qualities. Their speed in smooth water is from 11 to 13 miles an hour, and even in a heavy sea, and with a head wind, they seldom fall short of 8 miles an hour.

The returns made to the Provincial Parliament in 1859, exhibit the speed of the Canadian line of steamers, as follows. Average passages Westward 11 days and 5 hours: average passages Eastward, 10 days and 10 hours. The quickest passage Westward, made by the Hungarian in 9 days 14 hours. The quickest passage Eastward by the Anglo-Saxon in 9 days 5 hours. During the same year the Cunard line of steamers to Boston averaged West-ward 12 days 19 hours; East-ward, 10 days, 15 hours. The distance from Boston to Liverpool is 2823 miles; from Quebec to Liverpool by the Strait of Belleisle 2583 miles. It thus appears that the Canadian steamers maintained an average speed of $9\frac{1}{2}$ miles an hour, during the entire season of the St. Lawrence navigation. The Cunarders average $10\frac{1}{8}$ miles per hour, during the same months, namely from April till November.

The quickest passage on record across the Atlantic was made by the "Persia" of the Cunard line. In 1858, that ship made a passage from New York to Liverpool in 8 days, 22 hours, 23 minutes. The distance is 3013 miles, giving an average speed of over 14 miles an hour.

In 1860, there were twelve different lines of steamers, plying across the Atlantic, forming together a fleet of nearly 50 steamships ranging in tonnage from 1800 to 5,000 tons each, and affording almost daily communication between England and America by steam. The total number of passangers conveyed Westward by these steamers was 55,480; Eastward 27.597: in all 83,077. Of this number the Canadian line alone conveyed 8,637 passengers.

The projector of the *Cunard line* was preferred to the rank of a baronet of the United Kingdom, under the title of "Sir Samuel Cunard," in recognition of his enterprize in facilitating communication between England and the United States. We see no reason why, the equally spirited individual, who originated and so successfully sustained the Canadian line, plying between Britain and one of her own Colonies, should not in like manner be dubbed "*Sir Hugh Allan.*"

This Chapter nautical, would be incomplete without some allusion to the "*Great Eastern,*" that eighth wonder of the world which lately visited our shores. This Leviathan steamship, possesses a combination of features so entirely novel, in the art of naval Architecture, as to render her incomparable with any other vessel afloat; and as no one can fully realize her magnificent proportions without a personal inspection, we may say that she is indescribable. The *Great Eastern* differs from all other steamships in three particulars, viz., in size, in the method of construction, and in the arrangement of her motive power.

Her length is 692 feet, breadth of beam 83 feet, her depth 58 feet, and her actual capacity is 27,000 tons measurement. Let us suppose that we could divide the iron tube of the Victoria bridge into 9 equal parts, place them side by side, in a pile three deep and three tiers in height, we should have a mass of iron work, somewhat similar to the interior of the Great Eastern, precisely of the same length and depth, but only a little more than *one half* of her width. The weight of the tubes is about 8,250 tons : that of the *Great Eastern* with her machinery, 12,000 tons.

The *Great Eastern* differs in construction from every other ship in as much as she is built with double sides just as if one iron ship were placed within another, the inner and the outer hulls being of equal strength. The intervening space of two feet is divided longitudinally and transversely into a vast number of cellular apartments; this arrangement of the hull imparts immense strength to the ship, and her sides thus constructed are computed to be of equal strength, as though they were of solid iron, two feet in thickness : another advantage claimed is that in event of the outer surface being damaged by collision or otherwise, the only result would be that a few small cells would be filled with water, while the safty of the ship would not be in the least endangered. In addition to this she is divided internally into a great many water-tight compartments, any one or two of which might be filled with water, without detriment to the rest of the ship.

Her strength has already been put to the severest test, by an explosion which occurred in her hold, during her trial trip. The force of that explosion, was sufficient to have sent any other vessel to the bottom, yet the Great Eastern kept on her way, as though nothing had happened. The Great Eastern is propelled by paddle wheels at the sides, and also by a screw at the stern; in this she differs also from all other steam ships.

She is provided with eight steam engines, four of which work the paddle wheels and four, the screw; together working up to a nominal force of nearly 10,000 horse power the boilers are heated by 112 furnaces which consume daily, while on a vogage, 250 tons of coal.

The *Great Eastern* was commenced at Milwall upon the Thames in 1855, and in 1857 she was ready for launching. No such load had ever before slid down the ways of a ship yard, and every precaution, and appliance, that science could suggset, were adopted to ensure success. Correspondingly great was the disappointment, when " in the presence of Princes and savans, and an immense multitude of eager spectators, who had assembled to witness the mighty event of Leviathan rushing like a mountain into the waters of the Thames—the iron mammoth like a balky horse refused to obey the reins of the driver." It cost no less than $400,000, and constant labor from the 2nd November till the 31st January following before she reached her destined element.

The entire cost of the *Great Eastern*, when ready for sea, was about $4,000,000. She is fitted to carry 4,800 passengers; or an army of 10,000 men, in a superior manner to any other troop ship; in addition to her own crew of 400 men. After several experimental trips, and many vexatious delays, the *Great Eastern* finally ventured to cross the Atlantic. She left Southampton on *Sunday morning* the 17th of June, 1860, at 8 a. m. and arrived at Sandy Hook off New York at 7.30 a. m. on the morning of the 28th. The actual period of passage was eleven days, and two hours, or, allowing for the difference of time, 10 days 21 hours. This speed was less than had been expected of her, it had been far surpassed by the Persia. Nevertheless, it was considered satisfactory for a first trip. The distance run by Chart was 3242 nautical miles, the average speed of the voyage 12 knots an hour, the highest speed by the log was 14½ knots: the greatest day's run was 333 knots, and the lowest distance in one ship's day 254 knots, which was on the day defore arriving, when the ship was run slow for the purpose of sounding.

The arrival of the great ship in New York, was hailed with immense enthusiasm. She steamed majestically up the bay, amidst a fleet of boats of every description, so numerous, that it seemed a mystery how she was to get through them. Fort Hamilton saluted her with a discharge of 14 guns: the first time that ever a merchant-vessel had been saluted in America. "To this distinguished honor, the Great Eastern responded by stopping, and, dipping her ensign, replied gun for gun in a regular and seamanlike style." The Great Eastern remained in New York nearly two months, where she was visited by great numbers. She sailed for New York on the 16th August, called at Halifax, and made the run thence to Milford Haven, in 10 days and 4 hours. She was "gridironed" immediately upon her arrival, and her bottom thorougly cleaned off and painted. Repairs and alterations involving an outlay of £28000 stg. being required before she could be pronounced ready for actual service, it was resolved to lay her up for the winter—the hands were paid off and the great ship was left upon terra firma, a huge, and all but abandoned hulk.

As a steamship she has proved to be sea-worthy and managable. As a commercial speculation, as yet, an utter failure. What may be her future success, or how she is to be employed, no one seems to be acute enough to divine. In the meantime she is to be regarded as a gigantic experiment, and it is satisfactory to know that the problem to be wrought out in her future career, is in good hands and will yet be solved. We have great faith in the *great ship*, and firmly believe that her next passage across the Atlantic will be the fastest on record, and, so soon as her character is established as a reliable and fast medium of communication, her commercial success will commence, and will be followed up by the building of other ships of equal capacity.

THE GRAND TRUNK RAILWAY.—This railway traverses the county of Dundas at an average distance of about ¾ of a mile from the river St. Lawrence. The section of the road lying between Montreal and Brockville was first opened for traffic on the 17th of November, 1855, and the benefit already derived from it, by that part of the country, exceeds all calculation; indeed it may be said to have opened up a new era in its existence. Brought, at all seasons of the year, within easy access of Montreal, Boston, New York, Ottawa, Toronto, and the west, a ready cash market was at once afforded for every description of produce the county had to spare. Facilities for transacting business attracted numbers to the vicinity of the railway depôst, and opposition, the life of trade, came to the relief of the farmers who had previously been compelled to barter with a few old foggies upon their own terms. The travelling community too, experienced a relief that none may know who have not toiled the live-long day through mud and mire, knee deep, to reach their county town.

The Grand Trunk Railway was completed and informally opened for traffic, throughout its entire length, on the 17th of December, 1859. The simultaneous completion of the Victoria Bridge, and of a branch line from Port Huron to Detroit, at the extreme western limit of the road, opened, as it were, the sluice gates of commerce, which instantly rolled in like a flood. Not many days after, trains laden entirely with bales of cotton from Louisiana, and others with flour from Chicago, and pork from Cincannati, were passed through the iron tube, two miles in length, on their route to England. Since then the business of the road has steadily increased, the amount of freighting business, during winter especially, being frequently controlled only by the want of rolling stock to transmit it. This, one of the most extensive railway undertakings in the world, is 1112 miles in length, and was built at a cost of £10,000 sterling per mile, excluding the Victoria Bridge, he estimated price of which alone was, in round numbers as follows:—

For the approaches and abutments	$1,000,000
For the masonry in the piers between the abutments.	4,000,000
For the wrought iron tubular superstructure	2,000,000
Total	$7,000,000

This sum was afterwards reduced to $6,000,000, but subsequently, in consequence of a bonus of $300,000 paid to the contractors for having finished it one year in advance of the time agreed upon, the estimate cost of the structure came to be about $6,300,000.*

The entire cost of the Grand Trunk Railway, in construction, has thus been about *sixty two millions of dollars!* need we express surprise that this great enterprise, is financially, in a state bordering upon utter bankruptcy. The wonder is to see it there at all. It is truly astonishing that English capitalists who had but recently recovered from the effects of the railway *mania* at home, should so soon have relapsed into their besetting sin abroad. In so far as Canada is concerned, this magnificent railroad has been constructed at an outlay immeasurably disproportionate to the resources of the province. A much cheaper road, and much less of it might have been constructed with the *four millions* of dollars of Canada money swallowed up in the Grand Trunk, and would really have been more advantageous to all concerned. That it will ultimately become a paying enterprize, cannot for a moment be doubted, else, the oft expressed prediction of the future greatness of Canada, reasonably grounded upon its past progress, must be hopelessly falsified. If an economical and judicious system of management is now introduced and persevered in, the generation of stock-holders who shall succeed the present, will most likely reap all the advantages anticipated by the reckless and over sanguine capitalists of the present day.

---

*Glance at the Victoria Bridge by C. Legge.

There are two stations of the Grand Trunk Railroad in Dundas, viz., Williamsburgh and Matilda. In the neighborhood of each thriving villages are growing up apace, *Morrisburgh* near the former, and *Iroquois* adjoining the latter, whose combined railway freight traffic for 1859 was 2202 tons. Williamsburgh is distant, by rail, from Montreal 92 miles, from Ottawa City 70, and from Toronto 241 miles. The fares by first class, respectively, are, $3, $2.40, and $8. Iroquois lies 7 miles to the west of Morrisburgh. The station buildings at both places are first class, of handsome external appearance, being built of dressed stone and covered with slate. The station masters, Messrs. Purkis and Fell, are deservedly esteemed for their urbanity to the public, and their faithfulness to their employers.

Benjamin Chaffey and William Elliot were the contractors for the road throughout Dundas county. Mr. Chaffey subsequently took an extensive contract on the Victoria Bridge, where his extraordinary mechanical talents found scope for their full development. "The ingenuity which he brought to bear upon his work, showed him to be a man of rare genius. He had also acquired the reputation of being a most skilful mechanic, and what was of still greater consequence, had won universal confidence and esteem, for the probity which always characterized his dealings."* The steam traveller invented by him, and afterwards used by the other contractors, is described as one of the most wonderful inventions of the age; by means of it huge blocks of stone weighing twenty tons and upwards, were picked up and handled with the greatest of ease and precision, the whole machinery being under the control of an intelligent boy. Mr. Chaffey built one half of all the masonry of the bridge, besides a large portion of the coffer dams, tube staying, and other works connected with its construction. He earned for himself the "golden opinions" of his employers, and, in addition to that, the substantial reward due to his merit—an independant fortune—which the people of Dundas wish him long life to enjoy.

---

*Legge.

For many years he resided among us, and was ever conspicuous for his public spirit and generosity, no less esteemed for his unassuming manners, than his unostentatious christian worth. He now resides in Brockville. He was nominated as a candidate for Legislative Council honors by the liberal party of the St Lawrence electoral division in 1858, but retired from the field in favor of Dr. Brouse of Prescott, who lost the election. We have no doubt that the seclusion of private life, was, to Mr. Chaffey's naturally retiring disposition, infinitely more preferable than the highest Legislative honors that could have been conferred upon him.

U

CHAPTER XV.

Reminiscences.—The mound of Williamsburgh.—Early Methodist Missionaries.—The first Convert —The luke-warm Lutheran.—Record of the Grave-yard.—Eccentricities — Perpetual motion.—Novel Windmill.—Early mills in Dundas.—Auld acquaintance.

As the writer has resided but a few years in the County of Dundas, he cannot draw upon his own memory for such materials as are properly designated reminiscences. His limited intercourse with the old settlers added to his disinclination to draw upon his imagination, doubtless deprives the youthful reader of many interesting and humorous anecdotes "founded upon fact," which might otherwise have been introduced in this chapter. What he now offers has come to his hand from various sources, and to his mind has every appearance of truth. The reader must however judge for himself, "the tales we tell as they were told to us," and they are not without interest as illustrating the early history of the county.

THE MOUND OF WILLIAMSBURGH.—The following was communicated to us by a clergyman, an old resident of the county.

"When the first settlers took possession of the front part of lots numbers thirty and thirty-one in the fifth concession of Williamsburgh, they discovered there in the dense forest the remains of one of the tumuli, which abound in the peninsula of Canada, but here are seldom met with The wall of circumvallation of this mound was found on the southern bank of the eastern branch of the Fritz-Marklie creek on said lots near the bridge at the so called unfinished mill in that locality.

The enclosure covered an area of three or four acres of land; the wall was about eighteen inches high, and in the form of a semi-circle, obviously marked out the spot chosen for a camp.

The settlers found trees growing on this wall of earth, whose ages must have been about two hundred years or more. In ploughing the ground inside of the wall several skulls, some pieces of coarse earthenware, and a quantity of decayed parched maize were found. Altogether there have been found here six skulls; the bones of the cranium appeared to the settlers to have been twice as thick as that belonging to Europeans. They were surmised to have been Indian skulls, and were interred upon some less frequented spot on lot thirty-one.

Within this enclosure frequently has the absorbing love of money been evidenced in eager nocturnal searches for imagined hidden treasures, but we are not aware that the diggers have had their cupidity gratified in any instance. In 1830 the mound was still distinctly visible, but since 1833 when that part of these lots was permanently put under cultivation, almost every vestige of this ancient camp has vanished from the sight of the passing traveller. No doubt if a proper search were undertaken perhaps even at this day, other skulls and relics of the olden time might here be found.

Who built this mound? For what purpose was it built? On these themes and others equally interesting connected with the generation of past ages in Canada, history is silent."

EARLY METHODIST MISSIONARIES AND CONVERTS.—The habits and address of the early Methodist Missionaries in Canada were quite in unison with the characteristics of its inhabitants and their ministrations were none the less acceptable to their hearers that they were conducted in a simple, bold, and at times eccentric manner. Mr. Carroll in his observations upon "Methodism past and present," gives some graphic illustrations of the customs of pastors and people in its early days. "It was usual," he says, "for the missionary to travel on horseback or on foot to the remotest settlements. Alighting at the door of an isolated log shanty he commonly entered it with the salutation, "Peace be to this house;" he would then intimate that he wished the neighbors to assemble in that house the following morning.

The young members of the family would forthwith spread themselves out in different directions and make the novel announcement which was usually well responded to. Nathan Bangs' first meeting for religious worship is thus described,—"at the time appointed the house was filled, the Missionary rose up—told the people who he was, what he was, and the nature of his errand, concluding in the following manner. " I am a Methodist preacher, and my manner of worship is to stand up and sing, and to kneel in prayer: then I stand up and take a text and preach, while the people sit on their seats. As many of you as see fit to join in this method can do so, but if not, you can choose your own method. He gave out his hymn—they all arose, he keeled in prayer, they all without exception did the same. They then took their seats. He stood up and gave out his text. " Repent ye, therefore, and be converted, that your sins may be blotted out when the times of refreshing shall come from the presence of the Lord." His sermon ended, he then said, "All you who wish to hear any more such preaching, rise up," when every man, woman, and child stood up. An appointment was then made for another meeting in the same place, and they were dismissed with the benediction.

The first convert to Methodism in Dundas County was as we also learn from Mr. Carroll made under the following circumstances. "The first house which Losee entered in Matilda was that of one Mr. Wright a renegade Baptist. He introduced himself to the good wife as a Methodist Preacher." (a what? we can fancy her exclaiming), "and asked if she would not like to have preaching in her house; to which she replied that she would, as she could not understand the Germans. She ran to the barn to call her husband, and told him that there was a Methodist in the house. He expressed his surprise, and wished to know "how he looked," to which she replied that "he looked like another man, but that he wanted an arm." The preacher stopt to dinner, made an appointment to preach in the house on a certain day, and kept his word. Upon that occasion Mrs. Wright was awakened and became greatly concerned for the salvation of her soul. She spent the live long night in prayer and watching; for, as she expressed it, "she was afraid of being in hell before morning." The husband was less visibly affected, but the arrow of conviction had pierced him too. He went to the barn to pour out his soul in prayer to God. She literally fell upon her face on the floor, and "poured out strong cries and tears," suddenly a flood of light and joy broke in upon her soul, she sprang upon her feet crying out to her eldest daughter to run immediately for her father. She ran instantly and found him just getting out of the manger, where he had been at prayer. "Oh daddy, come quick, I never saw mamma look so before in my life," said the child. The husband and wife met at the door, and embracing each other glorified God with a loud voice. After walking accross the floor several times hand in hand in inexpressible rapture, away they flew like lightning to neighbor Doran's, and told them what the Lord had done for them. The woman was preparing for breakfast, but no sooner had she seen them and before they had spoken a word discovering their unusual and heavenly appearance, she threw herself into a chair, and began to weep bitterly on account of her sinful state. The husband who was smoking in the chimney corner, threw down his pipe and began to cry to God. They both bound themselves under a promise which was often made in those days, that they would not eat, drink, nor sleep till God should liberate their souls; and as the story runs the man obtained liberty that night, and the woman soon after."

The abrupt and enthusiastic declamations of the missionaries, seems to have had a corresponding effect upon the minds of their converts; and in imitation of their teachers, they were wont to upbraid their unbelieving neighbors, for their faithless and God-less lives. All minds were not, however, alike susceptible of impression by the new doctrines, and then as now, the missionaries had to contend with opposition. This was manifested by pointing the finger of scorn, calling opprobrious names, and, it is said in some instances, by throwing stones at the preacher, setting the dogs on his horse, and "*hurrahing*" for the Methodists. Others again ridiculed them in a quieter way.

A Methodist meeting had been held in a certain neighborhood, when a certain Lutheran had been stricken with a sense of his evil ways, had related his experience, and was admitted into the number of the faithful. He had occasion soon after to visit the blacksmith near by. Vulcan was a Lutheran too: brother A. believing that he was not in the right way, set himself to work in earnest to convert him to his new faith. A long discussion ensued, the Methodist waxed warm, and plied his adversary with arguments loud and long · the inexorable blacksmith remained as cool as a cucumber. With a sad countenance the Methodist took leave of him, commiserating the impenitence and lack of faith of this luke-warm Lutheran. Pointing to the river St. Lawrence, there a mile wide, he said, "as for me, now that I have got religion in real earnest, my faith is so strong, that I should not fear to walk across that river, were it necessary, even as Peter walked to the Saviour on the sea." With this exposition of his faith, he left the blacksmith to his meditations.

A few weeks after this, in the course of business, brother A. had occasion to cross the river to the American side—he had no canoe of his own, but the blacksmith was a good neighbor, and had a good canoe, which he had often borrowed before, accordingly to the smith's he went, and nothing doubting, requested the loan of his canoe. Our blacksmith was a wag in his way, and to the civil and neighborly request, he replied at once, and emphatically, "no sirree!" The other looked at him in amazement, and began to think over in his own mind what occasion of offence he had given him. "Surely you will not refuse to lend me your canoe." "Guess so," said the smith; "what do ye want it *furr?*" "Why, to go *over* the river to be sure." "What!" screamed out the blacksmith, "*you* want *my* canoe to go *over* the river! didn't you tell me jest tother day, that you had faith enough to walk right straight across that 'ere river, dry shod, without a-sinkin! No *sirree!* I dont lend my canoe to any sech men. I want jest to see you try that 'ere caper, you made your brags about, I don't believe in a man havin great faith one day, and a being a-scared the next." How the interview terminated we are not informed, no doubt, however, brother A. was a little more cautious in future, in representing the measure of his faith.

THE GRAVE YARD.—One cold winter morning the writer strolled into the burying ground in Williamsburgh, close to which had stood the first Protestant Church in Canada. His attention about that time being directed to the history of the old church, it occurred to him that the statements he had received, might find some confirmation in the record of the grave yard; but he sought in vain; a number of apparently old graves were there, but the headstones were chiefly modern, nearly all of them of white marble, carved and lettered in nearly every variety of style. Most of them bore the name of "Flynn," the Morrisburgh sculptor, who during the last few years has done a thriving business in thus perpetuating the names of passing generations, which, but for his chisel, had dropped into the grave "unlettered and unsung." The custom of inscribing high sounding epitaphs upon the tombstones of departed friends, is becoming yearly less prevalent, and although in many cases a few lines of some favorite hymn are still affixed, there is generally little more recorded than the name, the date of the birth, and death of the deceased. Occasionally we find a daguerreotype likeness of the person while living, set into the marble slab, the custom is an American one.

A few old and rudely carved dark gray limestone slabs were here and there scattered over the ground, but so marred by the severe frosts of oft repeated Canadian winters, that no vestige of inscription could be found on them. Our attention was directed to a group, said to contain some old stones in a retired corner of the grave yard; the oldest of them was bent over nearly to the ground, and held fast in that position by the frost; nothing could be learned from it beyond the fact that an inscription of some kind was chiselled upon its under side. In the ensuing summer we repaired to it again, with crowbar and spade in hand, and in mood akin to Old Mortality, raised the old stone to its original position; the inscription was somewhat elaborate, and far from legible, and it was with no small degree of interest we deciphered the sorrowful lament of a devoted husband, over the grave of a youthful and beloved wife. Thus it ran :—

To the memory of Katy,
wife of John Starnes. Married ye 8th Nove^m., 1785. she lived nine Years, five Months, and eleven Days with him. Was laid on a bed of Sickness four days and a half. she departed this life ye 3rd April, 1795. Aged 27 Years, six Months, and eighteen Days.

>Near this stone remains the mortal Part
>Of her who once delighted every Heart,
>How good she was, and what her virtues were,
>Her guardian angel can alone Declare.
>Rest precious dust, till heaven thy worth Reveal,
>Thy judge will publish what thy friends Conceal.

The stones adjoining this were of more modern erection, and their inscriptions quite legible. One was " In memory of the late Harriet Delisle, daughter of Margaret and David Delisle, late Rector of Christ's Church Montreal. Who departed this life October 8th 1791." Next to this was one inscribed " To the memory of the Hon. John Monroe, Esq. One of his Majesty's Legislative Council of Upper Canada, formerly Captain in the King's late Royal Regiment of New York, who died the 27th of October 1800 aged 72 years. Close by these, are the graves of the Revds Messrs. Swerdfeger and Weagant, formerly Ministers of Williamsbnrgh Church, the brief inscription on the head-stone of the latter we have already given. No lettered stone records the virtues of the other, but his memory is embalmed in the hearts of the few old Lutherans who lived in his time.

EARLY MILLS, AND ECCENTRICITIES.—The U. E. Loyalists were not without their eccentricities. Old Jacob Coons was a queer coon. An ingenious self taught mechanic, he delighted in nothing more than in exercising his handicraft. Generous in disposition, and the friend of every body, he was frequently to be found gratuitously employed, at the building of a Church, a mill, or a barn, merely that he might have a hand in it, and be in the way of learning something. His desire to be in this way usefully employed, was only exceeded by his delight at building "castles in the air."

At a very early period of the settlement, he conceived the plan of, and actually built, a grist mill, upon an entively novel principle. He had observed, that the mills driven by the stream of the St. Lawrence, were frequently interrupted by the rise and fall of the river, caused by sudden changes of wind, &c. To remedy this, he proposed to himself another plan, and erected a mill at some distance in the interior, which should alike be independent of the fluctuations of the river, and the caprices of the wind. The new mill, it was true, was to be somewhat costly, and its machinery rather complicated, but, the advantage of working the year round, without intermission, sunshine or rain, windy weather and calm, could not be overestimated.

The mode of propulsion was mysterious and original, and had been kept a profound secret from the inquisitive and we may add, the incredulous public. Its motive power, was in two words

"*Perpetual Motion*"! Over a deep well, was placed a large water wheel; over the wheel a pump, to be worked by the wheel, and to discharge into its buckets, water from the well, which, having turned the wheel, was again to have been turned into the well, and so on *ad infinitum*. We need scarcely add that the project was a failure, though it baffled the skill of its projector to tell the reason why. It stood for many a day, a monument of its builder's ingenuity and disappointment, and was seen and examined by many still living in the county. Jacob Coons was not the only one whose hopes had been similarly blasted. The theory of perpetual motion has engaged the life-time of many an aspiring mechanical genius, and not till recently has it been conclusively demonstrated to be an impossibility.

Our hero formed no exception to the tendency of minds like his, when baffled in one mode of procedure to fly off at once to the opposite extreme. His first mill had too much complicated machinery. His second, should have *none at all*, and supersede for ever all the gearing, spur and cog wheels of antediluvian millwrights. It was to be driven by the free winds of heaven.

To effect his purpose, he erected an octagonal building of about fourteen feet in height, and thirty-six feet in diameter. In the centre of this building, an excavation of two or three feet in depth was made, and in this was placed the nether mill stone. The upper stone received through its centre a wooden shaft, which extended perpendicularly to the top of the building, and passing through a circular hole in the tie-beam was free to turn in any direction. This shaft, having been morticed to receive the requisite number of horizontal arms, was equipped with wings, similar to the fan-boards of a fanning-mill. Eight openings were made, one on each side, the entire height of the building, to each of which was attached a door upon hinges. Thus the grist mill was complete.

Having free ingress and egress for the wind, from the four points of the compass, unlike windmills of the present day, the arms of his required no alteration of position to suit the breeze; all that was required to ensure success, was, that the wind should blow, no matter from what quarter. He took advantage of the first stiff breeze to start the mill. Opening the lee door first, no sooner had he opened the opposite one, than the stone began to revolve, the wings of course moving at a much higher velocity. It is said that he actually succeeded in grinding wheat with this paragon of simplicity—but "plague on it," when he had wheat to grind, the wind refused to blow. It is said too, but we will not stake our veracity on't, that upon one occasion, during the excitement of starting it, he was caught fast by one of the wings, and swept round and round the building, narrowly escaping with his life, at one of the open doors. If we have been rightly informed, the mill stones remained many years in their place, even after the building was removed. It must have been nearly on the side of the steam saw-mill at Iroquois.

In 1818 the first grist and saw-mills were put in operation, in the Township of Mountain, on the North branch, and nearly at the same time, another, in South Mountain on the Nation River.

Armstrong's Mills in Winchester, were commenced by two brothers named Merckley in 1825. As a *raising bee* could not be conducted in those days without *the liquor*, the two young men repaired to Waddington, purchased a barrel of whiskey, and set out on their return in a canoe. Whether or not before starting, they had too freely "preed" the contents of the cask, does not now appear, but by some mishap the canoe upset in mid-stream, the whiskey barrel rolled into the river, and both the young men were drowned. Thus too literally and unfortunately was exemplified the common saying of having "drowned the miller."

About the same time one Martinus Casselman, built an excellent grist-mill with fulling-mill attached, at Mariatown on the Rapid du Plat, driven by the stream. Shortly after its construction, the forwarders prosecuted him for obstructing the navigation. Being of a hasty disposition, and greatly averse to litigation, he tore it down in fit of passion, left the country, and took up his abode in "the land of liberty." He there erected another stream-mill, betwixt two islands, opposite Cook's tavern, and at the same time embarked in mercantile business. He was careless of money, and believing every one to be as honest as himself, he never thought of urging any body to pay his debts. After years of trading, as may be supposed, he acquired a great run of business, and soon accumulated a large amount of outstanding accounts. To his great surprise he received scarcely any payments at all . at length, he thought he would call and see a few of his old customers, and satisfy himself what the prospect was. It now appeared that being of a migratory turn, they had nearly all moved, "off West." His indignation knew no bounds, he denounced them as a parcel of thieves and vagabonds, and declared he would stay no longer in a country, whose people were so dishonest as to withhold payment of their just debts.

Accordingly he returned to Canada, and settled down among his friends. He attained a good old age, and we may add from personal knowledge, that a more honest and upright man or one more respected by his neighbors, never lived in the county than Martinus Casselman.

"Should auld acquaintance be forgot,
And never brought to mind."

There resided in the county an old lady and gentleman "of the olden time," a widow and a widower; the former 87 years of age, the latter 83. The old lady had been in her young days, wonderfully active and industrious, had raised a large family, and is reputed to have been the "smartest" woman of her time. She had from childhood been healthy and robust, and reached the goal of three score years and ten, before it could be said, that the woes of age had overtaken her. From that period the hardships of early life told upon her constitution, and she gradually declined in bodily strength and mental vigor until she became quite childish and oblivious to all that was past. She has now gone to her rest.

The other possesses still, all the vivacity and intelligence of youth. He has a distinct recollection of the advent of the first settlers to the county, and has been an attentive observer of the prominent occurrences that have transpired in it, from that time till the present. A warmer-hearted man does not breathe. More for him we cannot say, than that he is the type of that genuine U. E. Loyalist character, which elsewhere we endeavored to delineate.

The lines which we have placed at the head of this sketch, were never more forcibly brought to mind, than while listening to the recital of the affecting circumstances, under which these two aged U. E. Loyalists, met, after a separation of many, many years.

In days long gone by, their parents resided near to each other, and the little boy and girl attended school together. Time rolled on—the little boy became a lad of seventeen, and she, a buxom lass of one and twenty. A finer girl could not be, at least so thought our hero who about this time, it has been said, made her the offer of his heart and hand but she had " big feeling," and wouldn't marry a beardless boy, so much younger than herself; so his suit fell to the ground, and what was worse than all, his fair one was ere long wed to another. He too, was shortly afterwards married, and removed to another part of the township. What with constant occupation at home, and the distance between them, they came to be old man and woman, widower and widow, scarcely seeing each other in the interval. A short time since, hearing that the old lady was very poorly, the old gentleman resolved that he would go down and see her once more. She was informed that her old friend was in the house, and would like to see her. She heeded not. The old man entered her room, and took a seat beside her, for some minutes she gazed upon his once familiar features with a vacant stare. At last something in the tones of his voice arrested her wanderings thoughts. The key that had so long locked up every remembrance of the past, seemed to have turned in the chambers of her mind, and she became for the time perfectly conscious and rational. They warmly embraced each other, and the aged couple conversed for hours together upon old topics, with the greatest enthusiasm. Big tears coursed down their now furrowed cheeks, as they spoke of the days of " auld lang syne," when they had lived and loved together. Though not hand in hand, they had " clamb " the hill of life—they had both reached the summit and were now " met thegither at the foot." The meeting of these two hearts, whose natural warmth the snows of fourscore winters had not extinguished, was an affecting sight, and touched the surrounding friends, as nothing had ever done before.

How mysterious! How incomprehensible is the mind of man! No sooner had the old man taken leave of her, than the pleasing recollection of the scenes of childhood, which his presence had recalled, vanished from her memory. She relapsed into her wonted unconscious reverie, and not the most earnest assurance of her friends could convince her afterwards, that the interview had ever taken place.

CHAPTER XVI.

VISIT OF HIS ROYAL HIGHNESS THE PRINCE OF WALES TO CANADA.

> Lord, let War's tempest cease,
> Fold the whole Earth in paace
>   Under thy wings?
> Make all thy nation's one,
> And hearts beneath the sun,
> Till thou shalt reign alone
>   Great King of Kings.   O. W. HOLMES.

"It will be all the same one hundred years hence:"—is an expression too frequently uttered by inconsiderate and easy going men.

It is precisely one hundred years since an army of eleven thousand men, embarking on a flotilla of boats that must have covered the surface of the St. Lawrence for many miles, swept past the unbroken forests which then covered the County of Dundas. Will any one in the present day, looking back, say it was all the same one hundred years ago? As we trace the progress and mark the improvement of the Province during the past hundred years, is it not truly marvellous to contemplate the various changes that have hurried us rapidly on to the creditable position we have already attained?

Whether we regard Canada in respect of her natural situation, her fertility, her unequalled means of internal communication, her institutions, civil and sacred, or turn to the great public improvements that have already been effected, the enterprize of her merchants and the perseverance of her farmers, it becomes a matter of utter impossibility to determine, by any kind of calculation or with any degree of certainty, what she will be one hundred years hence.

In 1851 there were eighteen million of acres of land occupied in Canada. Of these only 7,300,000 were under cultivation; 138 millions of acres of territory were unoccupied and uninhabited. If the present ratio of increase continue, the population of the Province at the beginning of next century will have reached nearly twenty millions. " The future of Canada," says Mr. Morris " is a brilliant one; a great problem is being wrought out in her history, and on review of her immense resources, and a glance at her hardy, self-reliant population, the mind is irresistibly urged to the conclusion that her destiny is a grand one, and that on this American continent she may yet be destined to play no insignificant part among the role of peoples."

Several circumstances have of late years brought our country into public notice. The exhibitions in London and Paris during the years 1851 and 1855 respectively, contributed in no small degree to force Canada upon the attention of those who knew little or nothing of her before. But the recent visit of Victoria's eldest son, His Royal Highness, Albert Edward, Prince of Wales, to these North American colonies has been the crowning event of all.

The completion of the Victoria Bridge was deemed a matter of sufficient importance to induce both houses of the Canadian Parliament to invite the Queen of Britain to visit the Province in person. State reasons, and we may rely upon it, state reasons alone, prevented her from acceding to their request; but a literal compliance was approached as nearly as under the circumstances was possible. The gracious answer was returned, I will send you my son. It was accordingly intimated that the Prince of Wales would visit Canada during the summer of 1860, accompanied by

His Grace the Duke of Newcastle, Colonial Secretary, the Earl of St. Germains, Lord Steward of Her Majesty's Household, Major General Bruce, His Royal Highness' Governor, Major Teesdale, R. A., and Capt. Grey of the Grenadier Guards, equerries in waiting, and Dr. Acland, His Royal Highness' physician.

As soon as this became definitely known the President of the United States invited the Prince through the Queen to extend his visit to Washington. The following is the letter of invitation, and the unostentatious reply of the Queen.

Washington, June 4th, 1860.

To Her Majesty Queen Victoria:—

"I have learned from the public journals that the Prince of Wales is about to visit your Majesty's North American Dominions. Should it be the intention of His Highness to extend his visit to the United States, I need not say how happy I would be to give him a happy welcome to Washington. You may be well assured that everywhere in this country he will be greeted by the American people in such a manner as cannot fail to prove gratifying to your Majesty. In this they will manifest their deep sense of your domestic virtues, as well as their conviction of your merits as a wise, patriotic, and constitutional Sovereign."

Your Majesty's most obedient Servant,
JAMES BUCHANAN.

Buckingham Palace, June 22nd, 1860.

My Good Friend:—

"I have been much gratified at the feelings which prompted you to write to me, inviting the Prince of Wales to come to Washington. It will give him great pleasure to have an opportunity of testifying to you in person that these are fully reciprocated by him. He will thus be able at the same time to mark the respect which he entertains for the Chief Magistrate of a great friendly and kindred nation. The Prince of Wales will drop all Royal state on leaving my dominions, and travel under the name of Lord Renfrew, as he has done when travelling on the continent of Europe. The Prince Consort wishes to be kindly remembered."

I remain ever, your good friend,

VICTORIA R.

On the morning of the 10th July, 1860, the screw line of battle ship "Hero," 91, with His Royal Highness and suite on board, accompanied by the S. Frigate "Ariadne," 26, left Plymouth Sound, and directed their course for the Island of Newfoundland.

"On the evening of the 23rd the "Hero" steamed majestically into port between the abrupt and lofty headlands, forming the bold and picturesque entrance into the the fair haven of St. John's. The Ariadne followed, and both ships came to their moorings amidst the cheers of the inhabitants who lined the houses, wharves, and shipping, and amidst the pealing of Cathedral bells, whilst flags innumerable fluttered in the breeze." The following day at noon the Prince landed, and the dense crowds on shore made the air resound again and again with their cheers. The Ships of war thundered a Royal salute, and bands played the National Anthem. The streets were lined with enthusiastic and delighted multitudes, and the most perfect order reigned throughout.

Addresses of welcome were presented to the illustrious visitor; a grand dinner, supper, and ball awaited him at the Government-House. Before leaving, he was presented with a magnificent Newfoundland Dog, which the Prince received with evident pleasure, and named "Cabot" in honor of the discoverer of the Island.

On the 28th, the Royal Squadron entered the harbor of Halifax, Nova Scotia, and the illustrious visitor received from the inhabitants of that hospitable city a welcome, which none who witnessed it can ever forget, and which, for its hearty and unalloyed rejoicings, in some respects at least, was nowhere surpassed.

New Brunswick was next visited, and the tour of the Lower Provinces completed by a call at Prince Edward Island. Leaving this, the fleet steamed through the straits of Northumberland, crossing a portion of the Gulf, first sighted the shores of Canada on Sunday the 12th of August, and at sunset entered the Bay of Gaspé. Hither the Governor General of Canada and his ministry had come to meet the Prince. The Duke of Newcastle at once went on board their steamer, the "Victoria," to visit his Excellency, who was invited to breakfast with His Royal Highness the following morning. About noon the members of the Executive Council were introduced, after which, the squadron proceeded up the Gulf and came to anchor at the mouth of the Saguenay.

The weather was cold and rainy, but the Prince and his suite, wrapping themselves up in their waterproof coats, went on board the Victoria, ascended the river a distance of forty-five miles, and there spent two days, admiring the grand and romantic scenery, and amusing themselves the while with fishing.

On the 18th they arrived before the renowned citadel of Quebec. Their appearance, as the squadron rounded Point Levi, was the signal for a general salute from the "Nile" and "Valorous" in the harbor, and from the citadel and batteries on shore. "The scene then presented was very magnificent. Three fine ships of war were steaming up, under one of the strongest fortresses in the world. Clouds of smoke were enveloping the men of war, and capping the lofty steeps which frown down upon the water. The citadel, Durham Terrace, and the roofs of the houses, were black with multitudes of people; the yards of all the ships in port were manned by thousands of tars, the wharves covered with spectators, and the river was alive with steamers of all kinds plying to and fro."

A handsome pavilion had been erected on the market-wharf, carpeted with crimson, draped with flags and evergreens, and surmounted by the Royal standard. Here His Royal Highness landed and was received by the Governor, the cabinet ministers of Canada (in their new uniform, set off with heavy gold lace trimmings, and wearing swords and cocked hats,) the Mayor, attired in silken robes and attended by the corporation, and the English and Catholic clergy of the city in full canonicals. The Mayor read a lengthy but very excellent address, first in French, then in English, to which the Prince replied, and then taking his seat in the Governor's carriage, he drove to his Excellency's residence.

On the 21st, the Prince repaired to the splendid apartments that had been prepared for him by the Province in the Parliament buildings, there to receive the formal greetings of those whose real guest he was, the Legislative bodies of Canada. These, however, were not the first received at the Levee. The Roman Catholic Hierarchy, wearing purple robes and golden crucifixes, were first presented. The whole of the bishops belonging to that Church in the Province were present, and were separately introduced by one of their number: then the Judges of the Superior Courts in Lower Canada, in their silk robes and linen bands; next came the members of the Legislative Council and Assembly, who respectively presented, first in English, then in French, the following addresses.

To His Royal Highness, Albert Edward, Prince of Wales.

MAY IT PLEASE YOUR ROYAL HIGHNESS,—

"We the Legislative Council of Canada in Parliament assembled approach your Royal Highness with renewed assurances of our attachment and devotion to the person and crown of your Royal Mother, our beloved Queen.

"While we regret that the duties of state should have prevented our Sovereign from visiting this extensive portion of her vast dominion, we loyally and warmly appreciate the interest which he Majesty manifests in it, by deputing to us your Royal Highnes as her representative, and we rejoice in common with all her subjects in this Province at the presence among us of him, who at some future, but we hope distant day, will reign over the Realm, wearing with undiminished lustre the crown which will descend to him.

"Though the formal opening of that great work, the Victoria Bridge, known throughout the world as the most gigantic effort in modern times of engineering skill, has been made the special occasion of your Royal Highness' visit, and proud as are Canadians of it, we yet venture to hope that you will find in Canada many other evidences of greatness and progress, to interest you in the welfare and advancement of your future subjects.

"Enjoying under the institutions guaranteed to us all freedom in the management of our own affairs, and as British subjects having a common feeling and interest in the fortunes of the Empire, its glories and successes, we trust, as we believe, that the visit of Your Royal Highness will strengthen the ties which bind together the Sovereign and the Canadian people."

The Prince replied in English, then in French, his pronunciation of the French being as perfect as that of the English.

"GENTLEMEN,—

From my heart I thank you for this address, breathing a spirit of love and devotion to your Queen, and of kindly interest in me as her representative on this occasion. At every step of my progress through the British colonies, and now more forcibly in Canada, I am impressed with the conviction that I owe the overpowering cordiality of my reception to my connection with her, to whom, under Providence I owe every thing, my sovereign and parent.

"To her I shall with pride convey the expressions of your loyal sentiments, and if at some future period, so remote, I trust, that I may allude to it with less pain, it shall please God to place me in that closer relation to you which you contemplate, I cannot hope for any more honorable distinction, than to earn for myself such expressions of generous attachment as I now owe to your appreciation of the virtues of the Queen.

"Few as yet have been the days which I have spent in this country, but I have seen much to indicate the rapid progress and future greatness of United Canada. The infancy of this Province has resembled in some respects that of my native island, and as in centuries gone by, the mother country combined the several virtues of the Norman and Anglo Saxon races, so I may venture to anticipate in the matured character of Canada, the united excellencies of her double ancestry. Most heartily I respond to your desire that the ties which bind together the Sovereign and the Canadian people, may be strong and enduring."

The Assembly's address and reply are as follows:—

"The Speaker, with a sonorous voice, rolled out the address first in English then, in French; and, in reply, the quiet tones of the Prince's youthful voice were listened to in the deepest silence."

MAY IT PLEASE YOUR ROYAL HIGHNESS,—

"We, the Legislative Assembly of Canada, in Parliament assembled, approach your Royal Highness with assurances of our devoted attachment to the person and crown of our Most Gracious Sovereign.

"The Queen's loyal subjects in this Province would have re-rejoiced had the duties of state permitted their august Sovereign to have herself visited their country, and to have received in person the expression of their devotion to her, and of the admiration with which they regard the manner in which she administers the affairs of the vast Empire, over which it has pleased the Divine Providence to place her.

"But while we cannot refrain from expressing our unfeigned regret that it has proved impossible for our Queen to visit her possessions in Canada, we are deeply sensible of her gracious desire to meet the wishes of her subjects, by having permitted the opportunity of welcoming in this part of her dominions, the heir apparent of the throne—our future sovereign.

"We desire to congratulate your Royal Highness on your

arrival in Canada, an event to be long remembered, as manifesting the deep interest felt by the Queen in the welfare of her colonial subjects. On this auspicious occasion, when for the first time the colonies have been honored by the presence of the heir apparent, we receive an earnest of the determination of our most gracious Sovereign to knit yet more closely the ties of affection and duty which unite us to the British Empire, and enable us to share in its glories and its great historical associations.

" The approaching opening of the great Victoria Bridge by your Royal Highness, has been the more immediate cause of your present visit to Canada, and we trust you will find in that stupendous work the most striking evidence in which the capital and skill of the mother country have united with the energy and enterprize of the Province, in overcoming natural obstacles of the most formidable character; but we trust that in your further progress your Royal Highness will find in the peace and prosperity of the people, and in their attachment to their Sovereign, the best proof of the strength of the ties which unite Canada to the mother country, and of the mutual advantages to the Empire, and to the Colony, from the perpetuation of a connection which has been fraught with such great and beneficial results.

" We pray that your Royal Highness may be pleased to convey to our most gracious Queen, the feelings of love and gratitude with which we regard her rule, and especially of her condescension in affording us the occasion of welcoming your Royal Highness to the Province of Canada."

REPLY.

" GENTLEMEN,—No answer that I can return to your address will sufficiently convey my thanks to you, or express the pleasure which I have derived from the manifestations of loyalty and affection to the Queen, my mother, by which I have been met upon my arrival in this Province. As an Englishman, I recognize with pride these manifestations of your sympathy with the great nation from which so many of you trace your origin, and with which you share the honors of a glorious history. In addressing you, however, as an Englishman, I do not forget that some of my fellow-subjects here are not of my own blood: to them also, an especial acknowledgment is due, and I receive with peculiar gratification the proofs of their attachment to the Crown of England. They are evidence of their satisfaction with the equal laws under which they live, and of their just confidence, that whatever be their origin, all Canadians are alike objects of interest to their Sovereign and her people. Canada may be proud that within her limits, two races of different languages and habits are united in the same Legislature by a common loyalty, and are bound to the same Constitution by a common patriotism, but to all of you, and to the three millions British subjects of whom you are the representatives, I am heartily thankful for your demonstration of good will, and shall not readily forget the mode in which I have been received amongst you.

"With you I regret that the Queen has been unable to comply with your anxious desire, that she should visit this portion of her Empire. I have already had proofs of the affectionate devotion which would have attended her progress, but I shall make it my first, as it will be my most pleasing duty upon my return to England, to convey to her the feelings of love and gratitude to her person and her rule, which you have expressed on this occasion, and the sentiments of hearty welcome which you have offered to me, her son."

Now followed the most interesting ceremony of all; the Speaker of the Upper House knelt down on both knees in front of the Prince: His Royal Highness taking the Duke's unsheathed sword, laid it first on his left shoulder, then on his right, saying at the same time, "Rise, Sir Narcisse Belleau," who rose accordingly, and rose a knight. In like manner Mr. Henry Smith, the Speaker of the Assembly, knelt before the Prince, and rose a knight.

Unbounded enthusiasm had marked the progress of the Prince at every step, ever since he had set foot on the western hemisphere, but no where had preparations for his reception been made on so magnificent a scale as at Montreal. The corporation had erected fountains, created squares and gardens, and otherwise permanently embellished the city. A committee of the merchant princes, styled the Citizens' Reception Committee, had expended $43,490 on pavilions, arches, and other decorations. They had erected an octagonal ball-room, nearly 300 feet in diameter, of handsome exterior, lighted with gas, and embellished with palatial splendor. As if by magic it rose up in a few weeks, costing $16,000 in its construction. Ten thousand flags waved from the sparkling roofs of the silver city, or draped its principal thoroughfares. Ever since the Prince's landing on our shores, the weather had been damp and disagreeable, and for some days previous to his arrival in Montreal, the rain had not ceased to descend in torrents. Rivers of water flowed through the streets, and, in many places, the anxiously expectant spectators waded about in the mud ankle deep. The massive wooden arches were despoiled of much of their artistic colorings, and their gigantic proportions assumed a sombre and heavy aspect, as they loomed solemnly through the dark and drizzling atmosphere. Others of a lighter kind retained their freshness, and were even enhanced in beauty by the pearly rain drops which trickled from their pendant boughs of evergreen. As in Quebec, a gorgeous pavilion had been erected on the landing wharf, painted with crimson and gold, festooned with wreaths of evergreens, and surmounted by flags.

On the 24th of August, the steamer "Kingston," having the Prince on board, and with the Royal Standard floating from her mast-head, rounded Longue Point, 9 miles below Montreal. Many river steamers had gone down to meet her, trimmed with green branches, with colors flying and crowded with passengers. One by one, in regular file, they hove in sight, and a scene ensued which for its novelty and effect was very remarkable. Opposite

Longueuil, the "Kingston" dropped anchor, and the whole fleet of steamers, numbering over twenty, clustered around her in one dense mass, hugging and jostling each other in the most confused, yet friendly manner possible. From fifty funnels the pent up steam belched forth with indescribable noise, enveloping the whole in a cloud of fleecy vapor. Steam whistles screamed their shrillest notes, steamboat bells rang vociferously, the passengers cheered the *invisible* Prince till their throats were hoarse, and bands of music played the National Anthem till the musicians could blow no longer. Such a Babel of discordant sounds was surely never heard before. After a time the tumult subsided, and the attendant steamers, one by one, returned to the city, leaving the "Kingston" at anchor, and the Prince, "alone in his glory." The ceremony of landing was deferred till the following morning.

On Saturday the 25th, His Royal Highness attired in his colonel's uniform and attended by the suite, nimbly stepped from on board the Kingston, as soon as she came along-side the Bonsecours wharf, where the Mayor and the *élite* of the citizens were in waiting to receive him. The war Steamers "Styx," "Valorous," and "Flying-fish," anchored in the stream, roared a Royal salute from their great guns. Their crews manned the yards, and led by their commanders standing on the paddle boxes, sung out three lusty British cheers, and three times three, which wakened the echoes again for many miles around. The spectators, who crowded around the wharves, stood at the windows and on the roofs of the houses, and perched themselves high up in the rigging of the craft in the neighborhood, numbered 50,000. Here and there an effort was made by them to raise a cheer, but it was evident that cheering was not their fort, for it was taken up in a feeble and desultory manner, and died away unmistakably—*failure number one.*

Mayor Rodier in his scarlet robe trimmed with rich furs, magnificence personified, read the address of the Corporation, first in English, then in French. The Prince replied in English, and immediately after, proceeding to the state carriage and four which awaited him on the wharf, set out on his triumphal entry through the heart of the city, preceded by a band of painted Indians in their native costume, and followed by a numerous procession.

> " O, wud some power the giftie gie us;
> " *To see oursels as others see us.*"

Notwithstanding the glowing descriptions of some of the local newspapers, the procession, taken as a whole, was in our opinion, *failure number two.* But that was a very secondary matter; the crowds gathered to see the Prince, they did see him, and the most unbounded satisfaction prevailed. In the French Square, a company of American Volunteers, were drawn up in line, and presented arms as the Prince passed. Their handsome uniform, shining accoutrements, and martial bearing attracted the attention of the Prince, and elicited the plaudits of the spectators. A large number of Canadian Volunteers, cavalry, infantry, and artillery, joined in the cavalcade and made a good appearance; the Highland brigade with their plumes and tartans were particularly admired.

The exhibition building on St. Catherine Street, was first inaugurated. Then the all-important ceremony of laying the last stone, and clinching the last rivet of the great Victoria Bridge, was duly attended to, after which the Royal party were regaled by a sumptuous lunch at the Grand Trunk Railway Station. In the evening, a brilliant illumination exhibited the city in all the dazzling splendor of imagination's fairest fairy land. Whatever shortcomings there may have been, this was admitted by all to be a decided success. Great St. James Street presented on that night such a varied continuation of resplendent decorations, as perhaps no street of similar length, in any part of the world, had ever done before. At the same time, in the neighborhood of the Bridge from the wharves and the shipping, an unceasing and magnificent display of fireworks was sustained till midnight, revealing at intervals, the long lines of that wonderful structure, in alternate lights of red, white, and blue. On Monday a levee was held at the Court House, and during two hours the place was in a state of siege. 2000 citizens, in swallow tails, white neck-ties, and kids, thronged its halls, enduring all the tortures of an unmitigated squeeze, ere they succeeded in gaining the august presence, and the honor of presentation. The Anglican Bishop and Synod were first received, the Judges and Roman Catholic Clergy followed, and next the Presbyterians in connection with the Church of Scotland, headed by their Moderator, of venerable aspect, and portly mien. On reaching the presence, Dr. Mathieson unrolled his parchment, and was about to read the Synod's address, as the representative of the Anglican Church had done before him; at this point he was interrupted by the Governor General, who intimated that he could not read it, but must simply hand it in, without a reply, to the Prince. A scene now ensued, the full import of which did not at the time transpire, but it was evident to all that a screw was somewhere loose. The Doctor informed the Governor that such a course would neither be satisfactory to the deputation nor respectful to the Church, and that, under such circumstances, he must decline presenting it at all. With rare presence of mind and dignity, he rolled the parchment up, handed it to the Synod Clerk, and, being presented to the Prince, withdrew. " That's Scotch," whispered one of the mirth enjoying navy officers, who was standing near by. The position was rather an unfortunate one for all concerned. The *amende honorable* was however made, and the Synod's address was afterwards graciously received and replied to at Kingston. The true manliness of the Doctor, not only reflected upon himself showers of approbation from every Protestant body in Canada, but secured for each of them in Upper Canada, a similar recognition.

In the evening of the same day, the great event, upon which the citizens had rested their hopes of eclipsing every past and future demonstration, came off. The Ball, which above every thing else rendered the Montreal reception the most conspicuous, was upon a scale altogether unprecedented. It was attended by nearly 8000 persons, who enjoyed themselves in the presence of the Prince, till gray dawn of morning. The Prince danced, and talked, and enjoyed himself, to his own heart's content, and to the unspeakable admiration of all who saw him. Even the fastidious correspondent of the London "Times," acknowledged that success number two had been achieved.

On Tuesday, the 28th, the Royal party proceeded by the Grand Trunk Railway to Dickinson's Landing, where the Steamer "Kingston" was in waiting to convey them down the far famed rapids of the St. Lawrence. The inhabitants in this neighborhood had been kept in a state of excited suspense for some time by flying rumours of a contradictory kind, as to the precise locality which was to be honored by the embarkation of the Prince; but as soon as it became certainly known that this place had been decided upon, such preparations as the time permitted were made. The road from the station to the river was lined on both sides with spruce trees, and spanned by several light but tasteful arches of evergreens, bands of music were in attendance, the houses in the village were covered with flags, and Captain Dickenson's troop of Cavalry from Cornwall escorted the cortege to the wharf. Upon this was laid a carpet 80 feet in length, made of maple leaves sewed together, which although hurriedly got up by the ladies, its beauty and novelty yet attracted the attention of the Prince. But the most pleasing demonstration of all, was the presence of 10,000 farmers, who had poured in from the counties of Stormont and Dundas to do homage to the heir of Britain's throne. Here, as at almost every turn which his Royal Highness took, he was presented with an address, setting forth the loyalty of the inhabitants and their attachment to the crown and person of their sovereign. The Prince reached Montreal in the evening, greatly delighted with the excitement of "shooting" the rapids, and thoroughly fatigued with the unremitting ovations of the previous few days. On Friday morning the Prince took leave of Montreal, amidst a drenching rain, proceeded by the Grand Trunk Railway to St. Anne's, thence up the Ottawa, and reached the City of Ottawa at sunset.

No more royal squadrons, nor salutes from "sixty-four pounders," nor cheers from sailors on the manned yards, and yet their places are by no means inaptly supplied. As he approaches the heights on which the city stands, his steamer is met by a fleet of 150 bark canoes drawn up in two lines, manned by 1200 brawny lumbermen, all dressed in jackets of red or blue, white trousers, and jaunty straw hats. Steaming slowly through the picturesque lines, the "Phœnix" halted at their head, when they immediately ranged themselves in the form of the letter V, point foremost, the two wings stretching away behind to both shores, and the Prince's steamer leading in the midst.

"As this glorious aquatic procession passed New Edinburgh and the city, the enthusiasm became positively wonderful; the boatmen, and the 20,000 spectators who lined the slopes, raised the most vigorous cheers that had yet greeted the Prince in America, and this extraordinary demonstration excited the most intense interest of the whole royal party."

Excellent arrangements had been made at the landing place, but just at the auspicious moment, the customary rain set in and drenched the assemblage. The ceremony was hurried through, and the illustrious visitors drove off rapidly in close carriages to the Victoria Hotel. Sweet little children in white, singing the National Anthem, were driven like snow-flakes before the pitiless storm, and the disappointed multitude dispersed, finding their way as best they might to their homes, or the crowded hotels.

On Saturday the 1st of September, the sun shone propitiously on the gayly adorned and joyous little city. Numerous arches spanned the spacious streets. The arch at the entrance to the new Parliament buildings, was acknowledged to surpass anything of the kind seen in Montreal or elsewhere. The ceremony of laying the corner stone of the new Parliament buildings came off at eleven, and at noon the levee was opened. As it was somehow understood that one o'clock had been the hour named for this, not many had the honor of presentation. The Mayor and Corporation of Ottawa City were first presented, and then the deputation from the county of Dundas, who presented an address to his Royal Highness, which we give in full together with the reply, not from any supposed excellence in the address, but because to residents of the county it will be interesting hereafter, and to the general reader it will present a fair sample of nine-tenths of the addresses received and replied to by the Prince.

To His Royal Highness, Albert Edward, Prince of Wales.

MAY IT PLEASE YOUR ROYAL HIGHNESS,—

"We, the inhabitants of the County of Dundas, Canada West, approach your Royal Highness with sentiments of profound respect. We beg leave to assure your Royal Highness that it affords us unbounded satisfaction to avail ourselves of the gracious permission accorded to us, humbly to testify our devoted loyalty to the government of your august mother, our Queen; and to express to your Royal Highness our admiration of the many virtues which, adorning her character, have shed a lustre on the British Crown, and have distinguished our Queen as the most illustrious Sovereign that ever graced the British Throne

"Your royal ancestor, King George III, liberally rewarded those faithful soldiers who valiantly fought for their king and country in the first American war, with grants of land in Canada.

"Amongst the first counties thus settled, was Dundas in 1784, and we are proud to have an opportunity of declaring to your Royal Highness, that devotion to their Queen and to British institutions, in undiminished intensity, still animates the hearts of the descendants of the U. E. Loyalists of Dundas.

"In the visit of your Royal Highness to Canada at this time, we recognize an act of kindness and condescension on the part of our Sovereign demanding our deepest gratitude, while we trust it may gratify your Royal Highness to witness the loyalty of your future subjects; and while your visit inspires these subjects with increased admiration and respect for their beloved Queen, we also pray that it may have the effect of permanently cementing the friendly relations now happily subisting betwixt the citizens of our neighboring republic and the subjects of Her Majesty, in every portion of her vast dominions.

Dundas County, 30th July, 1860."

The following answer was transmitted:—

"OTTAWA, September, 1860.

SIR,—I have the honour to convey to you the thanks of His Royal Highness, the Prince of Wales, for the address presented to him by the inhabitants of the County of Dundas.

I am, Sir,
Your obedient servant,
NEWCASTLE.

Alex. McDonell, Esq."

A spirited canoe race terminated the proceedings of a day, memorable in the annals of Ottawa City and was followed at night by a torch light procession and general illumination. From Ottawa the Prince proceeded to Arnprior, and thence to Brockville, where he arrived at dusk. Here he was met by the most extraordinary enthusiasm yet witnessed. From the railway station to the steamer, the whole line of procession was lighted up by a continuous blaze of fire-works. "The halo of glory, the lots of smoke, and myriads of green, red, blue, and white fire-balls surrounding the Prince, made the whole thing look like some of the disappearances of H. S. M., (His satanic Majesty) in theatrical representations." The Prince slept on board his steamer anchored in the stream; next morning, he disembarked and drove through the town, and called upon the Hon. George Crawford at his residence. So much gratified was His Royal Highness with his hearty reception at Brockville, that he withdrew the short and formal reply given to their address, and conferred a double honor on the plucky little town, by the following *second* reply.

GENTLEMEN,

"I am deeply touched by the cordiality and warmth of feeling with which I have been welcomed to this town; for your address I thank you, and heartily appreciate the sentiments of attachment to your sovereign and her empire which you have expressed.

"The name of your town recals the memory of a brave man, and of brave deeds in times now happily past. May such men never be wanting to you, but may their services long remain uncalled for.

"I never doubted that the well known loyalty of the people would ensure to me a kind reception amongst you, but day after day convinces me that I had not fully estimated the strength and ardor of Canadian patriotism.

"Be assured that I shall not soon forget the scene of this evening."

On the 4th the Prince left Brockville and, passing through the Lake of the Thousand Islands, arrived off Kingston. Hitherto the populace had besieged the Prince; now the tables were reversed, and the Prince besieged the citizens. The Orangemen had repaired in great numbers to Kingston they had erected several arches decorated with the mottoes and devices, and other emblems of their order, and had announced their intention of joining in the procession dressed in their full regalia. The Roman Catholics, who are also numerous here, had protested loudly against these proceedings, in a communication to the Duke of Newcastle. The Duke intimated, that he could not advise the Prince to countenance any proceedings calculated to excite ill feeling amongst any portion of Her Majesty's subjects, and firmly announced his determination, that, unless these party emblems were removed, the Royal party would not land at all.

The Orangemen were immoveable, they had adopted as their motto "*no surrender,*" and it was unalterable. The Duke's decree was also irrevocable, hence the *contre temps*. For twenty-two hours the Prince and the Duke lay at anchor in the harbor; but finding them inexorable, they directed their course through the Bay of Quinte to Belleville. At this place a similar state of affairs existed, and the proposal to remove the obnoxious emblems was resisted. The Mayor of the town boarded the Prince's steamer, and expostulated with the Duke, but all in vain; no sooner had he turned to proceed to the shore, than the "Kingston" moved off down the bay, and was quickly out of sight. Now that the Prince had come and gone, the inhabitants of Belleville repented of their folly, and in a conciliatory address to the Prince at Toronto, besought him to come back again, but it was now *too late*.

His Royal Highness landed at Cobourg and Port Hope, and also visited Peterboro in the interior. "One of the enthusiastic throng there, thrust his hand into the Royal carriage, the Prince in the fulness of his good nature, shook it heartily—others followed the example, and he was soon busied shaking hands with all who came." From Port Hope he proceeded by rail to Whitby, where the people were literally mad with joy, and thence by steamer to Toronto.

The Orangemen had reluctantly promised to forego their party display here, and having given the Duke an explicit assurance that nothing of the kind would be presented, it was determined that His Royal Highness should land.

" The landing of the Prince in Toronto occurred an hour before dark. It was a spectacle which for magnificence has probably never been surpassed in the modern world. Just as the Montreal ball was the finest thing ever seen under a roof, so the display here was by far the finest thing ever seen out of doors. So exquisite and effective were the arrangements for landing, that when the Prince stepped ashore, he stood for several moments silently contemplating the scene. In front of him was an amphitheatre occupied by 12,000 people, rising tier above tier, and covering several acres of ground. The seats in front were occupied by over 5,000 school children, who after the presentation of the address, united their voices with the assembled multitude in singing the National Anthem. We believe we express the opinion of all competent judges when we say, that neither in England, France, nor the United States, did a more magnificent *coup d'œil* ever greet the eye of prince or potentate."

The Prince took an excursion to Collingwood on the Georgian Bay, and returned the same evening to Toronto, having travelled part of the way on the Northern Railway at the rate of 55 miles an hour. From Toronto he went to London, and thence to Sarnia, where an amusing and interesting scene took place. " The Indians —real red savages—majestic in mien, faces painted, heads adorned with hawks' feathers and squirrels' tails, silver spoons in their noses, moccasined, &c. One of them, a magnificent fellow named Kanwagasti, or the Great Bear of the North, advanced to the front, and striking out his right hand, yelled out an Indian address to the Prince, which was translated to him by an Indian interpreter, who, as the red chieftain finished each sentence and folded his arms, gave the meaning of what was said."

The harangue was as follows:—

GREAT BROTHER,

" The sky is beautiful. It was the wish of the Great Spirit that we should meet in this place. My heart is glad that the Queen sent her eldest son to see her Indian subjects. I am happy to see you here this day. I hope the sky will continue to look fine, to give happiness both to the whites and the Indians. Great Brother, when you were a little child your parents told you that there were such people as Indians in Canada, and now since you have come to Canada yourself you see them. I am one of the Ojibbeway Chiefs and represent the tribe here assembled to welcome their

Great Brother. You see the Indians who are around; they have heard that at some future day you will put on the British Crown and sit on the British Throne. It is their earnest desire you will always remember them."

"The Prince replied verbally, that he was grateful for the address, that he hoped the sky would always be beautiful, and that he should never forget his red brethren."

As each phrase was interpreted to the Indians they yelled their approbation. Then the name of each was called out by the interpreter from a list handed him by the Governor-General, and each one advanced in turn. Some had Buffalo horns upon their heads, some wore snake skins tied round their waists, and most of them were feathered on the legs like Bantam cocks."

From Sarnia the Prince returned to London, and next visited the Falls of Niagara, where he rested quietly for two days, enjoying the grand scene. He witnessed also Blondin's crowning feat of carrying a man upon his back over a slender rope stretched across the chasm below the Falls, and saw him return safely on stilts three feet in height, by the same narrow and fearfully hazardous path. On the 18th he was at Queenston heights assisting to lay the foundation of an obelisk, to mark the spot where General Brock received his death wound, and replied to an address from the veteran surviving heroes of 1812 as follows :

GENTLEMEN,

"I accept with mixed feelings of pride and pain the address which you have presented on this spot, pride in the gallant deeds of my countrymen, but pain from the recollection that so many of the noble band have passed away from the scene of the bravery of their youth, and of the peaceful avocations of their riper years. I have willingly consented to lay the first stone of this monument. Every nation may without offence to its neighbors commemorate its heroes' acts, their deeds of arms and their noble deaths. This is no boast of victory, no revival of past animosities, but a noble tribute to a soldier's fame—the more honorable because we readily acknowledge the bravery and chivalry of that people by whose hands he fell."

"I trust Canada will never want such Volunteers as those who fought in the last war, nor her Volunteers be without such leaders, but no less and most fervently I pray that your sons and your grandsons may never be called upon to add other laurels to those which you have so gallantly won. Accept from me, in the Queen's name, my thanks for your expressions of devoted loyalty."

Last of all, he visited Hamilton, where he bade an affectionate farewell to his Canadian fellow-subjects, in the following feeling reply to the address of the City Council.

GENTLEMEN,

"This is the last of the very numerous addresses which have flowed in upon me from the Municipal authorities, as well as other bodies throughout the Queen's dominions in North America, which I have now traversed from East to West, and I can say with truth that it is not the least fervent in its declarations of attachment to the Queen, nor the least earnest in its aspirations for the success and happiness of my future life, and in its prayers that my career may be one of usefulness to others and of honor to myself.

"You cannot doubt the readiness with which I undertook the duty which was entrusted to me by the Queen, of visiting in her name and in her behalf these possessions of her Crown.

"That task is now nearly completed, and it only remains for me to report to your Sovereign, universal enthusiasm, unanimous loyalty, all pervading patriotism, general contentment, and I trust no less general prosperity and happiness.

"I can never forget the scenes I have witnessed. The short time during which I have enjoyed the privilege of associating myself with the Canadian people must ever form a happy epoch in my life. I shall bear away with me a grateful remembrance of kindness and affection, which as yet I have been unable to do anything to merit, and it shall be the constant effort of my future years to prove myself not unworthy of the love and confidence of a generous people."

On the 20th His Royal Highness visited the show grounds of the Provincial Agricultural Association, and witnessed the largest exhibition of the industrial and agricultural productions of Canada that had ever been brought together. He had already had con-convincing proof of the devotion to his mother and himself, of the Canadian people; he now surveyed the unquestionable evidence of their industry and success in agricultural pursuits. Yet one more address from the farmers of Upper Canada—the farewell once more repeated, and the Prince of Wales has accomplished his mission.

The address of the Agricultural Association of Upper Canada was presented by Mr. Wade, its president.

To which His Royal Highness made the following reply:—

GENTLEMEN,

"I return you my warmest acknowledgements for the address you have just presented upon the occasion of opening the fifteenth exhibition of the Agricultural Society of Upper Canada, and I take this opportunity of thanking the agriculturists, artisans and manufacturers who are now assembled from distant parts, in this City of Hamilton, for the more than kind and enthusiastic reception which they gave me yesterday, and have repeated today.

"Blessed with a soil of very remarkable fertility, and a hardy race of industrious and enterprising men, this district must rapidly assume a most important position in the markets of the world, and I rejoice to learn that the improvements in agriculture, which skill, labor and science have of late years developed in the mother country, are fast increasing the capabilities of your soil, and enabling you to compete successfully with the energetic people, whose stock and other products are now ranged in friendly rivalry with your own within this vast enclosure.

"The Almighty has this year granted you that greatest boon to a people—an abundant harvest. I trust it will make glad many a home of those I see around me, and bring increased wealth and prosperity to this magnificent Province.

"My duties as representative of the Queen, deputed by her to visit British North America, cease this day, but in a private capacity I am about to visit, before my return home, that remarkable land which claims with us a common ancestry, and in whose extraordinary progress every Englishman feels a common interest.

"Before, however, I quit British soil, let me once more address through you the inhabitants of United Canada, and bid them an affectionate farewell.

"May God pour down His choicest blessings upon this great and loyal people."

The days of enthusiastic rejoicing in Canada have come to an end.—His Royal Highness the Prince of Wales assumes the garb and title of an English gentleman, and as "Baron Renfrew," hies to the west and alights on the shores of the Great Republic. He visits Detroit, Chicago, and St. Louis, cities of the West, and is idolized by their inhabitants. Fowling piece in hand he roams over the boundless prairie, traverses in perfect safety the long lines of railway connecting the Mississippi with the head waters of the Ohio, visits Cincinnati and Pittsburgh, and is received in the capital of the United States with Royal honors. We behold him paying homage at the tomb of the immortal Washington. We follow him to the regions of the 'sunny south.' New York the great commercial emporium of the continent opens wide her portals to receive and welcome him, and the hearty acclamations of half a million of republicans, reverberate from the Atlantic to the Pacific shores. In Boston he climbs the hill where the first blow for independence was struck, and his presence there, declares the nation worthy of the liberty which they achieved.

At Portland in the State of Maine, an armed fleet lies anchored where eighty-five years before a British squadron had hostilely bombarded the town. The cannons roar, but no hostile sound is there. Far and near the echoes ring, " give back thy priceless charge." A few words of parting spoken with moistened eye and quivering lip, and the illustrious visitor steps on board the royal barge. With vigorous strokes the jolly tars ply the oars, and soon, amid the thunders of a royal salute, the Prince of Wales is himself again, and he and his suite are, once more, on board the " Hero." " Up runs the royal standard to the main top, and once again the red flashes roll out, shaking the city and the heights of Mountjoy. Then up went the anchors, and the great ships, one after another, moved off majestically. Abreast of Fort Preble up runs another flag to the foremast head of the *Hero*, its folds spread out on the breeze, and lo! all eyes on shore perceive that it is the flag of the Union,—the stars and stripes—another discharge of distant artillery rolls heavily towards the land—the dense masses of smoke clear away—the American flag is no longer seen, it has been dipped in true man-of-war style." And now, like a dissolving view, the gallant ships are borne swiftly away to the blue horizon.

On the 15th of November, after a tempestuous voyage of twenty seven days, during which time serious fears for their safety had been entertained in England and in America, the *Hero* and the *Ariadne* came to anchor in Plymouth Sound. For the last time the ships manned yards and fired salutes as the royal standard came down from the *Hero*. Amid cheers from the crews of both ships, the Prince of Wales quitted the royal squadron, his long progress was brought to a close, and in a few hours more he was at home in Windsor Castle.

The time for moralizing had now come, and Canadians and Americans vied with each other in extolling the surpassing grace, and the princely bearing of him who was speeding o'er the deep to his native land, and in bright predictions of the eternal friendship that is to unite the kindred nations. Nothing, save the presence of the Queen herself, could have stirred to such depth these ocean floods of popular emotion; and we are almost tempted to bless our lot, that the son had been substituted for the mother, for had our gracious Queen visited us in person, we believe her Canadian subjects would have given vent to their feelings of admiration and respect in such exuberent demonstrations of devotion as had bordered upon insanity.

It may be asked, what is Canada the better for having been the theatre of events, which, during their occurrence, excited the most intense interest of the civilized world? What benefits are to accrue, what results to follow in the wake of the gorgeous pageant that so lately filled the hearts of millions of British subjects and of American citizens too, with joy and gladness?

The questions are more easily asked than answered, yet we shall attempt a reply;—In so far as Canadians were concerned, the invitation was dictated by a pure and lofty motive. It was nothing more nor less, than that the colonists might have an opportunity of testifying to their Sovereign in person, or to the representative whom she might appoint to visit them, their firm allegiance to the British throne, and their admiration of the virtues which conspicuously grace the monarch who wields the sceptre of Great Britain and under whose benignant sway the British North American Colonies have risen during a brief century to a position of prosperity unparalleled in the history of any other colony. The visit of the Prince of Wales has afforded such an opportunity, and the reception accorded to him has been such as to reflect credit upon the colonists, and has manifested to the world that they are worthy of the free institutions that have been conferred upon them, and that, while even now equal to the responsibilities of self government, they regard it as their privilege and their happiness to continue as subjects of the British Crown.

" The recent visit of the heir apparent of the British Crown to several of the noblest portions of his future empire, has not been without its influence in England. It has awakened interest, excited curiosity, and diffused information. The great ovation with which the representative of the British Monarchy and the British nation has been greeted, is an honorable acknowledgment of the obligations which the people of British North America owe to the land from which they derive their freedom, and to which they are indebted for much of their political importance and no inconsiderable amount of their prosperity.!' *

In another light it may be viewed, without doubt, as a means of bringing into notice our commercial, mechanical, and agricultural capabilities, and consequently we may reasonably anticipate an influx of English capital, and English skill, and what is of still more importance, of English *hands* to clear off our forests, and work out the destinies of what must yet become a great producing country.

That reasons of state policy, other than the mere gratification of loyal colonists, may have had their influence in connection with the royal visit, is more than probable, but in the absence of any authentic information on that head, it would be presumptuous to speculate upon them. It is, however, a generally received opinion that a union of all the British Provinces into one great North American Confederation, has, through the personal inspection of an acknowledged sagacious Colonial Minister, been suggested to the Imperial mind; and that although it will be left to the colonists themselves to decide upon the practicability of the movement, yet, that the influence of the British Government will be brought to bear upon its accomplishment.

There can be no doubt that the royal visit to the United States has been instrumental in cementing the friendly relations existing between England and that country, and the enthusiastic manner in which the Prince was every where welcomed by the American

---

* London Quarterly.

people, is a sure pledge that bygone national animosities are for ever buried in oblivion, and that the two countries, already one in origin, in religion, and in language, will become more than ever allied in their identity of interests, and will each at least view with impartiality the excellencies of the other.

FINIS.

John Lovell, Printer, St. Nicholas Street, Montreal.

ERRATA.

Page 241, line 10, for *and* read *each*.
" 301, " 15, " *for* read *from*.
" 302, " 14, " *depôst* read *depôt*.
" 304, " 29, " *staying* read *staging*.
" 315, " 15, " *side* read *site*.
" 320, " 7, " *million* read *millions*.
" 324, " 30, " *he* read *Her*.

INDEX.

	PAGE		PAGE
Abraham, heights of	62	Broeffle, Rev. Mr	258
Acadia	44, 46	Brouse, Jacob and Peter,	78
Adams, Samuel	94	Brown's Brigade	80
Addresses	325, 328, 335	Bunker Hill,	71
Aerolite	159	Cabot,	30
Agriculture in Canada	192	Calciferous Sandrock	174
Agricultural Societies	236	Campbell, Lying	279
Alexander, Sir Wm	46	Canada, 47, 52, 57, 59, 66, 105, 320
Allan's Steamers	297	Canals, St Lawrence	152, 287
Allan, Hugh	298	Canal, Rideau	97
America, discovery of	18	Cape Breton Island	55
" first settlement of	37, 43	Caroline, Steamer	111
" so named	29	Cartier, Jacques	33, 36
American War	71	Casselman, Martinus	316
Americus	27, 30	Census	241
Amherst, General	60, 65, 66	Chaffey, Benjamin	304
Animals, wild	189	Champlain	49
Arctic explorations	32	Chazy Rocks	175
Armstrong's mills	315	Chimney Island	66, 99
Assembly, Legislative	272-3	Church of England	256-7
Assimilation	150	Civil Courts	145
Backwoods	201	Clark, Duncan	78, 98
Balboa	33	Clergy Reserves	270, 164, 268
Battle of Crysler's Farm	85, 92	Colborne, Sir John	108
" Matilda	99	Collins Steamers	296
" Wind Mill	113, 119	Colony abandoned	40
Birds	189	Columbus, Christopher	19, 27
Bond Head, Sir F	51, 105, 108, 110	Common sense	217
Botany, study of,	188	Commerce	242
Boscawen, Admiral,	57, 59	Constitutional changes	271
Bouck's honey,	95	Conquest of Canada	51, 67
Boulders	178	Cook, John and J W.,	280
Brant	142	Cook's Point	81
Brock, General,	75	Coal Formation	168

INDEX.

	PAGE		PAGE
Coon, Queer	313	Dutch farmer	194
Coons, Mrs	157	Earthquake	160
Corn mills	132	Eastern District	219, 246
Cornwall	80	Eclipse	159
Cornwallis	48	Educational	230
Councillors	223	Elective Franchise	274
Cranberry marshes	154	" Legislative Council	275
Crawford, Hon. George	283	Elements of the soil	182
Crysler, Colonel	114, 130, 281	Elliot, William	203, 289
Crysler, John F.,	280	English Revolution	69
Crysler Farm	83	Exports and imports	243
Crystalline Rocks	168	Fish and fishing	189
Cunard Steamers	295	Flowers, native	187
Dairy, Farming	202	Foot prints	173
Dalhousie, Earl of	64	Forest trees	184
Declaration of Independence	71	Fossils	176, 181
" " War	74	Franklin, Sir John	32
De Monts	44	Frazer	279
Dickey, Rev. Mr	259	Free Church	260
Draining	208	French settlements	43
Duncan, Captain	145	" War	58
Dundas, County of	126	Geology	165
" early history of	127	Ghent, treaty of	93
" settled	129	Gilbert, Sir Humphrey	38
" intermediate history of	151	Glengarry Militia	114, 119
" soil of	153	Globe, first circumnavigated	33
" timber of	154	Gowan, Lieutenant Colonel	114
" climate of	155	Grammar School	234
" irrigation of	163	Grand Trunk Railroad	302
" roads of	164	Grant to Alexander, Sir Wm.	47
" Geology and Natural History of	165	Graveyard	311
		Great Eastern	299
" named	225	Grenadier Island	77
" population of	240	Grenville, Sir R.,	39
" Schools of	234	Hail storm	162
" Agricultural products	241	Halifax	48
" exports and imports	243	Hard times	134
" manufactures of	244	Harrison, General	77
" Militia of	123	Hayunga, Rev H	254
" houses in	246	Hennipin, Father	54
" Religion in	247, 270	Hispaniola	23
" Politics in	271, 286	History	17
" County, Members of	277	Hochelaga	35
" Canals in	287	Horses	204
" Address to Prince of Wales	335	Houses	246
		Hull, General	74
Durham Cattle	203	Hunters' Lodges	109
Durham, Lord	107	Hunting	191

INDEX.

	PAGE		PAGE
Iberville	54	Militia of Canada,	120-2
Implements	212	Militia, Dundas, 99, 115, 121, 123, 151	
Incident, affecting	217	Mills,	133, 140, 313
Indian Wars	50	Mineral spring,	163
Infernal Machine	213	Ministerial support,	267
Invasion of Canada	75	Mississippi discovered,	53
Irishman's life	200	Mohawk Indians,	142
Iroquois Indians	50	Montcalm,	61, 64
" Point	78, 263	Montreal,	35, 57, 77
Isle aux Noix	65, 128	Montreal, Prince of Wales at,	330
Kirk of Scotland	261	Montreal, Ball,	333
Kirk, Sir David	46	Morris, Alexander,	222, 320
Knighthood	328	Morrison, Col.,	82
Laborers	211	Mound of Williamsburgh,	307
LaSalle	54	Municipalities,	220
Laurentian Rocks	169	Murray, Brigadier,	62-67
Laws	273	Naval engagements,	73-76
Legal Institutions	227	New England,	40-42
Levee,	332, 335	Newfoundland 31, 35, 38, 48, 55, 322	
Levi,	61, 64	New France,	48, 50
Lindsay, Rev. Mr	256	New York,	42
Log shanty,	131	Nova Scotia, ...43, 46, 48, 68, 322	
Longue Sault,	67, 132	Ogdensburgh taken,	76
Louisiana settled,	54	Old age,	318
Louisbourg,	55, 59	Oldest inhabitant,	157
Lumbering,	152	Ottawa, Prince of Wales at,	334
Lunenburgh,	140, 219	Pacific Ocean discovered,	33
Lutheran Church,	250-5	Panther shot,	189
Lutheran, lukewarm,	310	Parliament, Canadian,	273
Magellan,	33	Patriot War,	109
Manufactures,	244	Peace,	93
Maple trees and sugar,	185	Pepperal,	56
Mariatown,	101, 145	Perpetual motion,	314
Marquette,	53	Phenomena,	158
Martial Law,	144	Pope, Rev. Messrs	263
Master and servant,	216	Pork.	133
Mathieson, Dr.,	332	Post-Tertiary deposits	180
Matilda,	79, 99, 253	Potsdam Sandstone	172
McMillan,	100	Practical farming	195
McKenzie,	110	Presbyterian Church	257, 261
Meadows,	197	Prescott	78, 82, 112, 119
Medals and Monuments,	96	President U. S	321
Merckley, Major H.;	86, 279	Prideaux, General	60, 65
Merckley, Jacob,	133	Primeval forest	130
Meteorology,	156	Prince of Wales	319-347
Methodist Church,	261-5	Prince, Colonel	119
Methodist missionaries,	308	Prince Edward Island	31, 56
Methodist converts,,	309	Proctor, General	77

INDEX.

	PAGE		PAGE
Profitable farming	197	Statute Labor	164
Protestant Church, The first in Canada	251	Steamboats	291, 302
Public Burdens	224	Steichmann	128, 148
Puritans	41	St Lawrence discovered	34
Quebec founded	49	" Rapids	66, 333
" taken by the English	64	Stock, Improved	203
" Prince of Wales at,	324–9	Sympathizers	116
Raleigh, Sir Walter	39	Systematic farming	194
Rebellion in Canada	107, 121	Taxes, Assessed	224
Reflections	149	Tertiary deposits	177
Religion	247	Thunder storm	162
Religious Statistics	266	Tile Draining	209
Renting land	206	Townships named	226
Representation	274	Trenton limestone	176
Rifleman's Song	125	Tried Sergeant	104
Right of Search	73	Types of ancient life	183
Riots in Lower Canada	108	U. E. Loyalists	130
Roanoke	38	" " character	136
Roberval	36	" " rights	135
Rocks, Grooved	179	Union of Churches	261
Roman Catholic Church	266	Union of Provinces	107, 273
Rose, J. W.	203, 280	Utrecht, treaty of	47
Ross, Christianne	137	Victoria Regina, reply to the President	321
Rotation, Crops,193-96-99, 202,	207	Victoria Bridge	303, 331
Sable Island	43	Virginia	38
Sackett's Harbor	77	Volunteer movement	124
Salmon River raid	102	Von Schoultz	113, 118, 120
Schools	141, 144, 232	War of 1812	73, 93
Scotch Settler	198	" Independence	71
Scott, General Winfred	117	Warren, Admiral	56
Seals	189	Washington, General	72
Siege of Quebec	60, 64	Weagant, Rev. J. G	252
" " Louisbourg	56	Weighing Horses	205
Separating Counties	221	" babies	205
Shares system	207	Wilkinson, General	77, 103
Shaver, Peter	157, 281	Williamsburgh, Americans land in and are defeated, 11th Nov 1813	80
Sheep	205		
Shrubs, Native	186		
Silurian Rocks	171	Wind-mill	113, 119
Slaves	273	Wolfe, General	59, 60, 64
Soil, Elements of	182	Wolves	133
Speedy, Wreck of the	148	York taken	76
Stadacona	34	Young, Colonel	115
Stamp Act	70		

CPSIA information can be obtained at www.ICGtesting.com
Printed in the USA
LVOW011924260413

331153LV00013B/640/P